O
P
E
R
A

PASSION, POWER AND POLITICS

O
P
E
R
A

PASSION, POWER AND POLITICS

Edited by Kate Bailey

V&A Publishing

Published to accompany the exhibition
Opera: Passion, Power and Politics
at the Victoria and Albert Museum, London,
from 30 September 2017 – 25 February 2018.

Sponsored by

SOCIETE
GENERALE

Sound partner

Bowers & Wilkins

With thanks to

BLAVATNIK FAMILY
FOUNDATION

THE TAYLOR FAMILY
FOUNDATION

In collaboration with

ROYAL
OPERA
HOUSE

V&A Publishing
Supporting the world's leading
museum of art and design,
the Victoria and Albert
Museum, London

First published by V&A Publishing, 2017
Victoria and Albert Museum
South Kensington
London SW7 2RL
www.vandapublishing.com

Distributed in North America by Abrams,
an imprint of ABRAMS

© Victoria and Albert Museum, London

The moral right of the authors has
been asserted.

Hardback edition
ISBN 978 1 85177 928 4

Paperback edition
ISBN 978 1 85177 946 8

Library of Congress Control Number
2017938447

10 9 8 7 6 5 4 3 2 1
2021 2020 2019 2018 2017

Staging an operatic performance is only possible
with the contribution of many different artists and
practitioners. Regrettably, space precludes the
crediting of every individual within the captions of
this book. For full information about productions
at the Royal Opera House, please visit roh.org.uk.

Foreign proper nouns have been translated
where appropriate; in some cases it has been
necessary to transliterate.

Designer: Praline
Copy-editor: Rebeka Cohen
Origination: DL Imaging Ltd, London
Index: Hilary Bird

New V&A photography by Robert Auton and
Paul Robins, V&A Photographic Studio

Printed in Singapore, with Pristone Pte Ltd

cover (detail)
Royal Opera House auditorium, London
© Rob Moore, 2005

p.2
Milano
From the series *Fratelli d'Italia*, Italy (2005–17)
Matthias Schaller
Courtesy of the artist © Matthias Schaller

p.8
Scene from *Król Roger*
Production by Kasper Holten with set designs
by Steffen Aarfing
Royal Opera House, London, 2015
© Bill Cooper/Royal Opera House/ArenaPAL

SPONSOR'S FOREWORD

SADIA RICKE
UK COUNTRY HEAD

From its earliest roots to the twenty-first century, opera has always been inspired by society.

Through this ground-breaking exhibition, the V&A takes you on an immersive journey through time, using opera to awaken all the senses and transport you to the societies of seven opera premieres in seven key European cities, with a finale that celebrates how opera is a thriving, international language for world cities today.

It is the notion of opera being a collection of art forms open to all demographics that inspired us to become lead sponsor of this exhibition. The V&A's commitment to promoting art, performance and culture across society as a whole mirrors our own support of the arts. In 2015, Societe Generale celebrated 20 years of support for contemporary art and 30 years for classical music in 2017.

Opera: Passion, Power and Politics brings to life an art form that has captivated audiences for centuries. We at Societe Generale hope many more audiences from around the world will continue to be captivated by this truly wonderful exhibition and discover their passion for opera.

DIRECTOR'S FOREWORD

TRISTRAM HUNT

Opera: Passion, Power and Politics is the first exhibition of its kind, offering new perspectives on a complex and innovative art form. Opera is both a medium which brings together a wide spectrum of artistic disciplines and a lens through which we can understand history, culture and society. Its richness, reach and influence make it an ideal subject for the V&A, the world's leading museum of art, design and performance.

Spanning nearly 400 years, the exhibition provides a soundtrack to the history of Europe. It examines key moments in the history of opera, focusing on seven premieres by seven renowned composers. It considers how these operas both reflect and shift the social, political and cultural life of the cities for which they were created, and presents opera houses as important cultural spaces where audiences, artistic passions and creativity meet.

The exhibition finale celebrates how opera constantly reinvigorates itself for new audiences, both locally and globally. Opera is now regularly performed in different locations across the world, and the great opera houses of the twenty-first century can be found outside its traditional homes in Europe – in Shanghai, Beijing, Seoul, Muscat and Dubai.

Today, opera can also exist beyond the walls of its traditional 'house'. In everyday life, we hear and see opera in different contexts: adverts, films and sporting events spring to mind, but personal music devices mean that we can take the music wherever we want to go. At a time when music is sometimes just 'background', this exhibition shows the context in which opera's masterpieces were created and invites us to explore the genesis of the music.

The drama and spectacle of opera makes it an especially suitable subject for the inaugural exhibition in the V&A's new landmark Sainsbury Gallery – one of the largest temporary exhibition spaces in the UK. Although the Museum has used pioneering audio technology in other recent exhibitions, this is the first time it has been applied to classical music. The result is a truly immersive visitor experience that constructs and deconstructs opera in seven distinct worlds, offering an accessible platform for many to experience opera for the first time.

This exhibition has provided a welcome opportunity to conserve and display objects from the V&A's diverse collections, including original Baroque theatre costumes and set designs, a selection of early musical instruments and a copy of Torquato Tasso's *Gerusalemme Liberata* (published in 1724) from the National Art Library. It has also benefitted from the generosity of numerous individuals and institutions who have loaned objects or contributed to the project in numerous different ways.

In particular, we are delighted to have collaborated so closely with the Royal Opera House, without whom this exhibition would not have been possible. Their expertise in the creation of live performance and knowledge of the subject matter has greatly enriched this project. We are also extremely grateful to our lead sponsor Societe Generale. Having provided invaluable support to the V&A for more than a decade, this is their second headline exhibition in a major two-year sponsorship agreement with the Museum, highlighting music as one of the cornerstones of their cultural activity.

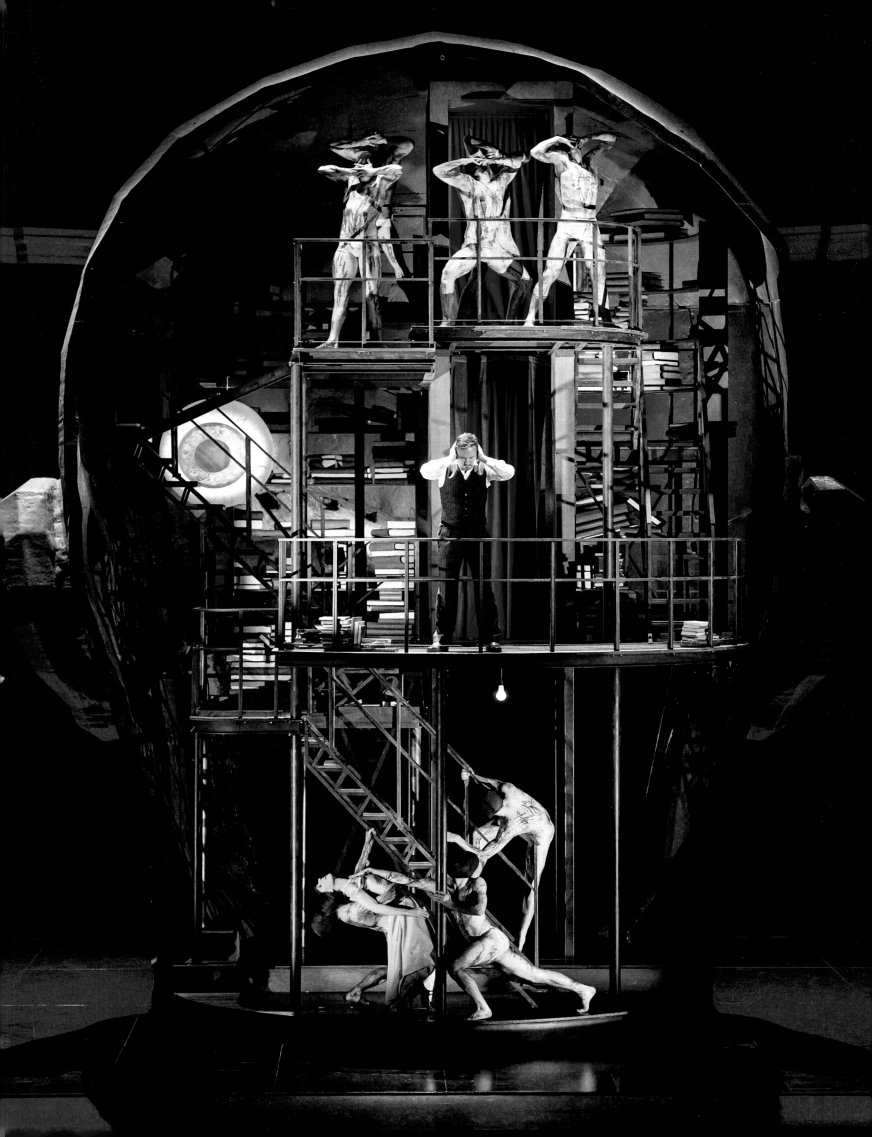

INTRODUCTION

KASPER HOLTEN

For me, opera is the ultimate art form. And yet, it isn't really an art in itself so much as a meeting of all other art forms: an overwhelming experience in which music, poetry, visual arts, theatre, movement and dance come together. There is nothing quite like it. In an era where we are digitally connected all of the time, and where impatience and restlessness seem to rule everything, I think we need opera more than ever before. It is an art form where highly trained professionals and artists collaborate to give us a live, unplugged, human experience, which we in turn experience with other people in a defined physical space and must concentrate on for a time, as we connect with their performance.

In this exhibition and publication we – the Royal Opera House and the V&A – want to dig deeper to understand the nature of opera, and share our learning with both opera lovers and newcomers. We want to understand how and why this art form can continue to survive and to surprise, thrill and challenge audiences around the world. And we want to examine the relationship between opera and the society that surrounds it. The museum offers us a platform from which to do this and a door through which visitors who are new to opera can find us.

When, years ago, I met the then-new Director of the V&A, Martin Roth, a short time after I had started as Director of Opera at the Royal Opera House in London, we agreed that it would be interesting to see what an ambitious exhibition could offer. We wanted to look at how opera, with its story-telling, theatrical effects and ever-changing expressions, could inspire an involving and immersive exhibition.

It has made a lot of sense for us to embark on this journey together. Opera is collaborative, bringing together art forms, skills and ideas that often appear to be contradictory or seem difficult to make work together. But go to any European city, and if you want to find the centre, just look for the location of its opera house: they have always been – because they must be – meeting places for ideas, expressions and people. As must museums.

Admittedly, in today's world, which offers so many other meeting places for ideas and for people, real or virtual, these roles may be under threat. The opera house must look at its roots, and find ways to continue to connect with the cities and the meeting spaces around us. An opera house should be in constant dialogue with the people and the world in which it exists and, if we want to change that world, we must be active participants in our cultural spaces.

Opera addresses life's biggest questions. Is anything more important to us in life than trying to understand the great themes of love and death, and to connect to these emotions, face them, embrace them, reflect on them – and maybe even have a chance to live through them, to rehearse them? Opera gives us a chance to put characters on stage; it forces us to relate to them, allowing the audience to share in their emotions through the combination of theatre, music and the raw, naked, unamplified human voice.

The human voice is at the core of opera, but it is presented with other art forms to make what is arguably the world's first multi-media art form. From birth until death, the voice is the carrier of our emotions and reflections. But our voices can be used expressively in ways that are more dramatic and more poetic than everyday speaking – just look at how we use our voices as children. Opera reconnects us with this original instinct, but in a highly controlled and sophisticated manner that takes years and years of training to achieve.

The history of opera is, in many ways, the soundtrack to the history of Europe. Opera excels in portrayals of suffering, and of doubt. These are possibly not things we normally care to celebrate in our modern world, where much focus is given to being successful and strong. But they are essential parts of the human experience, and of our existence, which we cannot deny or repress. The stories told in opera are often quite subversive, and critical of political and religious institutions and of people with power, money and privilege. In this way opera has also been an important mirror to hold up to society.

And so, opera can be seen as the essential expression of Europe's soul. It is founded on the original traditions of European theatre, as developed in particular by the Greeks. It brings together people in the seemingly impossible task of collaboration, and in the spirit of sharing. It explores the doubt and the suffering that has always been an inescapable part of the history of Europe, but in doing so, creates exquisite joy. My favourite example of this is the finale of the second act of Mozart's *Le nozze di Figaro* (*The Marriage of Figaro*) which links together seven people each with their own agenda. They sing, fight and debate with each other at the same time – and yet simultaneously create a beautiful harmony.

Opera is of course highly sophisticated, and requires the skills of a lot of very highly trained people. It is therefore both complex and expensive to deliver. But its roots are in fact in popular entertainment. There are also strong elements of circus and sport to opera – will the soprano make the right note? Will the tenor last the evening? Will everything work out? Performance carries risk, and we see that risk when we see opera performed live. It is precisely in opera's response to our primitive needs that its unique appeal is most wonderfully fulfilled.

In this exhibition and accompanying book, we have chosen to showcase seven world premieres across seven cities over a period of four centuries. We have had to make painful omissions, but it was never our goal to offer a comprehensive history of opera. Rather, in each of these moments in time, we hope to look at the interaction between artists, ideas, audiences and cities. By exploring these moments in European as well as operatic history, we hope to look at the relationship between the art form that is opera, and the world around it.

We begin our journey as opera moved from the private realm of Italian court entertainment to public life in Venice in the mid-seventeenth century. This popular performance genre was then disseminated and adapted across Italy and throughout the rest of Europe. Opera was presented in many languages, from Italian to French, Russian and English, and it used many different voices, from the popular castrato singers to the powerful heroic tenors and epic choruses. We will encounter divas and muses, rebels and rulers, politicians and impresarios, and will follow the sound of instruments including a renaissance ensemble of strings and a 100-piece orchestra with wind and brass. Opera librettos were inspired by many sources, including mythology, classics, the Bible and modern everyday life. The social experience of opera also varied considerably, from noisy, bustling eighteenth-century theatres to temples of music in the nineteenth century. Technology and innovation constantly pushed this art form forward, creating the spectacular scenery of the Baroque stage as well as the multi-media, streamed productions of the twenty-first century.

This book opens with Monteverdi, combining entertainment and social satire in his *L'incoronazione di Poppea* (*The Coronation of Poppea*) in mid-seventeenth century Venice. We then move on, investigating opera's theatricality, as developed spectacularly by Handel in the trade centre that was London in the eighteenth century. Mozart's *Le nozze di Figaro* is of course closely connected to both the Enlightenment and the social changes at the brink of the nineteenth century. We also consider operas such as Verdi's *Nabucco*, with its strong political significance in the wake of the Italian Risorgimento, and Wagner's redefinition of what opera could be with *Tannhäuser*, as the city of Paris was itself redefined. In the twentieth century, the role of women in opera changed significantly, and a whole new expressionistic depth emerged in operas such as Strauss' *Salome* and Shostakovich's *Lady Macbeth of the Mtsensk District* – which also raised questions of censorship and freedom of expression.

Reflecting on the close collaboration between the V&A and the Royal Opera House, this book brings the museum and opera worlds together, encouraging international discourse between institutions and stakeholders. Each section of this book discusses the social, political and cultural context for each opera, together with insights into how they are part of a continuing, living tradition. It includes essays from practitioners involved in performing or staging the works alongside scholarly essays on the historical background, linking composers and their masterpieces to the city of the premiere. This method recognizes the importance of the original setting and their enduring relevance in the world of opera today. And finally, as we get closer to our own time, we will reflect on the diversity of opera around the world, which has extended far beyond its European birthplace.

Through the exhibition and this book, we show the wonderful complexity needed to unite all kinds of expressions and skills into one story-telling venture, including the logistical effort involved in putting together an opera. We explore how different practitioners – from composer and librettist to designers, directors, conductors, musicians and singers – all come to opera from different specialisms, and must devote their individual skills to the service of a common goal. A performance where different elements support and challenge each other in a fruitful exchange can enrich the human experience.

Opera has always been reactive, but in doing so, it has never lost its power to change the world. It challenges people, engages them, forces them to discuss important issues, and it moves us emotionally. As the European art form of opera has gone global, and as social media connects us on a new scale, we need opera now, more than ever before, to connect us to the things that truly matter in life. Opera has become an international language, and we hope this exhibition and publication reach new audiences and stimulate contemporary conversations across cities, cultures and continents.

VENICE

1

CLAUDIO MONTEVERDI
1567–1643

L'incoronazione di Poppea

In Imperial Rome, the courtier
Otho is infatuated with the beautiful
Poppea, but she is Emperor Nero's
mistress and has ambitions to marry him.
Nero tells the philosopher Seneca of
his desire to leave his wife Octavia so that
he can marry Poppea. When Seneca
advises against this, Nero ruthlessly has
him killed. Uncovering a plot by Otho
and Octavia to murder Poppea, Nero
banishes them both and marries Poppea.

2

INTRODUCTION

DANIELLE DE NIESE

My role debut as Poppea took place in early 2004 for the inauguration of Chicago's Harris Theater in Chicago Opera Theater's new production, directed by Diane Paulus and conducted by Jane Glover. From the moment I began to explore the character of Poppea I have never stopped discovering and admiring this infamous and multifaceted woman.

The tale of Poppea Sabina and her blazing adulterous relationship with the Roman Emperor Nero is largely known as a cautionary tale: watch out, be careful what you wish for. Poppea, catching the eye of Nero, is drawn into an impassioned, enthralling affair when she becomes Nero's official mistress. But is it Nero she is drawn to, or his power? In my view, it's impossible to distinguish between either aspect of his personality: in Nero she finds both love and authority.

They are a perfect match — she builds him up when he is insecure, entreating the young ruler to think for himself and take his power into his own hands; he puts her on a pedestal, exalting her beauty and brains, and turning her into a human goddess — she becomes his muse in every sense. Poppea, however, not content to be mistress alone, desires formal recognition as Nero's wife. She achieves her ambition and is finally crowned empress of Rome — but at what cost?

This remarkable piece of music was composed when the format we now know as opera was in its infancy. Although the leading as well as the supporting characters in this anti-morality tale were well known figures in Roman life, Busenello decided to represent the actions of the characters in his libretto in a new light ('But here things will be represented differently'/'Ma qui si rappresenta il fatto diverse').

And so, as I do with all roles, I started with the libretto — and therein I discovered the key to interpreting Poppea herself. Busenello's great accomplishment was to construct characters who defied history, and personalities that refused to date. Out of legendary historical figures, he created actual people with traits we can see in ourselves even today. The challenge for me was to make Poppea real in the twenty-first century.

Where Busenello's libretto gave audiences access to the interwoven relationships and inner life they might have imagined for these figures, the weaving musical lines of Monteverdi imbued them with a soul, adding a splendorous, almost transcendental nature to their dialogue. This new combination of textual realism and musical ethereality redefined theatrical musical boundaries.

But it would be wrong to assume that this rich and textured opera started out written in this way. In the Baroque era (c.1600–1750), music was annotated in a bare-bones style, allowing performers to decide instrumentation and vocal ornamentation for themselves, which allowed for vastly different styles within the same passage of music. Over time these developed into a number of different versions. Although I have performed the Venice premiere version, the second Naples version, and every official combination in between, because of the freedoms written into, and allowed by, the score, none of my musical interpretations of Poppea have resembled one another. Rather they have taken completely different forms, which in turn allow for the dramatic creation and management of her persona.

And ultimately it's the music that drives the opera and determines the interpretation of the libretto. I love Poppea's exposed lines — there is one moment when she asks Nero: 'How delicious did you find the sweet kisses from my mouth … how did you find the apples of my bosom … and the embrace of my arms?' These are some of the most sensuous phrases I have ever sung — yet they are neither sumptuous in their melodic line nor in their instrumentation. Rather, they are simple, almost naked in their composition, with very little movement in the melody. This allows the text to remain intimate and gives the performer an opportunity to personalize it — and I do: filling the phrases with voluptuous vocal tones and Baroque ornamentations that pulse with internal desire. This is the gift of Baroque music — the freedom within a structured form to create, improvise and compose alongside Monteverdi himself in an almost jazz-like way, making the performer's contribution very personal.

But beyond the music, and beyond the vocal challenges of the score, lies the more difficult task of rendering a fully fleshed-out dramatic portrayal of the character in question. From my role debut to this day, I find that Poppea polarizes audiences — everyone has an opinion about her. When I start exploring a character, I usually take into account the ways in which she is described by those surrounding her, which helps me to understand the character from an external perspective. All these small pieces of information fit into the complex puzzle of the final, complete portrayal.

Yet with Poppea I decided to do the opposite. For the first time in my career, I put aside all the salacious adjectives that history has used to describe her: duplicitous, evil, greedy, driven, ambitious, ruthless, conniving, cynical, temptress … the ultimate manipulator. I wanted to find Poppea myself; I refused to incarnate her in the way that others saw her. I wanted to recreate her in the way she saw herself. This decision has always been at the very heart of my Poppea and it has allowed me to form a rounded character rather than a caricature of the archetypal female seductress and schemer.

When I portray Poppea on stage, it is my intention to invite the audience into my mindset so powerfully during the opera that they discard their own notions of Poppea, and find themselves inside my own head. I want people to root for Poppea, to feel for Poppea, and to live the story from Poppea's point of view. If I can get the audience on my side, so that they almost forget they know the ending to the story, then they can experience her trajectory from the inside out, rather than from the outside looking in. One of my greatest joys as a performer is to feel a connection with the audience; to know that they are tethered to your every thought and reaction, and that they are living in the present story-telling sphere. This steers the audience away from judgement and towards empathetic understanding.

At its 1642 premiere, Venetian audiences were scandalized by *L'incoronazione di Poppea* and I suspect people remain scandalized by her story today. Whenever I'm on a press tour, I am almost always asked: 'What is it like to play someone so bad, in an opera where the "bad guys" win and are somehow rewarded with that sublime duet?' My response is complex. I have learned a lot from getting to know Poppea. In wanting audiences to shed their judgement of her, I have come to change my own perspective of her. As people say about *L'incoronazione di Poppea*, virtue is condemned and vice is rewarded. But it all depends on your point of view. The world has judged historical figures through third person accounts of their lives, but I like to consider how this story might have been written down if Poppea had authored the annals instead of Tacitus.

Society passes judgement on people, classifying them as good or bad based on their actions (Nero and Poppea would most certainly fall into the latter category), and people accept the tag by which society labels them even if they have not seen it themselves. This is still true today. But bad people still live lives filled with the mundane and the exceptional. They have wives, husbands, sons, daughters. They have birthdays like everyone else, they fall in love, they marry, celebrate milestones, they protect their loved ones and their own interests. They believe themselves worthy of the happiness they have attained (no matter the cost) — and their badness doesn't affect that conviction. Do the bad people in *L'incoronazione di Poppea* consider themselves to be immoral? I don't think they do.

It is somehow fitting for me that the 'bad guys' get to sing this sublime duet. In one crystallized moment in time, Poppea and Nero are so synchronized with each other that even though people and circumstances may conspire to pull them apart, they forge ahead undaunted and united in their common desires, and become almost one person. This is beautifully reflected in the multiple dissonant suspensions between their two vocal lines which continuously push against one another, only to perpetually resolve, finally ending in one unison note where (when sung well), it becomes impossible to distinguish one voice from the other.

Long before terms like 'Brangelina' were coined for the celebrities of modern times, we had Poppea and Nero — the first century's famous power couple. Roman audiences knew all too well that they didn't achieve their 'happily ever after' — indeed, Nero kicked a pregnant Poppea to death. But at the end of this opera — their 'happily ever after' seems to be entirely plausible. Why shouldn't they sing a sublime duet?

3

4

THE TRIUMPH OF POPPEA: VIRTUE, VICE AND SONG IN THE VENETIAN REPUBLIC

WENDY HELLER

6

Now that Seneca is dead,
Lucan, let us sing
amorous songs
in praise of that beautiful face
whom the hand of love has engraved on my heart.[1]

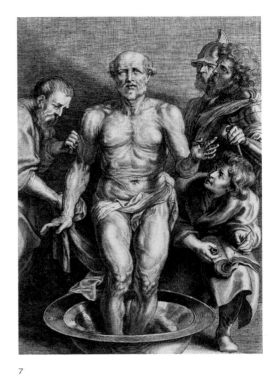

7

In Act II, Scene VI of *L'incoronazione di Poppea* by Claudio Monteverdi, the Roman Emperor Nero and his companion Lucan sing a virtuosic and sensual duet in which they fantasize about the pleasures that might be enjoyed with the beautiful Poppea. Most operas feature such diegetic episodes, in which the characters are understood to be actually singing, be it a lullaby, a serenade, a lament or a drinking song. However, *L'incoronazione di Poppea* may be the only work in which song is used to celebrate the death of a central character: the philosopher Seneca (pl.7), whose suicide Nero orders to enable the Emperor to banish his wife Octavia and subsequently marry his mistress Poppea. The opera ends with another lush duet that vividly enacts this union: their vocal lines wrap around one another, sometimes sweetly, other times with biting dissonances, creating a sonic image of the physical pleasure Nero and Poppea eagerly anticipate. In this clever manipulation of Roman history contrived by the librettist Giovanni Francesco Busenello (1598–1659) and made audible through Monteverdi's music, we are left with the happy ending that convention required; however, it is one in which ambition, lust and self-indulgence triumph over morality, wisdom and restraint.[2] Although many of the operas produced in the public theatres in seventeenth-century Venice would celebrate the pleasures and freedoms for which the carnival city was renowned, it is arguably *L'incoronazione di Poppea* that most perfectly captures the ambivalent forces that were at the heart of political realities, myths and fantasies associated with, and promulgated by, the Most Serene Republic.[3]

VENICE AS VIRGIN AND GODDESS

For the many travellers who published accounts of their visits to Venice, it was inevitably the city's singular topography that was so arresting (pl.6).[4] Foreigners and natives alike extolled the watery city that had emerged as a natural phenomenon on top of structural pilings in a lagoon off the Adriatic Sea. Writing in the early seventeenth century, the English visitor Thomas Coryat (*c*.1577–1617) lamented the inability of his 'unpolished pen' to capture fully the city's splendours, lauding *La Serenissima* as 'so beautiful, so renowned, so glorious a Virgin'.[5]

Coryat's description of Venice as a virginal lady was by no means unusual, for indeed tales of the city's special association with the Virgin Mary had been a part of Venetian mythology from the very beginning.[6] Venice was presumably founded on the Feast of the Annunciation on 25 March in the year 421, designated as a Christian realm built upon the ruins of Rome. Along with Saint Mark, whose relics were among Venice's most treasured spoils from the Holy Land, Mary was Venice's patron saint. These special relationships would be captured by Tintoretto (1518–94) in a painting for the Sala del Senato in the Ducal Palace, where both the Virgin Mary and Saint Mark kneel before Doge Pietro Loredano (pl.8).

Yet, Mary was not the only female entity to represent the Republic. Venice was also associated with the allegorical representation of Justice, the goddess Roma, and even Juno, the royal wife of Jupiter.[7] But of all the pagan goddesses it was Venus, the goddess of love, also born of the sea, who was perhaps best suited to stand with the Virgin Mary as the enduring symbol of all the Republic had to offer.[8]

5 (pp.20–1)
La Fenice, Venice
Main building and auditorium rebuilt
in 2001–4 after the 1836 design

6
Piazza San Marco at Carnival Time
Joseph Heintz (1600–78)
Oil on canvas, mid-17th century
Doria Pamphilj Gallery, Rome

7
Death of Seneca
Cornelius Galle (c.1570–1641)
Designed by Rubens from an antique
statue of the work entitled *Philosopher*
Print on paper, late 16th–mid-17th century
V&A: DYCE.2225

8

9

THE MASCULINE REPUBLIC

Despite the extensive use of female imagery to represent Venice, this durable, impermeable Republic was a decidedly masculine institution. While Venice boasted of, and was lauded for, her many freedoms, in reality rule was restricted to men of the noble classes, and controlled through a pyramidal structure: on the bottom was the Great Council, which included all the noble males over the age of 25; there was the senate, elected from the Great Council; at the top sat the doge, elected for life, whose largely symbolic power was limited by an elaborate system of checks and balances.[9] The lack of a monarch or ruling family meant that Venice had no central court that controlled patronage or in which women might assume a public role. Power was shared by the male representatives of the relatively small group of patrician families, many of whom could boast of having produced a doge or even a pope.

Venice's unique form of government inspired admiration and envy in foreigners. For James Howell (c.1594–1666), writing in the 1640s, Venice's republican government was perfection itself: 'Were it within the reach of humane brain to prescribe Rules for fixing a Society and Succession of people under the same Species of Government as long as the World lasted, the Republic of *Venice* were the fittest pattern on Earth both for direction and imitation'.[10] Among the explanations that he offers is the lack of Church involvement in the secular councils and the fact that Venice was never 'subject to the authority of Women'.[11] Writing in the 1680s, the French nobleman Alexandre-Touissant de Limojon de Saint-Didier (1630–89) compared the government of the Venetian Republic to a 'great an Ingenuous Engine, whose many secret Springs have an exact agreement with the least of its External motions', and in particular he lauded the balance between various segments of the population – old and young, rich and poor – that resulted in a 'perfect union, and Fervant Zeal for the Common Welfare, which are the basis of the lasting Foundation of this Republick'.[12]

10

STAGING VENICE

Saint-Didier's notion of Venice as an 'Ingenuous Engine' was inspired not only by his investigation of her political system, but would have been continually reinforced by the city's special modes of self-presentation: her splendid art and architecture and her many sumptuous civic and religious rituals, not to mention the recreational activities (gambling, theatre and music) enjoyed with particular relish during carnival season.[13] The Virgin-Venus dichotomy helps us to understand how Venice could present herself simultaneously as pure and sinful: a city of virtuous men and women, but one in which every pleasure might be had. Venetians were particularly adept at using the city's natural scenery as a backdrop for its rituals. Processions could be seen throughout the liturgical year, and often featured retinues of gondolas or makeshift bridges made of boats that provided a way for the faithful to cross the lagoon. Perhaps the best example is the Sensa, celebrated on Ascension Day, when the doge, accompanied by the nobility and members of the Senate, would journey out into the lagoon in a special golden barge to toss into the water a ceremonial ring that symbolized Venice's marriage to (and domination of) the sea (pl.10).[14] These tensions between the sacred and the secular – between temporal and heavenly power – are imbedded in the very heart of Venice: the Piazza San Marco (pl.9).[15] Here spectators could gaze both upon the exotic Byzantine splendor of the Basilica San Marco (the doge's private chapel) that housed the remains of Saint Mark and the refined Renaissance elegance of the Ducal Palace, the seat of Venice's political power.[16] Thomas Coryat called it the 'fairest place in the citie … so stupendous that at my first entrance thereof it did even amaze or rather ravish my senses'.[17]

8
The Doge Pietro Loredano kneeling before the Virgin Mary and Saint Mark
Jacopo Robusti Tintoretto (1518–94)
Oil on canvas
Venice, 1581–4
Sala del Senata, Ducal Palace, Venice

9
Procession in the Piazza San Marco
Gentile Bellini (1429–1507)
Oil on canvas
Venice, 1496
Gallerie dell'Accademia, Venice

10
La Serenissima Dogaressa dal suo palazzo (The Dogaressa Leaving the Palace on the Bucintoro)
Giacomo Franco (1550–1620)
Engraving from *Habiti d'huomeni et donne Venetiane*, 1610
The Metropolitan Museum of Art, New York

11

Coryat's senses were also ravished by the music that he heard in Venice ('so excellent, that I thinke no man could surpasse it');[18] indeed so many of the Venetian institutions linked to worship – churches, convents, orphanages, the confraternities (the lay religious orders that played a central role in Venetian life) – produced elaborate music for special feasts.[19] Monteverdi (pl.12), after having worked for many years at the Mantuan court, might have briefly regretted not having won the post in Rome that he had initially sought, but he would spend the majority of his career in one of the most prestigious positions for a musician on the Italian peninsula – as *maestro di capella* at San Marco.[20] In so doing, he became part of an esteemed Venetian musical tradition established in the sixteenth century, composing the sumptuous music for multiple choirs and instrumental ensembles for which the Basilica was so renowned.[21] The musicians employed at San Marco were some of the best in the city, and were heard not only in the opera theatres, but also in the many academies and private concerts sponsored by Venetian nobles throughout the sixteenth and seventeenth centuries, such as the one represented in this painting (pl.11) by Bernardo Strozzi (1581–1644).[22]

The Piazza San Marco was also a hub of international activity; Coryat marvelled that 'so many distinct and sundrie nations' met there: Venetian patricians, clad in long black gowns, mingled with the 'Polonians, Slavonians, Persians, Grecians, Turks, Jews, Christians ... each distinguished from another by their proper and peculiar habits'.[23] For indeed, the Piazza was the epicentre for what was assuredly the best costume party in all of Europe – Venice's famous carnival, which began the day after Christmas and ended with the beginning of Lent. It was not enough, as the French traveller François Misson (*c*.1650–1722) observed, that Venetians could wear masks during carnival and gamble or attend the theatre. These revellers, he wrote:

> ... are not satisfied with the ordinary Libertinism, they improve and refine all their Pleasures and plunge into them up to the Neck ... Vice and Vertue are never so well counterfeited, and both the Names and Use of 'em is absolutely chang'd.... You would swear, that all the World were turn'd Fools in an instant.[24]

11
The Concert
Bernardo Strozzi (1581–1644)
Oil on canvas, c.1635
Royal Collection Trust, London, RCIN 404978

12
Portrait of Claudio Monteverdi
After Bernardo Strozzi (1581–1644)
Oil on canvas, c.1633
Private collection

12

VENICE

13

14

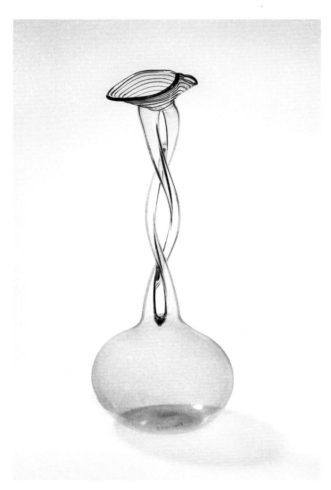

15

16

Was Venice as glorious or as free in the seventeenth century as many Venetians and foreigners would have had us believe? Given the relative instability of so much of Europe during this time, Venice, with its unique form of government, the absence of a court and its associated intrigues, its pleasures, and relative peace with its neighbours (with the exception of the Ottoman Empire) may well have seemed idyllic.

Nonetheless, Venetians faced any number of challenges. A certain degree of economic decline began in the sixteenth century, though there is some disagreement as to the causes of the recession, which also affected much of Europe during this period.[25] As Venice lost her dominance as a maritime power, focus shifted to the *terra firma*: to agriculture, ship-building, and the manufacture of textiles (silk and wool), leather and Venetian glass, an industry that remained relatively strong well into the seventeenth century (pl.13–16).[26] The production of luxury goods, however, may only have enhanced Venice's reputation for decadence, underscoring the notion that the Republic had become a consumer rather than a producer of expensive goods, while the increased commercial activity on the mainland likely reinforced a growing anxiety that Venice was no longer at the centre of the world.

Meanwhile, the ongoing battles with the Ottomans showed no signs of abating; despite the Venetian victory in Lepanto in 1571, the war of Candia (1645–69) would prove less successful.[27] The two devastating bouts of the plague – one between 1575–7 and the other between 1630–1 – took their toll on the Venetian population. By 1581, the population, which had swelled to approximately 170,000 in 1570, had fallen to under 135,000. Demographics stabilized somewhat in the early decades of the seventeenth century, but the effects of the plague in the 1630s were even more catastrophic, causing a drop in the population from around 140,000 to 102,000 or less.[28] Masks, such as the one pictured here, were therefore not only part of the carnival celebrations, but rather were also designed to protect doctors who treated plague patients from airborne infection (pl.17).

Then there were the struggles with Rome, manifest in the Interdict of 1606–7, when some relatively minor squabbles between the Papacy and Venice escalated, resulting in the temporary excommunication of the entire Republic.[29] This conflict seems to have had less to do with doctrine than has traditionally been assumed; nonetheless the notions about political liberty and anti-Roman perspectives expressed by writers caught up in the controversies – Paolo Sarpi (1552–1623), Giovanni Botero (1544–1617), and Traiano Boccalini (1556–1613) – established Venice's reputation as a source for political wisdom, another valuable commodity that could be exported.[30] Venice may no longer have enjoyed the economic expansion, naval power, and military successes of the fifteenth and early sixteenth centuries, but she could still boast of her unmatched liberties, her religious tolerance, and, of course, the pleasures she offered her cosmopolitan visitors.

Not every commentator took Venetian propaganda at face value, however. Misson, whose comments about carnival are above, alleged that despite 'stuffing their heads' with 'notions of liberty', Venetians were – like all people – 'slaves to their masters':

> I will tell you in Two words, what that liberty is: You must never in the least meddle with the Affairs of State: you must commit no enormous Crimes punishable by Justice, which by their notoriety may oblige the Government to call you to an account; and in all other respects you may do what you please, without so much as fearing to be censur'd. This is the Summ of the Venetian Liberty.[31]

17

13
Bottle
Filigree glass, mould-blown with a gilded copper mount
Venice, 1550–1625
V&A: 1913-1855

14
Tazza
Glass, moulded, tooled stem, applied blue rim
Venice, 17th century
V&A: C.497-1936

15
Bottle (Kuttrolf)
Blown glass with applied blue trailing
Venice, 17th–18th century
V&A: C.371-1928

16
Goblet
Blown glass, moulded and twisted stem
Venice, 17th century
V&A: 5527-1859

17
A Masked Lady
Luca Carlevarijs (1663–1730)
Oil on canvas, c.1700–10
V&A: P.72-1938

Misson's comments capture something of the contradictory elements of conservatism and libertinism that typified seventeenth-century Venetian thinking. The growing awareness that Venice's best days may have been in the past only intensified the patriotic sentiments of its citizens, who advocated for protectionist policies designed to protect the status quo. At the same time, a certain moral permissiveness – at least for its male citizens – was not only acceptable, but an indication of loyalty to the Republic.

WIVES, NUNS AND COURTESANS

Venice's women, on the other hand, did not enjoy the same freedoms as their husbands, fathers and brothers.[32] Because of the high costs of dowries and the necessity of preserving wealth in noble families, only some daughters had the option of marrying; many others were obliged to become nuns, often against their will. This was the case with the Venetian writer and nun Arcangela Tarabotti (1604–52), who complained bitterly about being forced into an 'inferno monacale' – a monastic hell – and in her *Tirannia paterna*, published posthumously, she condemned the fathers who forced their daughters into the convent, claiming that they were worse than the most infamous tyrants of history, citing no less a figure than Nero.[33]

The wives of Venetian patricians may have enjoyed far more luxuries than their counterparts in the convent, but as Misson and other commentators observed, they were accorded relatively little freedom:

> At present the Women of Quality are shut up so close, that you can scarcely see their Face; not even in the Churches, which are the only places where they usually appear in Publick. When they go abroad, they are shut up in their Gondola's, and accompanied by Two or Three old Women, who never leave them.[34]

In most civic ceremonies, elegantly dressed patrician women were visible, but placed in the background, much like extras on a movie set. Occasionally the wives of the doges were accorded a more prominent role; this was the case, for instance, in 1597 when Dogaressa Morosina Morosini was given a highly theatrical coronation, complete with a female procession.[35]

Coryat attributed this protective attitude toward Venetian wives to anxiety about another segment of the female population: the numerous courtesans who presumably were tolerated both because they helped protect the chastity of Venetian wives and also contributed to the city's revenue.[36] Indeed, courtesans provided a valuable service for the many young men who – like their sisters – were forced to delay or forego marriage altogether in the interest of preserving family wealth.[37] Coryat may have exaggerated when he stated that Venice and the adjacent areas contained at least twenty thousand courtesans, 'esteemd so loose that they are said to open their quivers to every arrow'; regardless, they were surely part of Venice's appeal to male tourists, for 'these amorous Calypsos', as Coryat dubbed them, attracted visitors from 'the remotest part of Christendome'.[38] Coryat was particularly fascinated by the sensory delight provided by the most accomplished and well-bred courtesans: her physical beauty, her elegant gowns, the chains of gold and orient pearls that she wore 'like a second Cleopatra', the perfumed bedding and precious objects in her 'chamber of recreation' – and he was utterly fascinated by the accomplishments of the courtesans in the realm of music and literature:[39]

18

Cortigiana Veneta · *Cortigiana Veneta*

19

Moreover she will endevour to enchaunt thee partly with her melodious
notes that she warbles out upon her lute, which shee fingers with as
laudable a stroake as many men that are excellent professors in the noble
science of Musicke; and partly with that heart-tempting harmony of her
voice. Also thou wilt finde the Venetian Cortezan (if she be a selected
woman indeede) a good Rhetorician, and a most elegant discourser, so
that if she cannot move thee with all these foresaid delights, shee will
assay thy constancy with her Rhetoricall tongue.[40]

We see something of the fascination with the courtesan's body in this engraving from
1594, in which the viewer is allowed to peek under her dress and see the masculine
breeches that some reputedly wore (pl.19). We see here as well the famous chopines
or *zoccoli*: the high wooden platforms, covered with coloured leather, worn by both
courtesan and wives, which made even the shortest woman appear tall (pl.18). James
Howell recounts a story of a gentleman, after having contracted to spend the night with
a courtesan whose height was artificially enhanced by *zoccoli*, awoke the next day and
immediately demanded a refund, since 'she was but half the Woman that had appeerd
to him formerly'.[41] Courtesans may have used all kinds of tricks to fool their clients, but
the astute gentlemen of Venice apparently knew how to bargain for their pleasures and
get the most value for their money.

18
Pair of chopines
Punched kid leather and carved pine
Venice, c.1600
V&A: T.48&A-1914

19
A Courtesan with her Charms Revealed
Pietro Bertelli (d.1621)
Engraving from *Diversarum nationum
habitus*, 1594
V&A: National Art Library

By the fourth decade of the seventeenth century, public opera was becoming one of those pleasurable commodities. John Evelyn (1620-1706), another traveller to Venice, provided this glowing description of a performance of the opera *Ercole in Lidia* at the Teatro Novissimo in 1645:

> That night ... we went to the opera, where comedies and other plays are represented in recitative music by the most excellent musicians, vocal and instrumental, with variety of sceanes painted and contrived with no lesse art than perspective, and machines for flying in the aire, and other wonderfull motion; taken together it is one of the most magnificent and expensive diversions the wit of man can invent.[42]

While opera had been born in the Northern Italian courts in the late sixteenth century, also gaining a foothold in Rome under the patronage of Urban VIII, it was in Venice that it acquired many of the conventions and characteristics that would forever shape the art. There were in fact a number of reasons why Venice provided such fertile ground for opera.[43] Lacking a central court, the prominent families of Venice saw opera as a means of enhancing their own prestige and that of the Republic to which they were so devoted. History may tell us that producers of opera lose money more often than not; however, in Venice opera was a flourishing business in which many eagerly participated, despite the fact that investors rarely reaped significant returns.[44] The noble owners of the theatres, their investors, and the impresarios, poets, musicians, set designers, dancers, cashiers and carpenters they hired, were all part of an industry dedicated to the production of an entertainment that only added to the already substantial allure of Venice's notorious carnival.[45] While Venetian and foreign nobles were certainly enthusiastic consumers of opera, the public theatres in Venice were designed to accommodate a diverse audience. The multiple rows of private boxes stacked on top of one another made it possible for spectators of different classes to enjoy the evening's entertainment without having to mingle with one another, as shown in this diagram of the Teatro SS. Giovanni e Paolo (pl.20).[46] The visual spectacle that John Evelyn so praised was also an important priority. Venetians were particularly fortunate to have a number of their productions designed by the brilliant Giacomo Torelli (1608-78), whose stage machinery made it possible to create the fabulous visual effects so praised by John Evelyn. Our understanding of stage design in early Venetian opera is indebted to the surviving engravings of Torelli's productions, such as this set from the 1643 opera *Venere gelosa* by Francesco Sacrati (1605-50) (pl.21).[47]

Musically, Venice was also well-positioned to support the new genre. Monteverdi had had considerable experience with it during his tenure at Mantua, and his young student, Francesco Cavalli (1602-76) was among the first to write operas for the Venetian stage, ultimately becoming the most esteemed opera composer of the century.[48] It may also have been Cavalli who persuaded Monteverdi not only to revive his *Arianna* (originally presented in Mantua in 1608) for Venice, but also to compose three new operas for the Venice stage, the final one being *L'incoronazione di Poppea*.[49] Notably, archival documents reveal that the Venetian opera orchestra did not include the lush woodwinds, brass and multiple continuo instruments that Monteverdi used in his *L'Orfeo* or would have been heard in Venetian churches on major festivals. Unlike the colourful orchestration used in most modern performances and recordings of Venetian operas, the orchestras in the theatres would typically have included only a small group of strings (pl.23), a couple of theorbos or archlutes (pl.24), several harpsichords (pl.22) and an occasional trumpet.[50]

20
Floor plan for the Teatro SS. Giovanni e Paolo
Carlo Fontana (1634/38–1714)
Print from c.1690 (original made 1654)
Sir John Soane's Museum, London, vol.117/34

21
Set design for Bacchus' temple in the opera *Venere gelosa*, or *Jealous Venus*, performed at the Teatro Novissimo in Venice in 1643
After Giacomo Torelli (1608–78)
Etching, late 17th century
V&A: S.3079–2009

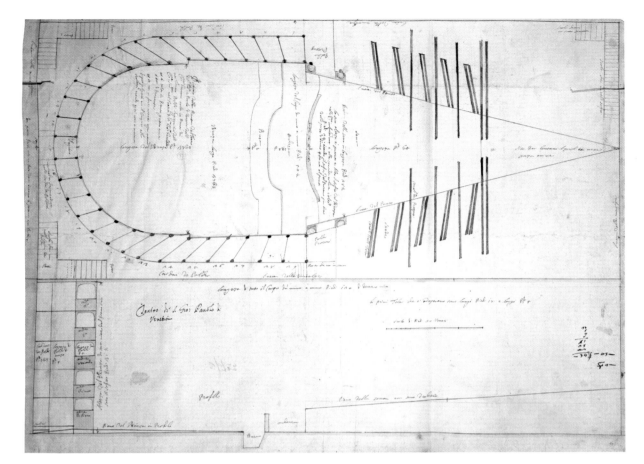

20

Le Temple de BACCHUS dans l'Isle de Naxos, C'est une decoration du premier Acte de l'Opera de VENUS IALOUSE representé a Venise. Inventé par Jacques Torelly de Fano en Italie, et Gravé par Aueline a Paris

21

23

24

22 (and detail)
Harpsichord
Giovanni Baffo (active mid-16th century)
Pine case, inner face veneered with rosewood,
partly inlaid with boxwood, cypress soundboard
Venice, 1574
V&A: 6007:1 to 3-1859

23
Viola
Antonio (b.1540) and Girolamo Amati (1561–1630)
Cremona, c.1620
Royal Academy of Music Museum, London,
2002.863

24
Archlute (theorbo)
Cristoforo Choc (active 17th century)
Pine, ivory, rosewood and ebony, 1650
V&A: 7756-1862

VENICE

Intima si cantum simulat præcordia mulcet,
Ipsam animam sensim si canit Anna rapit.
Iacobus Picinus Venetus faciebat Venis

25

LE
GLORIE
Della Signora
ANNA RENZI
ROMANA·

IN VENETIA, M. DC. XLIV.

Appreſſo Gio: Batiſta Surian . Con Licenza de'Sup.

26

The emphasis, thus, was less on rich orchestral timbre than on the drama, the visual effects, and, above all, on the quality of the singers. While there was no shortage of male singers among the freelance musicians in Venice, women – who were forbidden from singing in church – were more of a novelty and thus became objects of fascination.[51] Anna Renzi (1620–61) (pl.25) became so popular that her admirers published a book of poems in her honour, noting in particular her performance as Octavia in *L'incoronazione di Poppea* (pl.26).[52] The contract that she signed with the impresario Girolamo Lappoli in December of 1643 shows not only that the best female singers could demand high salaries, but could demand other benefits: Renzi would still earn half her salary even if she were ill or the performance was cancelled, and the theatre also paid for all of her costumes and provided her with a box in the theatre that she could use throughout the carnival season.

Many of the writers who praised Renzi's performances with laudatory sonnets had also become involved in another essential part of opera composition: the crafting of librettos. Arguably the most important member of the dramaturgical team, the librettist was not only responsible for constructing the plot and characters and creating a text, but also made fundamental decisions about the visual elements – sets, special effects and dance. While professional librettists would assume this responsibility in the second half of the seventeenth century, initially the task was undertaken as an avocation by nobles, diplomats and lawyers (such as Busenello), who were members of one of the period's most important academies, the Accademia degli Incogniti.

Founded in 1630 by the Venetian nobleman Francesco Loredano, the Incogniti dominated Venetian publishing in the middle part of the century, penning histories, poems, letters and academic discourses, as well as writing librettos for Venetian public opera.[53] Known for their heterodox and libertine views and their championship of forbidden books, the Incogniti also included among their members a number of poets who had experience writing poetry intended for music. It was a subgroup of the academy, the Accademia degli Unisoni, who welcomed Barbara Strozzi (1619-77) into their meetings.[54] The adopted (and perhaps illegitimate) daughter of the poet and librettist Giulio Strozzi (1583–1682), Barbara was a superb singer and composer, whose eight volumes of printed music represent some of the best vocal chamber music of the period. Her portrait (pl.27) by the painter Bernardo Strozzi (no relation), interpreted by some as

27

VENICE

SABINA POPPÆA

28

evidence that she was a courtesan, provides more than a hint of why (as apparent in the gently misogynistic accounts of Unisoni meetings) the members might have found this combination of female beauty and musical skill both seductive and intimidating. Strozzi's brilliant settings of poetry by her adoptive father and colleagues, on the other hand, reveals an awareness of her power as a singer and composer, a sardonic sense of humour, and an ability to manipulate the men who both championed and mocked her.[55]

L'INCORONAZIONE DI POPPEA

Given the allure of female singers, it is perhaps not surprising that Busenello would have turned to Poppea Sabina (CE 30–60) as the heroine for his one and only collaboration with Monteverdi (pl.28). In basing his opera on an episode in Roman history (CE 58–65) as described by Cornelius Tacitus, Suetonius and Dio Cassius, Busenello eschewed the mythological topics that had dominated Venetian opera initially (his previous two operas set by Cavalli were inspired by Ovid and Virgil respectively), perhaps seeing in Roman imperial history an opportunity to make a different sort of political statement. Venice had long viewed herself as the true heir of Rome's considerable glory – 'another Rome on the water' – as Busenello himself once described the city.[56] Imperial Rome could be invoked to proclaim another Venetian trope: a Christian nation that had never been conquered, resisted the pull of monarchy and avoided female rule was not merely Rome's equal, but was her superior. In fact, just prior to the premiere of *L'incoronazione di Poppea* (pl.29), several Incogniti writers penned novels and plays that focused on the crimes of Poppea's predecessors: the promiscuous Messalina and the overly ambitious Agrippina, mother of Nero.[57] Busenello would emulate his colleagues by casting aspersions on the only character in the historical narrative that was utterly blameless – Nero's wife Octavia.[58] In the opera, the Empress Octavia coerces Poppea's husband Otho into disguising himself as a woman so that he might sneak into the garden and murder the sleeping Poppea; the plot is thwarted by the fortuitous appearance of Love, Poppea's guardian angel. Moreover, throughout the opera the invented characters – soldiers, servants, nurses and even the allegorical figures in the prologue – provide a subtle, but damning commentary on court life and its associated intrigues, which only underscored Venice's superiority to her noble ancestor.

It may have been the moral flaws of virtually every character in the opera that so inspired the elderly Monteverdi. By this time, he had proven his mastery over every musical genre and nuance of musical and dramatic expression, bringing to his final opera profound insights into human nature and an ability to plumb the depths of human passions with every note (pl.31). Monteverdi vividly portrays Poppea's eloquence and powers of persuasion, her ability both to seduce and to feign virtue, contrasting her rich vocalism and sensual erotic dissonances with the austere laments sung by the rejected and ostensibly frigid Octavia.[59] He captures as well the inevitable impact of Poppea's charms on the men who desire her, finding musical equivalents for Otho's outbursts of jealousy, indecision and self-hatred and Nero's (pl.30) petulant eruptions of anger and erotic excesses. Even the Stoic philosopher Seneca evoked a complex and ambivalent response from Monteverdi: appearing at first as a peddler of platitudes represented with an exaggerated and often pompous musical rhetoric, Seneca, on the verge of suicide in the second act, sings movingly to his followers, who subsequently lament his passing with heartrending chromaticism, all the while acknowledging their considerable relief at not having to give up their own lives.[60] Indeed, the death of this ostensible guardian of morality signals the beginning of music's ostensible triumph. It is no coincidence that Seneca's suicide is followed immediately by two of Monteverdi's most marvellously erotic duets. First, a young servant couple celebrates their sexual awakening; then, as we

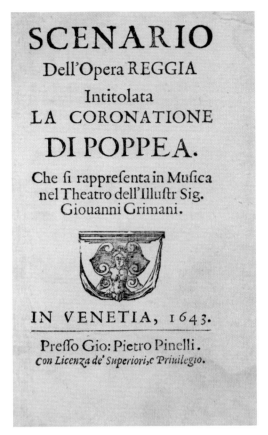

SCENARIO
Dell'Opera REGGIA
Intitolata
LA CORONATIONE
DI POPPEA.
Che si rapprefenta in Mufica
nel Theatro dell'Illuftr Sig.
Giouanni Grimani.

IN VENETIA, 1643.

Preffo Gio: Pietro Pinelli.
Con Licenza de' Superiori,e Priuilegio.

29

28
Sabina Poppaea
Fontainebleau School
Oil on canvas, c.1570
Museum of Art and History, Geneva, 1841-0001

29
Scenario dell'opera reggia intitolata
La Coronatione di Poppea
(Scenario of L'incoronazione di Poppea)
Francesco Busenello (1598–1659)
Published by Pinelli, Venice, 1643
Marciana National Library, DRAMM 910.8

noted at the outset, Nero gleefully announces the death of Seneca to his companion the poet Lucan; the two young men, exulting in the sheer pleasure of singing, abandon themselves to an obsessive, erotically charged ostinato bass in which they meditate upon the beauty of Poppea's mouth. And it may be here as well that we can understand something of the opera's political message: the real Lucan, Seneca's nephew Marcus Annaeus Lucanus (CE 39–65) and author of *Pharsalus*, a history of the Roman civil war, was much admired in seventeenth-century Venice as a champion of Republican causes.[61] The evils of monarchy, the dangers of female power, and the rights of men to enjoy sensual pleasures – principles dear to Venetians – all find expression here.

Critics have long argued about the morally ambivalent message in *L'incoronazione di Poppea*; indeed, it may well be that ambiguity – along with the glorious music – that has inspired so many revivals of the opera in recent decades. Are we to rejoice in the happy ending, despite the death of Seneca and the banishment of Octavia? Or are we to assume that audience members, who would have known that Nero would later kill the pregnant Poppea with a violent kick, might have extracted a moral from the story – namely that unrestrained female ambition and lust always proves fatal? Or maybe we should simply view this as the triumph of Love, who proclaims her superiority in the prologue and who even appears as the *deus ex machina* to prevent Poppea's murder, thus enacting the counterfeiting of vice and virtue that Misson would later observe during carnival. As we hear Nero and the newly crowned empress intertwine their voices in the opera's luscious final duet, it is hard to condemn the sensual delights and imperial crimes that inspired Monteverdi to write some of his most remarkable music.[62] That Venice's purity could be celebrated by transferring her voices to Imperial Rome shows something of the enduring capacity of the Republic to weave seductive myths about herself. The goddess Venus would surely have approved.

30
Bust of Emperor Nero
Bronze and ormolu
Italy, 17th century
V&A: 991-1882

31
Il Nerone, beginning of Act II
Manuscript copy of Monteverdi's opera
today known as *L'incoronazione di Poppea*
Acts I and III copied by Francesco Cavalli's
wife in the early 1650s
Contains additional notes by Cavalli
Marciana National Library, 1641-1660 MSS
(=09963) It. IV, 439

30

31

VENICE

32

32
Card players and fortune teller
Nicolas Régnier (1591–1667)
Oil on canvas, 1620–5
Museum of Art and History, Geneva, 1974-0011

This everyday subject depicts the darker side of
Roman and Venetian society in the seventeenth
century. The theme of gambling and fortune
tellers is directly inspired by the paintings of
Michelangelo Merisi da Caravaggio, as is the use
of chiaroscuro (alternating light and shadow).

33 (and detail)
Games board for chess and backgammon
Woods, including chestnut, with ivory inlay
Spain or Italy, 16th century
V&A: 7849-1861

This elaborate games board would have been
used by rich patricians either at home or in a
Ridotto (a public house in Venice used as a casino
or place of entertainment).

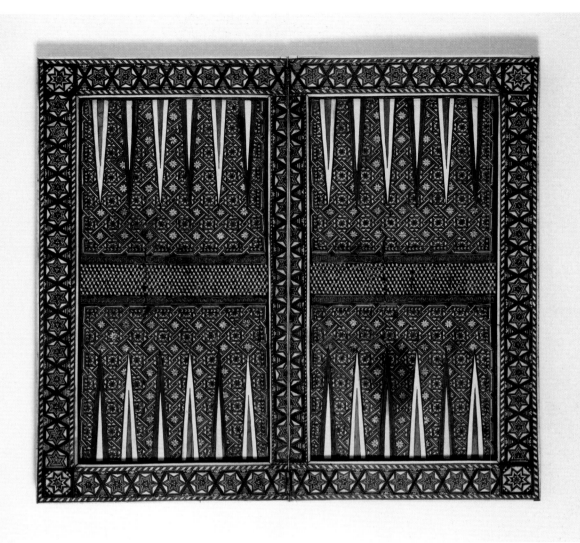

33

VENICE

34

VENICE

35

34
Ewer
Bronze, engraved, with dragon handle, depicting busts in medallions and signs of the Zodiac
Venice, c.1540
V&A: 8430-1863

Luxurious dining was part of the Venetian way of life; for the nobility, meals were an occasion to show off good taste in food and dining accessories. This ewer would have been used to clean the diner's hands between courses. Although forks were more commonly used in the seventeenth century, the ewer continued to be displayed in the dining room as a symbol of wealth.

35
Necklace
Rose-cut diamonds set in gold, the backs of the settings enamelled
Western Europe, late 17th century
V&A: M.88-1975

This necklace is typical of luxury Venetian jewellery made during the mid-to-late seventeenth century. The enamel catch is a later addition.

Femina Veneta,

36

37

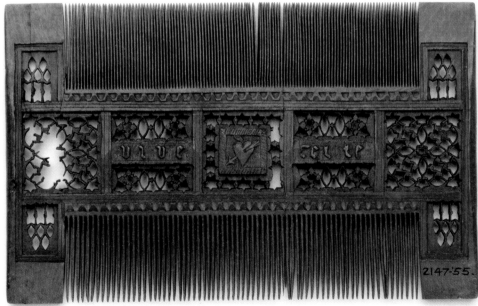

38

36
Femina Veneta
Pietro Bertelli (d.1621)
Engraving from *Diversarum nationum habitus*, 1589
V&A: National Art Library

37
Box (Casket)
Softwood, veneered with woods and bone (some pieces stained green)
Venice, 16th century
V&A: 2568-1856

38
Comb
Carved boxwood, inscribed 'Vive celle/ que jayme' (Long live the woman I love)
France, 16th century
V&A: 2147-1855

Pietro Bertelli's *Diversarum nationum habitus* depicts the costumes and habits of different Venetian women in the sixteenth century, including courtesans, widows and married women. This young, fashionable noblewoman sits in the sun on the *Altana* (a Venetian roof terrace) in order to bleach her hair. Caskets, jewellery and combs were typical of the accessories belonging to a courtesan. These combs were often used as love tokens or gifts. Made in France, they were later prized by collectors throughout Europe and often formed part of curiosity cabinets.

39
Scene from *Les Fêtes Vénitiennes*
Opéra-ballet by André Campra and directed
by Robert Carsen, with costume designs
by Petra Reinhardt
Théâtre National de l'Opéra Comique, 2014

These costumes, designed by Petra Reinhardt,
were inspired by the engraving in plate 19 (p.31),
which shows a Venetian courtesan lifting her skirt.
The designer created similar skirts that could
be opened or closed, revealing high platform
shoes reminiscent of chopines (pl.18).

Uxbridge

Southampton House

Grays Inn fields

Clarkenwell

South fields

Montague house

Holborn

Lincoln Inn fields

Lower Lincoln Inn fields

St James's field

Piazza

St James s fields

the Mase

RIVER THAMES

Scotland yard

St James's

Parke

Westminster Bridge

Parlement staires

Whitehall staires

Privy Stairs

Lambeth marsh

Bank side

Green Walk

High Street

LAMBETH

Lambeth

Horse Ferry

Lambeth bridge

Lambeth Ferry

THE RIVER

Kennington

SOUTHWARK

Places of Southwark
1 St Mary Overs
2 St Olaves
3 St Thomas's
4 St George's
5 St Magdalen's
6 The Old Abby
7 Winchester house
8 The Kings Bench
9 The Marshallsea
10 The Bare garden

St George's Field

Blackman St

Kennington

LONDON

2

GEORGE FRIDERIC HANDEL
1685–1759

Rinaldo

Rinaldo and Goffredo are Christian noblemen engaged in a war against the Saracen King of Jerusalem, Argante. In a bid to defeat the Christian army, the sorceress Armida kidnaps Goffredo's daughter Almirena, who is engaged to marry Rinaldo. While Rinaldo resolves to rescue Almirena, Argante starts to fall in love with her, enraging Armida. She tries and fails to seduce Rinaldo. Helped by Goffredo, Rinaldo eventually rescues Almirena and the Christians conquer Jerusalem.

41

INTRODUCTION

ROBERT CARSEN

When Glyndebourne Festival asked me to direct *Rinaldo* for the 2011 festival, I had already staged several Handel operas (including *Orlando* and *Semele* for the Aix-en-Provence Festival and *Alcina* for the Paris Opéra), and, like one of the characters in his operas of enchantment, I had fallen completely under the composer's spell. His unique ability to create intense, complex, psychological theatre, set to music of often breath-taking beauty, turned me into an addict from my first encounter.

Audiences often come away from performances of a Handel stage work (I use this term to include the oratorios as well as the operas), with the feeling of having been in contact with the characters, their desires and ambitions in a more intense way than with almost any other composer's work. When Handel is composing his most intimate psychological studies, he almost invariably uses the *da capo* aria form (meaning 'from the beginning', involving an 'A' section followed by a 'B' section followed by the repeat of the 'A' section, but this time usually with additional vocal ornamentation), to create arias that are sometimes much longer than normal. In *Alcina,* for example, the sorceress' great Act II aria 'Ah mio cor' can last between 10 and 14 minutes (depending on who is conducting and singing). Since some of the principal characters may have more than six arias over the course of an evening, the audience spends a great deal of time in their company, and can gain great understanding of their often contradictory desires and actions: the audience, if you like, has a chance to psychoanalyse the characters.

Handel also developed what I like to call 'the theatre of the lie'. Often in Handel's theatre world, characters find that they cannot tell the truth to the person in front of them, perhaps because they once reciprocated that person's love and have recently ceased to do so. And so, perhaps to spare the other person's feelings, or out of cowardly motives, they prefer to lie to them — usually to the most exquisite and heart-breaking music. This prevents their true feelings from being discovered, at least for the time being, while making the emotional situation of the opera richer and more complex. Action in a Handel opera tends to be advanced through the recitatives, whereas the arias are the moments for psychological introspection. As we have seen, the *da capo* aria form (which almost invariably results in a character leaving the stage after his or her aria), creates an emotional landscape of its own, but it is important for the director not to lose sight of the rhythm of the whole piece and to be careful about the way in which the individual moments of emotional development are knitted together to make the whole.

Handel often employs a post-Shakespearean structure of alternating tragic scenes with comic ones. This is another reason why so many modern directors love to work on his operas. The characters are frequently drawn from archetypes (for example a queen, a prince, a magician, a knight and a shepherdess), and the plots are often complex and not always easy to situate. This may lead to a liberal use of irony in a staging, not only as a response to the dramatic situations but also as a tool for creating a world within which to set them. We know that in Handel's day audiences did not take the dramatic content of their operas as seriously as we do today. We know also that during performances they didn't remain in their seats, that the lighting and costume may not have changed, that realism played no part in the theatrical experience and that certain people came into the auditorium simply to hear a particular star singer shine in a bravura aria. But despite these massive differences in performance practice, I cannot believe that Handel could have had the prolonged and intense success that he had (particularly in London), if audiences had not recognized what a magician of the emotions he was.

Rinaldo was composed in 1711 and was Handel's first opera for London. It took the city by storm and was the most popular of his works to be performed during his lifetime. Giacomo Rossi's libretto (set to a scenario prepared by Aaron Hill), explores the popular theme of duty versus desire. It is taken from Torquato Tasso's epic *Gerusalemme Liberata*, following the adventures of a knight of the First Crusade, Rinaldo, in his attempts to follow his duty and resist sensual temptation. This theme was much explored by other composers both before and after Handel, such as Lully (in his masterpiece *Armide*), Campra, Vivaldi, Traetta or Gluck. According to Rossi,

Handel composed the opera in record time — about two weeks. In fact Handel borrowed music he had previously composed for other stage works, such as *Agrippina* and *Acis and Galatea*, as was quite common practice at the time. Indeed the most famous aria of all, Almirena's 'Lascia ch'io pianga', had already appeared in Handel's oratorio *Il trionfo del tempo e del disinganno*.

Although the opera contains some of Handel's greatest music, Rossi's libretto is universally considered to be one of the weakest Handel ever had to compose to. I remember once describing it to Gideon Davey, the designer of the production, as being like a china plate that someone had accidentally dropped, picked up the pieces and stuck together in any old order. There are so many dead ends and false starts in the narration that it seemed to me as if it were a child who was telling the story. This observation led us to the idea that we could perhaps imagine our Rinaldo as a bullied schoolboy who escapes into his own fantasy world, imagining himself to be a great hero. This immediately helped us find a tone for telling the story: we could take Rinaldo seriously as a hero and explore his heroic ambitions when we needed to, but also not have to make sense of the numerous implausible sections in the libretto.

We first developed these ideas in our staging of the overture, where a pupil is being teased and bullied by his classmates for being sweet on a girl. In a further injustice he is then punished by two teachers for his classmates' misbehaviour. In the day-dream which follows his punishment, the schoolboy becomes the heroic knight Rinaldo, in whom all the other knights' hopes lie. His girlfriend is now called Almirena and in the first scene her father Goffredo begs Rinaldo to lead the Crusaders to victory against the Saracen army, promising the young knight his daughter's hand in marriage if he should succeed. The Saracen army become frightening girls, by turns wicked and wild or seductive and inviting. They are led by the two teachers who punished Rinaldo, who become the villains Armida and Argante. In the schoolboy's fantasy it is natural that Armida should hate Rinaldo and try everything in her power to seduce him, while ending up madly in love with him instead.

We thought that setting this production in an English public school would be amusing and recognizable to the audience. Having chosen that as our starting point, we then decided how the space could develop, from the school room to a bicycle yard, a dormitory, a science lab and a locker room. The opera reaches its climax in a huge battle scene between the opposing forces. There is no chorus in *Rinaldo* and as we were only able to have a relatively small number of actors/dancers in our show, we decided to stage this final battle as a football game. This allowed us to make reference in a light-hearted way to some of the important issues present in the opera of opposing cultures and religions: our game was therefore played with the globe of the world being kicked around as the football (which originally started life on the teacher's desk). Perhaps the schoolboy's class was studying the First Crusade when the day-dream began, and so we ended the show with Rinaldo, having won the game, the girl and the day, now alone in his classroom pensively turning the globe on the teacher's desk while looking questioningly at the audience....

Directors are story-tellers. We are a bridge between the stage and the audience, and our attempts to bring stories to life for a particular night (or even for a particular knight), can lead us to adventures which are as complex as those which Handel's eponymous hero undergoes. We have to meet and destroy our monsters and try and rescue the heroine. It is a thrilling responsibility to have and a very rewarding one too.

40 (pp.50–1; detail)
Londini Angliae Regni Metropolis Delineatio, Accuratissima Autore F. De Witt Cum Privilegio
Frederick de Wit (1629–1706)
Engraving on paper
Amsterdam, 1689–1702
V&A: 24431

41 (p.54)
Brenda Rae as Armida in *Rinaldo*
Directed by Robert Carsen with set designs by Gideon Davey
Glyndebourne Festival, 2011

42
Scene from *Rinaldo*
Directed by Robert Carsen with set designs by Gideon Davey
Glyndebourne Festival, 2011

43
Final battle scene from *Rinaldo*
Directed by Robert Carsen with set designs by Gideon Davey
Glyndebourne Festival, 2011

42

43

LONDON: WORLD CITY–
HANDEL AND *RINALDO*

DANIEL SNOWMAN

45

'London [is] the chiefest Emporium, or Town of Trade in the World ...
the fairest and most opulent City at this day in all Europe, perhaps in
the Whole World.'[1]

It would have been hard to take issue with this judgement from 1707. Or that from
A Foreigners Guide to London some years later which pronounced London 'the Metropolis
of Great-Britain, the Seat of her Monarchs, the greatest, richest, most populous and most
flourishing City in Europe'. This was the city in which the 25-year-old George Frideric
Handel (born Georg Friedrich Händel) arrived for the first time in autumn 1710
(pl.45 and 46).

Handel (pl.48) was born and raised in Halle, a small town in Saxony in eastern
Germany, not far from Leipzig.[2] In his late teens, he travelled north to play in the opera
orchestra in Hamburg and went on to spend his early twenties in Italy where he further
honed his gifts as performer and composer, absorbing the rich musical culture of Florence,
Venice, Rome and Naples. He returned to Germany in 1710, armed with recommendations
to several of the most brilliant courts, notably that of the Elector of Hanover who took
the gifted young man into his service. A few months later, Handel requested and obtained
permission to visit that great commercial hub of the musical world and of much else
besides – London.[3]

46

LONDON – WORLD CITY

With a population approaching 600,000, London was the largest city in Europe at the
time.[4] Its closest rival, Paris, seems to have had a population of well under half a million,
while other great European cities such as Naples or Amsterdam were smaller still.[5]
Norwich, England's second city at the time, had a mere thirty thousand or thereabouts.[6]

In some ways, London in the early eighteenth century was not unlike that of the
early twenty-first century. Packed, busy, a great commercial and cultural capital then as
now, London was a vast, sprawling, bustling metropolis, a city with worldwide interests
and connections, home to a huge and growing mixed multitude. As in our own times,
the city housed (or failed to house) many who struggled to survive in considerable poverty,
while others, endowed with great wealth, would sometimes undertake ambitious but
risky investments that might issue in huge profits or economic débacle. Gin gradually came
to prove as addictive to some as heroin or cocaine today, while a newly combative and
partisan press would gleefully report on the doings, misdoings and undoings of prominent
social, cultural and political leaders, reinforced by such sharp-penned satirists as
Jonathan Swift (1667–1745), Alexander Pope (1688–1744) and Daniel Defoe (1660–1731).

For a 'person of quality' (the kind Handel no doubt set out to meet), life could
take on an appearance of unprecedented comfort and opulence. By the early eighteenth
century, the old-fashioned doublet and hose had long been discarded and any
fashionably-minded gentleman in London would by now be appearing in the latest
three-piece suit of coat, waistcoat and knee-breeches (pl.47), topped by an elegant and
expensively powdered wig, his wife sporting a tall headdress and perhaps wearing
a mantua with elbow-length cuffed sleeves and ruffles hanging down to the wrists. Both
men and women might be wearing perfumed gloves and carry a pocket 'mouchoir'
as they welcomed visitors to their townhouse, in or adjacent to one of the smart new
squares springing up in what would come to be called London's 'West End'. Once inside,
an impressive sense of light would have been created by long sash windows, brightly
painted plastered walls and an abundance of sconces, candlesticks and mirrors. Personal
comfort was enhanced by cushioned couches, settees and sofas, the silk coverings perhaps
imported from India or the Levant, and guests might be invited by their hosts to take a

44 (pp.58–9)
Royal Opera House auditorium, London
Main building and auditorium built in 1857–8

45
Fresh Wharf, London Bridge
William Marlow (1740–1813)
Oil on canvas, 1762–3
Museum of London, 50.31

46
*St Paul's Cathedral by Sir Christopher Wren
(1632–1723): Elevation of the West front*
Colen Campbell (1676–1729)
Engraving from *Vitruvius Britannicus*, 1717, pl.2
Royal Institute of British Architects, London

47

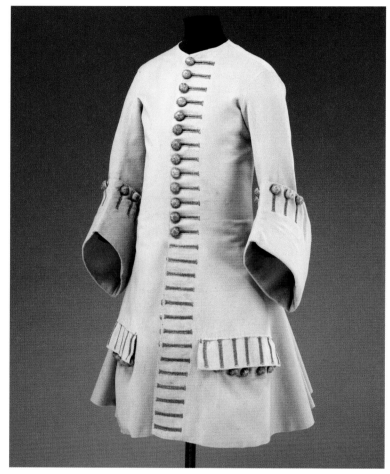

47
Coat
Wool, silk, linen, linen thread, silver thread;
hand-woven broadcloth, silk and buckram,
passementerie, hand-sewn
England, 1695–1705
V&A: T.30-1938

48
G.F. Handel
After Bartholomew Dandridge (1691–c.1755)
Oil on canvas, after 1720
Fitzwilliam Museum, University of
Cambridge, PDP 693

48

LONDON

49

49
Interior of a London Coffee-house
Unknown artist
Gouache on paper, 1650–1750
British Museum, London, 1931,0613.2

50
Tea-pot
TL (unidentified maker's mark)
Engraved: 'This Siluer tea Pott was presented
to ye Com[mi]tte[e] / of ye East India Cumpany
[sic] by ye Right Honou[rabl]e / George Lord
Berkeley of Berkeley Castle / A member of that
Honourable & worthy Society and A True Hearty
Louer of them'
Silver with leather handle
London, 1670–1
V&A: M.399-1921

51
Thomas Britton
John Wollaston (active c.1742–75)
Oil on canvas, 1703
Foundling Museum, London

50

seat and have a drink – from the most elegant china or silverware – of tea, chocolate or above all, coffee – all of which were luxury products of a developing empire (pl.50).

Coffee houses abounded in the London of Handel's time, and many of the best-known were to be found in and around the rapidly growing Covent Garden area. At some of the more elegant establishments, lawyers would congregate, while at others, men of the cloth. Tories here; Whigs there. In 1706, the merchant Thomas Twining bought Tom's Coffee House in the Strand; there he sold not only coffee but also the finest tea in London, a reputation that was maintained for centuries thereafter by the company that still bears his name. Will's, on the corner of Bow Street and Russell Street, was where the poet John Dryden (1631–1700) had regularly held court, though by Handel's time its popularity was being overtaken by Button's across the way.

51

These were, in effect, gentleman's clubs where, according to the satirist Tom Brown (1662–1704): 'several knights-errant come to seat themselves at the same table without knowing one another, and yet talk as familiarly together as if they had been of many years acquaintance'.[7] Some were essentially gambling dens where the latest beaus would assemble to show off their finery to each other (and might be waited upon 'by beautiful, neat, well-dressed, and amiable, but very dangerous nymphs').[8] Ned Ward, typically, relished the seedier side of things. 'There was a rabble going hither and thither,' he wrote in *The London Spy*, 'reminding me of a swarm of rats in a ruinous cheesestore'.[9]

Here, the gentlemen would relax, eat, drink, smoke their clay pipes and take snuff (pl.49). And if the mood took them, they might sing a few bawdy catches together. Music making? Hardly. But more fun – and cheaper – than an evening going to the opera or listening to professionals.

> MUSICK'S a Crotchet the Sober think Vain;
> The *Fiddle's* a Wooden Projection;
> *Tunes* are but flirts of a Whimsical Brain,
> Which the Bottle brings best to Perfection.
> *Musicians* are Half Witted, Merry, and Mad;
> The same are all those that admire 'em;
> They're Fools if they Play, unless they're well Paid;
> And the others are Blockheads to Hire-'em.[12]

London also provided for those with more elevated musical tastes. Not only opera, but inexpensive public concerts pioneered by a modest, cultured charcoal maker (or 'small coal-man') called Thomas Britton (pl.51) who adapted the loft in his Clerkenwell home into a small concert hall and for 30 years presented regular concerts there until his death in 1714. Handel was said to be a regular visitor and he may well have met – and perhaps played alongside – the versatile German-born composer Johann Christoph Pepusch (1667–1752), one of Britton's regular performers (chiefly remembered today as arranger of the music in *The Beggar's Opera*). These concerts, wrote the diarist Ralph Thoresby (1658–1725) in 1712, were 'the best in town' and were attended by, among others, 'most foreigners and many persons of distinction'.[11]

People poured into London: young men from all over the country looking for work; young women seeking husbands to sustain them or any other form of livelihood available; and uncounted visitors – immigrants some of them – from across the water. Many of these in Handel's time were Protestant Huguenots, originally from France who, having settled in and around the Spitalfields area of town, set themselves up as silk weavers. Then there were the Dutch and Spaniards, as well as the Italians, and Jewish merchants such as the Duke of Marlborough's friend Solomon de Medina – the first Jew to be knighted in England. Others hailed from the German-speaking world: Pepusch, for example, or the Swiss impresario of German descent, John Jacob Heidegger, who ran the new theatre in the Haymarket (pl.52) in Handel's day but who was better known for the masquerade balls he promoted there than for opera (pl.53).

The Lübeck-born Godfrey Kneller (1646–1723), court painter since the time of King Charles II, was still fulfilling this role under Queen Anne when Handel arrived in 1710. For a truly vivid account of life in London at the time – the bull-baiting, the footpads who might rob you after dark, the latest kind of alarm clock, the spas people liked to visit or what it was like walking across London bridge or buying a book in the vicinity of the newly-completed St Paul's Cathedral – Frankfurt-born traveller and scholar Zacharias Conrad von Uffenbach details it all in his account of *London in 1710*.[12] Many of the Germans in London were poor, ill-educated refugees, among them the 12,000 or more (mostly Calvinist) from the Middle Rhine region who, fleeing the European wars of the time, turned up in London by the boatload in 1709–10. Handel was far from the only foreigner in town when he disembarked in 1710.

London's river was regarded then much as its airports are today: the Thames was a busy gateway for goods and people, and an important link to and from the wider world. The nation's very lifeblood – its extensive and growing international trade – depended to a considerable extent upon the navigability of the waterway. But this was that same river that (as some saw it) led to the city being overcrowded by immigrants: unwelcome foreigners who arrived to take 'our' jobs and feed off 'our' welfare benefits. Sound familiar? This was how a broadside ballad of the time put it:

> It once was Decraed,
> to make a Collection,
> for Strangers protection,
> In order to feed,
> and nourish them here:
> Which encourag'd them so,
> That from hence they'll not go,
> but live on our shore;
> And ruine all Labour,
> And ruine all Labour,
> which pinches the Poor.[13]

However, Defoe poured his satirical scorn upon those who imagined there had ever been, or could ever been, some kind of 'pure' Englishness. On the contrary, said Defoe defiantly (in *The True-Born Englishman*), we English were the product of wave upon wave of immigration.[14]

> The Romans first with Julius Cæsar came,
> Including all the nations of that name,
> Gauls, Greeks, and Lombards, and, by computation,
> Auxiliaries or slaves of every nation.
> With Hengist, Saxons; Danes with Sueno came,
> In search of plunder, not in search of fame.
> Scots, Picts, and Irish from the Hibernian shore,
> And conquering William brought the Normans o'er.
> All these their barbarous offspring left behind,
> The dregs of armies, they of all mankind;
> Blended with Britons, who before were here,
> Of whom the Welsh ha' blessed the character.
> From this amphibious ill-born mob began
> That vain ill-natured thing, an Englishman.

52
Exterior view of the Italian Opera House at the Haymarket 'as it appeared before the fire June 17, 1789'
William Capon (1757–1827), engraved by Charles John Smith (1803–38)
c.18th century
V&A: S.4171-2009

53
A Masquerade at the King's Theatre, Haymarket
Giuseppe Grisoni (1699–1769)
Oil on canvas, c.1724
V&A: P.22-1948

52

53

The customs, surnames, languages, and manners
Of all these nations are their own explainers:
Whose relics are so lasting and so strong,
They ha' left a shibboleth upon our tongue,
By which with easy search you may distinguish
Your Roman-Saxon-Danish-Norman English.

And he might have added 'German'.

THEATRE, MUSIC AND THE ARTS

In much of continental Europe, cultural life was essentially financed and controlled
by the local ecclesiastical or political authorities: what we might today dub the church
or the state. Thus, Handel's early musical training came from the organist at Halle's
Liebfrauenkirche, the late Gothic church that still dominates the Halle marketplace (and
where you can still see the Reichel organ on which he played as a youngster). Aged 17
he went on to become the organist at the nearby Calvinist church. During Handel's
all-important years in Italy, this shrewd young German Protestant managed to have his
experience and career (and purse) enriched by the attentions of a succession of Catholic
dignitaries. The Venice-born Cardinal Ottoboni, for example, whose protégés included
Antonio Vivaldi (1678–1741) and Alessandro Scarlatti (1660–1725), and who famously set
up a friendly keyboard competition between Handel and Scarlatti's son Domenico. It
was through Ottoboni that young Handel also met Arcangelo Corelli (1653–1713). While
in Rome, Handel was also 'much and often at the palaces of two Cardinals, Colonna and
Pamphili' according to his first biographer John Mainwaring.[15] As for state control of the
arts, this was evident on the grandest scale at the court of King Louis XIV in France,
and Handel's first professional appointment (like that of his exact contemporary Johann
Sebastian Bach (1685–1750) and many another of the time) was as Kapellmeister to a
local ruler: in his case, Prince George, the Elector of Hanover.

In England, things were different. Here, the monarchy had undergone a series
of formidable disruptions, starting with the civil wars of the 1640s, the execution
of the king and the brief Cromwellian Protectorate. Some rulers, it is true, enjoyed
patronizing the arts and theatre, notably King Charles II after the restoration of the Stuart
monarchy in 1660 or King William III's co-regnant Queen Mary 30 years later. In the
early 1700s the frail Queen Anne (see pl.65) could be kindly towards the leading artists
of her time (including Handel, to whom she allotted a pension). But none of these
monarchs – much less the shakily established Protestant church – was in any position to
take serious control of the arts. Thus, the London to which Handel came was going
through a period of considerable political turmoil: a commercial capital in which the
arts, like much else, had to respond to an invigorating and sometimes chilly market
economy, allied to an emerging system of aristocratic patronage.[16]

One can see why Handel wanted to come to London. The city would have been
an obvious target for any talented, adventurous young man from small-town continental
Europe. But there is no evidence that Handel had any particular contract to draw him
to London and we are not even sure when he arrived, where he stayed, or with whom – if
anyone – he had had any prior contact. Looking back to the London of Handel's first visit,
we celebrate the theatrical imagination of playwrights William Congreve (1670–1729)
and William Wycherley (1641–1716), the satirical pens of Defoe and Swift, the portraiture
of Kneller and the buildings of Christopher Wren (1632–1723) and Nicholas Hawksmoor
(1661–1736). But the leading creative figures of the period were essentially independent
entrepreneurs selling their talents as best they could in a cultural marketplace that

remained for the most part largely unregulated. If wealthy aristocrats chose to patronize your work you might thrive; if not, you were in danger of being thrown back on the economic scrapheap.

One person who learned this the hard way was that formidably talented soldier, playwright, architect and landscape gardener John Vanbrugh (1664–1726; pl.54). Vanbrugh had a vision: he would design, build and run a new theatre – the 'Queen's Theatre' in the Haymarket – and make it the first in Britain to be devoted to the public performance of all-sung opera.[17] There was of course nothing new about having music on the English theatrical stage. Shakespeare had written songs into his plays, while Nell Gwyn was as renowned for her singing as for her acting and her other accomplishments. During the Restoration era (1660–90), opera – or drama-with-music – had been produced by London's two officially licensed theatres in Dorset Garden and Drury Lane, and a shrewd promoter could mount a popular comedy and, with the profits, put on a few performances of a multi-media extravaganza (or 'semi-opera') such as *King Arthur* or *The Fairy Queen*. For a few years following the premature death of composer Henry Purcell (1659–95), sharp-eyed promoters such as Christopher Rich were not slow to note the growing popularity in the great courts of the continent of all-sung Italian opera. But could this complex art form, with its singers and dancers, its 'scenes and machines' and its props, costumes and orchestra, transfer successfully to England? Common sense suggested at best only the occasional production of opera alongside a more regular (and profitable) diet of spoken drama.

Vanbrugh was nevertheless determined to make his new theatre the home of opera in London. Not quite 'Italian' opera, perhaps, but Italianate. His announced intention was to open his new theatre in 1705 with two operas, both of them based on English versions of Italian-based texts. One was to be *Orlando furioso* derived from Ariosto and composed by Daniel Purcell (1664–1717) – the brother, or cousin, of Henry. The other was *Arsinoe, Queen of Cyprus*, 'a confection of weak plot and Italian tunes "borrowed" by Thomas Clayton' (according to Christopher Hogwood).[18] In the event, the Purcell opera was never completed. But *Arsinoe*, set to an English-language libretto but advertised as being 'after the Italian manner' (in other words, with recitative rather than spoken dialogue) proved something of a triumph. Not that Vanbrugh received any benefit. It seems his arch rival Christopher Rich, an aggressive man who clearly enjoyed power and money, had lured Clayton away to the Theatre Royal, Drury Lane, and it was here on 16 January 1705, and not in Vanbrugh's new theatre in the Haymarket, that London audiences were offered what was in effect their first experience of all-sung, full-length, Italian-style opera (see pl.76 and 77).

Three months later, Vanbrugh was finally to open his theatre with an Italian opera, sung in Italian. It was entitled *Gli amori di Ergasto*. One observer, 'Roscius Anglicanus' (aka John Downes), noted drily that the Italian singers were 'the worst that e're came from thence' and that the opera 'lasted but 5 Days'.[19] The following year, Vanbrugh ill-advisedly plunged further towards possible bankruptcy by producing at the Queen's Theatre not one but three full-dress, Italian-style (English-language) operas. Meanwhile, the more savvy Rich at Drury Lane mounted just one, *Il trionfo di Camilla*, a work by the Italian composer Giovanni Bononcini (1670–1747) and as such the first authentically Italian opera to be produced in London, albeit to a text rendered into English by Owen Swiney.

Many of the supposedly Italian operas of the day were what had come to be called *pasticcios*: amalgamations of items from various pre-existing works, loosely knitted together by some kind of plot and the addition of a few extra items all (or mostly) translated into English. Vanbrugh's ambition, to produce authentic, integrated Italian opera in Italian, remained undiminished. Eventually, after much complex politicking, he achieved what perhaps he had been aiming for from the start: an official pronouncement by the Lord Chamberlain of a division of labour, to start in 1708, whereby Rich would take

54

54
Portrait of Sir John Vanbrugh
Thomas Chambars (c.1724–89), after a portrait by Sir Godfrey Kneller (1646–1723)
Engraving, c.18th century
V&A: S.2896-2009

55 (pp.70–1)
Rinaldo (opera seria by Giacomo Rossi after a scenario by Aaron Hill)
George F. Handel (1685–1759)
Autograph score, 1711–31
British Library, London, RM.20.C.3

il mio ben dite dov'è?

dite dov'è o zeffiretti che spirate aure dolci intorno ... dite

56

control of London's two licensed acting companies while Vanbrugh would be presented with an opera monopoly at his theatre on Haymarket. Vanbrugh immediately set to work, but was soon spending far more than he could afford. An application to the Queen for a subsidy to help finance his losses was turned down and in any case Vanbrugh's attention was by now increasingly turning towards the construction of Blenheim Palace. Management of the Queen's Theatre was passed to Swiney who, like Vanbrugh, somehow hoped that the cost of the overpaid Italian stars he had on his books – notably the celebrated castrato Nicolini (1673–1732) – would be offset by raised ticket prices. Swiney was ousted in 1710 by an ambitious MP named William Collier who handed day-to-day management of the theatre to the young and inexperienced writer Aaron Hill (pl.56).

Hill in turn was ousted less than a year later – but not before he had mounted *Rinaldo*, an opera for which he had drafted a basic text and stage directions. An Italian libretto was provided by the Italian-born poet Giacomo Rossi (d.1731) and the music by the 25-year-old Handel, recently arrived in London. Handel's reputation had preceded him (perhaps among members of the nobility who had encountered him while on the Grand Tour), and his music had been included in the celebrations of Queen Anne's birthday on 6 February 1711. *Rinaldo* followed 18 days later – and it was evidently something of a rush to get it ready in time.

RINALDO

In many ways, *Rinaldo* followed in the tradition of Italian *opera seria*: music drama often based on uplifting themes derived from classical sources (in contrast to the lighter *opera buffa*). But Hill, in dedicating the work to the Queen, emphasized its domestic provenance and his determination 'to see the English OPERA more splendid than her MOTHER, the Italian ... I resolv'd,' says Hill, 'to frame some Dramma, that, by different Instances and Passions, might afford the Musick Scope to vary and display its Excellence, and fill the Eye with more delightful Prospects, so at once to give Two Senses equal Pleasure'. As for the librettist, Rossi, he poured praise upon his musical colleague 'Mr Hendel' as 'the Orpheus of our Century'. In setting the work to music, he said, Handel 'scarcely gave me the Time to write, and to my great Astonishment I saw an entire Opera put to music by that sublime Genius in only two Weeks, and to the highest degree of Perfection'.[20] If Handel wrote the score in a fortnight (pl.55), that was not perhaps quite as remarkable as it sounds, for it contains some 15 numbers he had previously composed for other works (including the famous aria 'Lascia ch'io pianga'). *Rinaldo* opened at the Queen's Theatre, Haymarket, on 24 February 1711, a day after Handel's twenty-sixth birthday (pl.57).

Rinaldo was loosely based on *Gerusalemme Liberata*, a highly mythologized epic about the 'liberation' of Jerusalem during the First Crusade by the Renaissance Italian poet Torquato Tasso. Goffredo (Godfrey de Bouillon), leading his Christian troops outside the walls of Muslim-occupied Jerusalem, has promised the hand of his daughter Almirena to the knight Rinaldo once the city has been conquered. A temporary truce is called by the Saracen king Argante, during which Almirena is abducted by the Queen of Damascus – a wicked sorceress named Armida. Rinaldo vows revenge. In due course, he finds himself in Armida's enchanted palace where she makes every effort to win him over, even to the point of assuming the form of his beloved Almirena. But Rinaldo remains obdurate. In the third and final act, the noble Goffredo and his brother rescue Almirena, Rinaldo leads the Christian forces in a final assault and captures Jerusalem and he and Almirena marry. Finally, Armida, now robbed of her magic powers, becomes a Christian and she marries the former Saracen king Argante.

57

58

The production of *Rinaldo* at the Queen's Theatre aroused considerable attention. Just as Hill had promised, the production was designed to please not just the ear but also the eye with a series of spectacular stage effects: Armida entered in a chariot drawn by dragons, magic gardens and castles materialized on stage while men sailed across turbulent oceans and climbed mountains that disappeared with a stroke of a wand. Particularly impressive, it seems, was the presence of Nicolini in the title role (pl.58), who, we are told, could act as well as he could sing (which possibly helps explain the huge fees he demanded).[21] And yet, then as now, satirical journalists had no difficulty making fun of opera and its (to many people) exaggerated pretensions.[22] Thus, one may imagine the kinds of gossip that went the rounds – and continued to do so for many a decade – especially regarding the cult of the castrato (see pl.73-5).

As for all those 'Scenes and Machines', the editors of the original *The Spectator* magazine, Joseph Addison and Richard Steele, lambasted what, for all Hill's protestations, seemed to them like an overblown, over-expensive, over-elaborate and essentially foreign form of art.[23] How, they wondered 'would the Wits of King Charles's time (Charles II) have laughed to have seen Nicolini exposed to a Tempest in Robes of Ermin, and sailing in an open Boat upon a Sea of Paste-Board?'[24]

56
Head and torso portrait of
Mr. Aaron Hill in 1709, at the age of 24
Hendrick Hulsbergh (active in
London from 1709, d.1729)
Etching cut within the plate, paper
and printing ink, early 18th century
V&A: S.2066-2009

57
Songs in the Opera of Rinaldo
Words by A. Hill, translated by G. Rossi,
full score printed by J. Walsh … & J. Hare
London, 1711
British Library, London, R.M.7.h.24

58
Rehearsal of an Opera
Marco Ricci (1676–1729)
Gouache on paper, c.1709
Private collection

THE OPERA HOUSE or the ITALIAN EUNUCH'S GLORY

Humbly *Inscribed to those Generous Encouragers of* FOREIGNERS, *and Ruiners of* ENGLAND. { *From France, From Rome we come; To help Old England to to b'undone*

ET CANTARE PARES ET RESPONDERE PARATÆ

HARMONY

A List of the rich Presents Segnor Farinello y Italian Singer Condescended to Accept, off y English Nobillity & Gentry for one Nights Performance in y Opera Artaxerxes

A pair of Diamond knee Buckles Presen ted by .... A Diamond Ring by .... A Bank Note enclosed in a Rich Gold Lace by .... A Gold Snuff Box Chaced with the Story of Orpheus Charming y Brutes by T: Rakewell Esqr. £ 100. 20. 100.

Brittains attend — *view this harmonious Stage*

And listen to those notes which charm the age

How sweet the Sound where Cats and Bears,	*Were such discourag'd, we should find —*
With brutish Noise, offend our Ears!	*Musick at Home to charm the Mind!*
Just so the Foreign Singers move,	*Our Home Spun Authors, must forsake the Field,*
Rather contempt than gain our Love.	*And* Shakespear *to the Italian* Eunuchs *Yield.* 1728

59

Addison poured his amused wrath upon the extravagance of *Rinaldo* and of Italian opera in general. He reported how he had encountered a man in the street carrying a cage full of birds evidently destined for the opera and had naughtily imagined the birds making an entrance 'in very wrong and improper Scenes, so as to be seen flying in a Lady's Bed-Chamber, or perching upon a King's Throne' – not to mention the 'inconveniences' the birds might drop upon the heads of those in the audience.[25] In the same report, Addison told his readers reassuringly that:

> The Opera Rinaldo is filled with Thunder and Lightning, Illuminations, and Fireworks; which the Audience may look upon without catching Cold, and indeed without much Danger of being burnt; for there are several Engines filled with Water, and ready to play at a Minute's Warning, in case such Accident should happen.

Addison's co-editor, Steele, noted that while *Rinaldo* was on at the posh Haymarket theatre another big 'Diversion' in town was a much cheaper one in the piazza at Covent Garden put on by the puppeteer Martin Powell. Powell seems to have deliberately contrasted the two – the 'high' and the 'low' theatrical genres – by promoting his own show as a contrast to Italian opera. Steele went along to sample them both. And pretty similar he found them. By the 'squeak of their voices', he said, the heroes of both the opera and the puppet show were evidently eunuchs. And he added, sniffily, that the wit in both pieces was 'equal'. But, on balance, 'I must prefer the performance of Mr Powell because it is in our own language'.[26]

Opera, in other words, was derided as 'foreign'. It was a foreign genre, performed by foreign singers (led by one who was a eunuch) in a foreign language that no-one in the audience could understand. Worse, the genre, language and performers were Italian – and that meant Catholic. The story of operas like *Rinaldo* were mostly over-stated tales about the moral superiority of great kings and conquerors and high Christianity (Catholicism again) told through a succession of equally grandiose emotions that nobody could possibly believe. As for all those absurd scenes and machines, the fire-eating dragons and crumbling castles – what true Englishman could possibly want to spend his time and money on such a farrago of nonsense when he could, with Richard Steele, be enjoying Martin Powell's puppets performing *Whittington and his Cat*, which contained no eunuchs and was performed in English? What was wrong with putting on our own theatrical entertainments, with our own actors and singers performing in our own language? And when the opera was taking a break, why did the Haymarket theatre put on – of all things – Venetian-style 'masquerades'? This was what Addison and Steele wanted to know. As, in due course, did the painter and satirist William Hogarth (1697–1764) and many another patriot (pl.59 and 60).

How should we assess the impact or success of *Rinaldo*? On a good night, the Queen's Theatre on the Haymarket held an audience of perhaps 600, often rather fewer, in a city with a population of well over half a million. The audience would have been almost entirely composed of 'the quality', or in other words, people choosing to pay for an expensive evening of what we would now call 'elite' entertainment.

Did *Rinaldo* also draw in members of the rising 'middle class'? Hardly. As Mainwaring was to write: 'There were few persons of any other class, besides that of the Nobility, who had much knowledge of the Italian, any notion of such compositions (operas), or consequently any real pleasure in hearing them'.[27] And it is probably anachronistic to imagine a substantial 'middle class' in England before the onset of industrialization in the later eighteenth century. Back in 1711, the overwhelming population of England – and of London – consisted of people far too poor to afford tickets to the opera or to have any interest in it.[28]

59
The Opera House or the Italian Eunuch's Glory
Unknown artist, after William Hogarth
(1697–1764)
Etching, 1735
British Museum, London, 1868,0808.3526

60
Masquerades and Opera or
The Bad Taste of the Town
William Hogarth (1697–1764)
Engraving, c.1790s
V&A: S.952-2010

61

By the end of the 1710/11 season, the opera company at the Queen's Theatre was in dire straits. Box office receipts proved scarcely enough to pay the basic expenses of all involved. Handel himself received only £186/7/11 of an agreed payment of £430, while the copyist took away the score after every performance until Collier was able to pay him. True, *Rinaldo* was given 15 performances between February and June, taken to Dublin the following year and revived in subsequent London seasons as Handel's fame grew. But, as the scholar Robert D. Hume reminds us, *Arsinoe* had run 36 times in its first three seasons and *Camilla* 47 (and 112 times by 1728).[29]

Should we therefore write off *Rinaldo* as a minor event in the artistic calendar of London? It may not have been the overwhelming success some have regarded it in retrospect, nor was it the first Italian-style opera to be presented on the London stage. But it was the first to be created especially for London and sung throughout in Italian, with the composer himself presiding over the production. As such, it claims an important place in the history of opera and that of its composer. 'Few débuts have been so auspicious as the première of Rinaldo', wrote Curtis Price in the mid-1980s, adding that this event 'ushered in the Augustan musical age and helped to effect a basic change in English aesthetics' while to Christopher Hogwood, writing around the same time, *Rinaldo* could be said to have 'settled the course of Handel's career and the future of opera in England'.[30] Long before, Mainwaring had noted that while members of the nobility might have encountered opera in Italy, 'the conduct of them here, ie: all that regards the drama, or plan, including also the machinery, scenes, and decorations, was foolish and absurd beyond imagination'. And he concluded: 'The arrival of Handel put an end to this reign of nonsense' (pl.61).[31]

Handel, having stayed in London longer than he originally intended, left at the end of the season, returning to Hanover. But he was back a year later, in 1712, settling in London for the rest of his life. He watched as the popularity (and potential profitability) of Italian-style opera periodically rose and fell, and shrewdly adapted his work to the fluctuations in the market, gradually flowering into one of the most prolific and successful composers of his time. At first, he produced a succession of Italian operas, which, for some 20 years after *Rinaldo*, were premiered at the same theatre (re-named the 'King's' after the death of Queen Anne in 1714 and the accession to the crown of Handel's former employer, now King George of England).

But Italian opera, already in decline, received a major setback when, in January 1728, the actor and theatrical manager John Rich (son of Christopher) took over the popular theatre in Lincoln's Inn Fields for a production of a new English-language musical entertainment called *The Beggar's Opera*. Based on the music of already familiar ballads arranged by Pepusch, and a storyline about a highwayman and his girlfriends to words by John Gay, *Beggar's* proved far more popular than anything ever achieved by Handel in *opera seria*. It ran for over 60 performances and Rich was able to use the proceeds to build an entirely new theatre. The first of three on the north-eastern corner of the Covent Garden piazza, Rich's theatre opened to great acclaim in 1732. For a few more years, Handel continued to compose Italian operas, some of which premiered at Rich's Covent Garden theatre. But the taste for Italian opera was by now on the wane, and Handel found himself turning more and more to English texts whilst also looking away from stage works towards the great liturgical compositions of his later years, notably *Messiah*. By the time of his death in 1759, Handel had become a hugely celebrated and admired composer (pl.62). But it would scarcely have occurred to anyone to mount a revival of *Rinaldo*.

61
Rinaldo, Drama in Music
Libretto by Giacomo Rossi (active as Handel's librettist 1710–29)
Translation by Barthold Feind (1678–1721)
Printed by Friedrich Conrad Greflinger (d.1717)
Hamburg, 1715
Berlin State Library, Yq1903

62
George Frideric Handel
Louis François Roubiliac (1702–62)
Terracotta, pre 1738
Fitzwilliam Museum, University of Cambridge, M.3-1922

62

LONDON

LONDON

LONDON *eertits genaemt* Lundonia *een groote hosostadt de vver.* LONDRE *auparavant appellé* Lundonia *une grande ville ...* LONDEN *vor dheem genahnste* Londonia *ein groe huistade die* LONDON *Formerly called* Londonia *a City of great English the* ... *in groot Britanien een Setel des Koninckx is gelegen am de Rivier* ... *et la plus celebre en grand bretaine une Siege d'u Roy ...* ... *vernahmste in gross Britanien ein palleis des Koninckx is gelegen am die* ... *Chiefest in great britain the throne of the Kingdom is Scituated on the* ... *de Teems geschlt door* Britius Constantinus *de groote hoofdse met* ... *situe sur la riviere du* Thomas *edifie par* Brit. ... Constantin *le Rivier de* Theems *gefondert durch* Britius Constantinus *die gesse hade 90 Rivir* thames, *and Founded of* Britius Constantinus *the great Compassed a* ... *muiren ensiangele verciert met 122 kercken* St Paulis *is de hoost* ... *grand l'at siensse de muirailles orne de 120 eghlis St Paul oste* ... *die 120 eighlis St Paul* ... *to kircken Sanct Teith wall, beautipied th with 120 Churches St Paul the Cathedrall and a Sta* ... *kerck en hoost een Trefflicke Boussie en* Tower *98 Arsenael en andere dele et a vne tresceleber boussie, et vn* Tower *in* Arsenael *et autres bass'* ... Paulis *is de heiste kirchen mit hadt en hospitelchen breisse oder kaupmans ven wly exchange* Tower *and other Stately buildings beeing by the last great fire* ... *t'meeste deel der* Stat *maor vu door de groote rijckdem des inwoenders herboit grande partie de la ville mais ashier par la grande richesse des Citoyens rebastes* ... *brant hyna alle verbrant weshens die greotse deyl der stade vnde wider wider, the great wealth of the Citizens builds again*

geduckt tot
AMSTERDAM
by F. de Wit

64

65

63
View of London
Frederick de Wit (1629–1706)
Engraving, 1694–1704
V&A: 24429

Part of Frederick de Wit's *Townbook*, showing
views of famous European and Asian cities,
this aspect of London is taken from south of the
river Thames. It includes scenes of everyday life
in the foreground, several prominent buildings
rebuilt after the Great Fire of London in 1666,
and boats laden with imported goods, reflecting
the prosperity of the city.

64
Terrestrial Globe
Richard Cushee (1696–c.1734)
Brass, silver, paper and card
Science Museum, London, 1910-161

The maker of this globe was based in Chancery
Lane, close to the Royal Exchange. A fashionable
item in the eighteenth century, globes demonstrated
the owner's knowledge of the world and often
depicted the most recent discoveries; this one
includes Australia. Globes were often sold in
pairs, one terrestrial and the second showing
the layout of the stars.

65
Model of Queen Anne
Panel of modelled wax and curled paper on
a paper ground, with gilt and coloured detail
England, 1705–10
V&A: W.25-1955

Reigning between 1702 and 1714, Queen Anne
was one of Handel's patrons and his music was
used for her birthday celebrations in 1711. This wax
and paper depiction was originally intended
as a shop sign; it shows her in a theatre setting
that emphasizes the elaborate nature of the
Baroque stage.

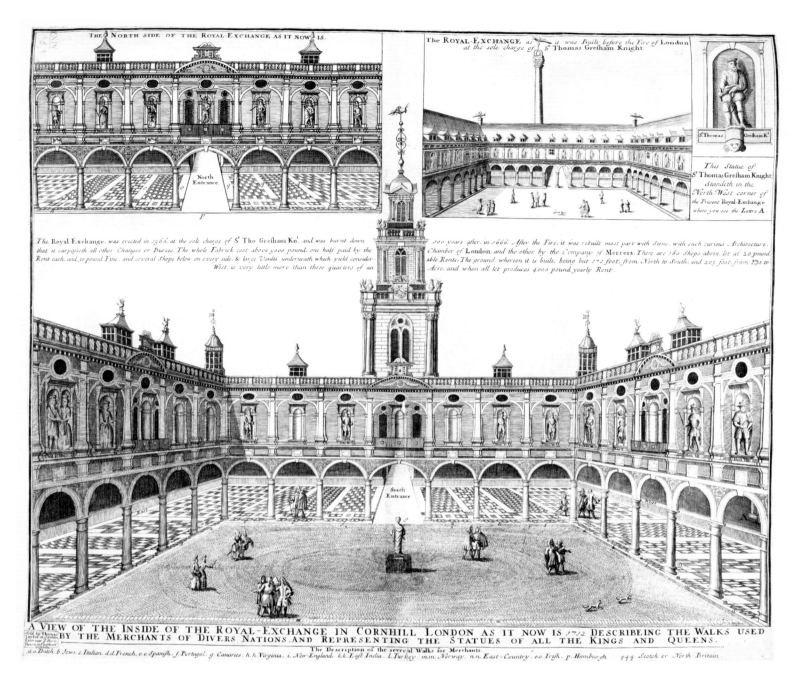

THE NORTH SIDE OF THE ROYAL EXCHANGE AS IT NOW IS.

The ROYAL-EXCHANGE as it was Built before the Fire of London at the sole charge of Sᵗ Thomas Gresham Knight

This Statue of Sᵗ Thomas Gresham Knight Standeth in the North-West corner of the Present Royal-Exchange where you see the Letter A.

A VIEW OF THE INSIDE OF THE ROYAL-EXCHANGE IN CORNHILL LONDON AS IT NOW IS 1712 DESCRIBEING THE WALKS USED BY THE MERCHANTS OF DIVERS NATIONS AND REPRESENTING THE STATUES OF ALL THE KINGS AND QUEENS.

66

66

*A view of the inside of the Royal Exchange in
Cornhill London as it now is*, Sold by Thomas Taylor
Sutton Nicholls (1680–1740)
Print, 1712
British Library, London, Ktop 24 11-k

The Royal Exchange on Cornhill was rebuilt
after the Great Fire of London in 1666. Written
underneath this image is a list of all the nations
that traded at the Royal Exchange (including
Italy, France, East India and Turkey), reflecting
London's central role in international commerce
during the eighteenth century.

67

Covent Garden Market
Balthazar Nebot (active 1730–65)
Oil on canvas, 1737
Tate Britain, London, N01453

At the beginning of the eighteenth century, Covent
Garden was a 'known place of sexual resort', as
well as an area full of small commerce and coffee
houses such as Will's on Russell Street. This is
where artists, politicians and businessmen would
meet to discuss the news of the day or the latest
theatre shows. Each profession had its own
preferred coffee house.

68

*Rich's Glory or his Triumphant Entry
into Covent Garden*
Workshop of William Hogarth (1697–1764)
Engraving, after 1732
Royal Opera House Collections, London

After the success of *The Beggar's Opera* in 1728,
John Rich moved his theatre from Lincoln's
Inn Fields to Covent Garden, establishing regular
musical performances on the current site of the
Royal Opera House. He is seen here triumphantly
leading the crowd to the new building through
the colonnade on the right, reflecting his status,
fame and wealth.

67

68

LONDON

70

71

72

71
Snuffbox decorated with the sacrifice of Iphigenia
Mark of Burel
Gold, raised and chased, c.1720
V&A LOAN: GILBERT.318-2008

The mythological figure depicted on the lid of this snuff box is Iphigenia, a character from the Greek play written by Euripides in around 400BC. Such subjects were often used as inspiration for the decorative arts as well as in music; Iphigenia was also a character in Handel's opera *Oreste* (1724).

72
Snuffbox decorated with Aesop's fable of the Fox and the Crow
Michel Cabaret Lagarene
(recorded as a Goldsmith in 1709)
Chased gold
London, c.1710
V&A LOAN: SNOWMAN.7-1997

Taking snuff (powdered tobacco) was a fashionable habit in eighteenth-century British society. Snuff boxes were made from a variety of materials such as gold, silver, tortoiseshell, mother-of-pearl, lacquer and enamel.

70
Silver cup and cover
Paul de Lamerie (1688–1751)
Raised, cast, pierced, punched and engraved silver with applied cut-card calyx, 1717–18
V&A LOAN: GILBERT.649:1, 2-2008

Following the revocation of the Edict of Nantes (which granted Huguenots freedom of religion in France between 1598 and 1685), several hundred French Protestants found refuge in England. Among them were gifted goldsmiths such as Pierre Platel and his apprentice Paul de Lamerie, who became very successful in London. They introduced fashionable French styles, technical innovations and higher standards of craftsmanship.

69
The Coffehous Mob
Unknown artist
Engraving, 1710
British Museum, London, 1880,0807.301

This satirical frontispiece to *The Fourth Part of Vulgus Britannicus: or the British Hudibras* shows the interior of a well-appointed coffee house. Journalists and other gentlemen are disputing the Sacheverell riots and related events of the day; the title appears on the ceiling.

The Ladies Lamentation for ỹ Loss of Senesino.

G. Bickham jun. fc.

Set for ỹ German Flute &c.

As musing I rang'd in the Meads all alone, A beautifull Creature was making her Moan,

Oh! the Tears they did trickle full fast from her Eyes, And she peirc'd both the Air and my

Heart with her Cries, Oh! the Tears they did trickle full fast from her Eyes, And she peirc'd both ỹ

Ritt

Air and my Heart with her Cries.

I gently requested the Cause of her moan,
She told me her sweet Senisino was flown,
And in that sad Posture she'd ever remain,
Unless the dear Charmer wou'd come back again.

Why who is this Mortal so Cruel said I,
That draws such a stream from so Lovely an Eye,
To Beauty so blooming, what Man can be blind,
To Passion so tender, what Monster unkind.

'Tis neither for Man, nor for Woman, said she,
That thus in Lamenting I water the lee,
My Warbler Cælestial sweet Darling of fame,
Is a Shadow of something, a Sex without Name.

Perhaps 'tis some Linnet, some Blackbird, said I,
Perhaps 'tis your Lark, that has soar'd to the sky;
Come dry up your Tears, and abandon your grief,
I'll bring you another, to give you relief.

No Linnet, no Blackbird, no Skylark, said she,
But one much more tunefull, by far than all three,
My sweet Senisino for whom thus I cry,
Is sweeter than all the wing'd Songsters that fly.

Adieu Farinelli, Cuzzoni, Likewise,
Whom stars, and whom Garters, extol to the skies,
Adieu to the Opera, adieu to the Ball,
My darling is gone, and a fig for them all.

FOR THE FLUTE.

74

75

73
Song sheet for *The Loss of Senesino*
George Bickham Junior (1706–71)
With words and music for keyboard
and flute, and engraved heading
Ink on paper, 1737–8
V&A: S.1137-1986

The fashion for Italian operas sung by foreign
stars in London was started by the castratos,
who were the equivalent of modern day popstars
and apparently much admired by female fans.
However, castratos were often mocked by the
press and rumoured to have low morals. This song
sheet commemorates the frenzy that resulted
when the famous castrato Senesino (Francesco
Bernardi, c.1680–1750) left London in 1730.

74
Gaetano Berenstatt as Flavio, Francesca Cuzzoni
as Emilia and Francesco Bernardi (Senesino)
as Guido in Act III, Scene IV of 'Flavio' by Handel
First performed on 20 February 1723 at
the King's Theatre Haymarket
Unknown artist
Engraving, 1723
V&A: S.4254-2009

Castratos were male singers who had been
castrated in order to preserve the purity and
pitch of a young boy's voice. Italian-style opera
had favoured the voice of the castrato for the
leading male roles since the seventeenth century.

75
Portrait miniature of Carlo Broschi,
known as Farinelli (1705–1782)
Christian Friedrich Zincke (1683–1767)
Enamel and painted, c.1735
V&A: S.1682-2014

Carlo Broschi, otherwise known as Farinelli,
was a successful castrato in the eighteenth century.
Miniature portraits such as this one might have
been worn as a brooch by an admirer or lover.

Arsinoë on a Couch

Act 1st Sc. 3d
A Room of State, wth Statues & Busts

D. 28. 91.

76

Act. 2nd Sc: 3d Arsinoë in a fine Garden, wth Ships, Harbrs &c in
Distance

D. 27. 91

77

78

79

76
*Design for Act I, scene 9, Queen's apartment
for 'Arsinoe, Queen of Cyprus', as produced
at Theatre Royal, London, 1705*
James Thornhill (1675–1734)
Paper, pen, ink and wash, 1705
V&A: D.28-1891

77
*Design for Act II, scene 8, Garden,
for 'Arsinoe, Queen of Cyprus',
as produced at Theatre Royal, London, 1705*
James Thornhill (1675–1734)
Paper, pen, ink and wash, 1705
V&A: D.25-1891

These images are some of the earliest surviving
designs for British theatre. They demonstrate
the influence of Italian design on the London stage,
with the use of grand perspective and Baroque
aesthetic, echoing the style of Italian designer
Giacomo Torelli (1608–78). Usually the stage
design for an opera comprised one grand
architectural setting, which could be adapted for
interiors or garden settings, as depicted here.

78
Bodice of a theatre costume
Cream and silver tinsel brocade
Italy, c.1750
V&A: S.798&A-1982

79
Male theatre costume
Brown, pink and silver brocade
Italy, c.1750
V&A: S.796-1982

These male and female costumes come from
the private theatre of Meleto Castle in Italy.
Originally made in the mid-eighteenth century,
these costumes have been altered over time
to suit different performances, fashions and
characters. The tinsel embroidery would have
been illuminated by the candles on stage,
emphasizing the gestures of the singers and
helping to create the spectacular stage setting
of a Baroque opera.

Der Bibliothec Platz.

Der Neue Marckt

Der Michaeler Platz

Die Seiler Straße

Die Anna Gaße

Die Iohanites Gaße

Die Kärntner Straße

Die Rauhen Stein Gaße

Auf dem Graben

auf dem Peter

Der Stock im Eisen Platz

Die Singer Straße

Die Wollzeile

Die Schuler Straße

Der hohe Marckt

Die Wiplinger

Die obere Becken straße

Die untere Becken Straße

Der alte Fleisch Marckt

Das Stuben Thor

Das Schwyel

Das Iacob Thor

Das Thor

Donau Arm.

VIENNA

3

WOLFGANG AMADEUS MOZART
1756–91

Le nozze di Figaro

The servants Figaro and Susanna are engaged. Their employer Count Almaviva wants to seduce Susanna and attempts to cancel their wedding. He tries to force Figaro to marry Marcellina, a woman old enough to be his mother, until it is revealed that she really is, in fact, his long-lost mother. Figaro, Susanna and Countess Almaviva succeed in their plot to expose the Count's womanizing. The Count begs the Countess for forgiveness and Figaro and Susanna can finally marry.

81

INTRODUCTION

ANTONIO PAPPANO

Giving the up beat to *Le nozze di Figaro* overture is the quintessential split-second decision to commit mischief. Tense, eyebrows raised, the whites of the bassoonists' eyes in front of me, with a flick the music flies past. Wait for me! Cherubino, breathless, late perhaps, it's a wedding day. The occasion is announced politely, no, haughtily by oboes and horns (we are in the house of the Count and Countess!), the whole band explodes indecorously in celebration. Bursts of instrumental colour, peals of laughter, much showing off, scales, fanfares, a musical party. Ah, but wait, there are clandestine goings on, too. Darting eyes, secrets, the sudden shutting of doors, hiding. Will they be found out? Oh my God, the preparations — and we're so late!!! Run!

Susanna and Figaro, servants in a fine manor house, are about to get married, and they are both busy. The orchestra tells you exactly what's going on. The second violins' semiquavers give you the prenuptial 'buzz' in the room, while the cellos and double basses pronounce a long 'Mmm!' Figaro is taking measurements in the room for the marriage bed, the first violins pecking out metronomically the centimetres. He is pleased with himself. A vaguely erotic atmosphere pervades. The bassoons join in and concur that Figaro is a genius, such a genius, as they climb higher and higher. Susanna looks to see what the fuss is about (flutes and oboes, inquisitively). He dances a quadrille! Men! The oboe preens, joined by the flute, the fiddles shiver in admiration — what a gorgeous Spanish woman is Susanna! She admires the fit of her new hat, triplets complimenting too. Woodwinds just so!

Figaro and Susanna sing over each other at cross purposes, now together, a fractious Latin couple, and so in love, tumbling into a bawdy embrace. It goes on: in something akin to actual speech rather than song (we call this *recitativo secco*, dry recitation being the rather dull translation — it means no orchestra, just a keyboard) we find out that their room is in close proximity to the Count's rooms. Alarm bells! 'You stupid Figaro, don't you know why he's given us this room?' (This dry recitation can be very spirited and certainly pushes the action forward.) Figaro launches the most delicious little duet, with the orchestra imitating bells:

'Come here, go there' — the life of the servant. Susanna reverts to the minor key (uh-oh!), the bell imitations become dangerous and plaintive. 'You'll be sent off on an errand (din din!) and I'll be a sitting duck for the Count's predatory advances (DON DON!!!!!). Do you want to hear the rest?' Musical hesitations everywhere. Figaro becomes dark and vengeful. Now alone, he sings to the invisible Count: 'if you want to dance this dance, then I'll play along' (pathetically he is shadowed by the horns, the traditional theatrical symbols for the cuckold), pretending everything is fine, but then (the music becomes turbo-charged with impossible trills, and impossible Italian!) 'I'll turn your world upside down!' Revolution is around the corner....

Have I conveyed my love for this piece and its energy with the descriptions I've given above? I hope so. This is how I need the Mozart experience to be for me. Every word, every gesture: pure theatre.

No one comes close to his awareness of human motivation, nor the knowledge that life is an adventure to be experienced, often dangerous, often painful, but exhilarating and essential at the same time. The only way I know how to engage with his operas, and in particular this one, is by considering every detail (there are myriad) from every angle and perspective, and through the prism of every character. Let me tell you that every character is, in the end, out for himself or herself. The other name for this opera is *La Folle Journée*, or *The Crazy Day*. This household is most certainly dysfunctional, and Mozart has truly thought of all the preposterous ins and outs of this impossible wedding day with the help of his rogue-genius librettist Lorenzo da Ponte (1749—1838). The rascals must have had such fun!

Either sitting alone at the study table or in the midst of the hustle and bustle of rehearsals (there is no opera that is more fun to work on), I'm constantly trying to understand or fathom what the wordless orchestra is trying to say. It has perhaps the loudest voice, but it has in my mind the most secrets to reveal if one listens really carefully.

The mirth of Act I is balanced by its polar opposite, Act II. We meet the Countess for the first time, a show biz trick of introducing a new character comparatively late on. Four stately chords followed by three tired semiquavers and then a heart-breaking melody (Beethoven stole this musical signature over and over) that truly weeps, then a cry of anguish followed by secret sobs, another cry and 'why me'. All of this before any words have been sung. The Countess languishes (she is married to a serial philanderer), she sings in exquisite pain to love itself, asking for some remedy for her sighing melancholy. There is a feeling of wallowing in her sadness, but how profoundly human that is, and the orchestra sighs for her. She wants to die, she goes to a musical precipice. We stop ... no, she doesn't do it. She finishes in a whimper, the clarinet and bassoon trying to console her.

The young scamp Cherubino enters and sings a lovely song, the fiddles plucking cheekily, mandolin-like, the accompaniment, the clarinet and the bassoon amorous, the oboe sighing exaggeratedly. The boy is nervous, but he sings well. He steals furtive glances at the Countess — he is in love he thinks. The big surprise of the night is that the Countess is aroused; how could she not be by THAT modulation into A flat major: 'one minute I'm freezing, another my soul is on fire, and then back again'. (The horns bathe this phrase in a warm glow.) Mozart and Cherubino are innocent and sly seducers. The sexual tension is palpable, and honestly, who can blame the Countess for being tempted out of her gloom, despite her languishing aria having been sung only a few moments before. Marriage, infidelity, constancy, first love, class warfare — it's all here.

I could go on forever. See this opera, listen to this opera. It will teach you so much. And you will laugh and cry, and laugh and cry....

82

83

VIENNA AND THE ENLIGHTENMENT

NICHOLAS TILL

85

THE ENLIGHTENED DESPOT

In November 1780, upon the death of his mother Maria Theresa, the Holy Roman Emperor Joseph II (b.1741) acceded to the dispersed thrones of the Habsburg Empire, which he had hitherto ruled as co-regent with his mother (pl.86). Joseph was a man in a hurry who embarked on a whirlwind programme to modernize the still backward Habsburg lands, having long been frustrated by his mother's more cautious approach to reform. His project was broadly based on the teachings of the eighteenth-century French Enlightenment: in a double portrait of Joseph and his brother Leopold by Pompeo Batoni (1708–87) of 1769, the princes are depicted standing beside a table on which there rests a copy of Montesquieu's *L'esprit des lois*, the Enlightenment's bible for principles of government according to the law.

The ideas of French thinkers like Montesquieu (1689–1755) and Voltaire (1694–1778) (pl.87) were themselves often derived from progressive thought in England. Indeed, when Voltaire and Montesquieu visited England in the 1720s, they were presented with striking evidence of the relationship between social, political and religious freedoms and economic growth. 'Where there is not liberty of conscience' concluded Voltaire, 'there is seldom liberty of trade'.[1] While his pious mother lived, Joseph had often argued with her about the need for religious toleration. Within a year of taking the reins of power he had introduced a wide-ranging Patent of Toleration, giving freedom of worship throughout his kingdoms.

Joseph's adoption of such ideas was based upon pragmatism rather than any ideological commitment. He certainly had little faith in Montesquieu's ideal of constitutional government, believing that the most effective way of changing things was by personal fiat, and refusing to allow the representative bodies of his kingdoms to meet. To this extent he was the quintessential 'enlightened despot'. And expectations of Joseph were high, for his reputation as a son of the Enlightenment had been well trailed; in the year of Batoni's portrait, Voltaire was assured that the young Emperor was 'one of us'.[2] In 1777 Joseph had made an incognito visit to Paris, where he met and engaged with many of the most prominent Enlightenment *philosophes*. And within a very short time of assuming power he introduced a series of measures that appeared to meet in one fell swoop all the main demands of the *philosophes*. Press freedom was introduced, and literary censorship relaxed. Education and healthcare were improved, and as absolutist monarchs had done before him, Joseph launched a virulent campaign against the feudal powers, and the social and financial privileges, of the nobility. 'For industry, for commerce' Joseph argued, 'nothing is more necessary than liberty, nothing more harmful than privileges and monopolies.'[3] The law was progressively re-codified to introduce the principle of equality, and the nobility – to their horror – found themselves subjected to the same penalties as commoners for crimes, and eventually to the same taxation. Feudal serfdom was abolished. Joseph's programme seemed to encapsulate everything that the Enlightenment had fought for so vigorously, and Joseph himself was lauded as 'the *philosophe* on the throne'.[4]

THE PUBLIC SPHERE

One of the most characteristic features of the Enlightenment was the creation of an autonomous social sphere for the dissemination of the new intellectual consensus, leading to the development of the familiar institutions of eighteenth-century society that constituted what has been called 'the public sphere', where people of different social status could mix freely without violating the essential social hierarchies. Hence there sprang up the parks, pleasure gardens, public assembly rooms and concert halls, that met

84 (pp.98–9)
Vienna State Opera auditorium
Main building extensively rebuilt after the war, between 1949 and 1955, following the design of the previous theatre built in 1861–9

85
The Freyung in Vienna,
View from the South West
Bernardo Bellotto (1721–80),
also called Canaletto
Oil on canvas, 1758–61
Kunsthistorisches Museum, Vienna, 1654

86
Emperor Joseph II with
Grand Duke Pietro Leopoldo of Tuscany
Pompeo Batoni (1708–87)
Oil on canvas, 1769
Kunsthistorisches Museum, Vienna, GG 1628

87

the leisure demands of an expanding urban bourgeoisie, whilst in coffee-shops, clubs and salons, political, social and intellectual gossip might be traded. In an early edition of his new weekly periodical *The Spectator*, founded in London in 1711, Joseph Addison wrote of his desire to bring philosophy 'out of Closets and Libraries, Schools and Colleges to dwell in Clubs and Assemblies, at Tea Tables and in Coffee Houses'.[5] Seventy years later in Vienna, one of Addison's spiritual heirs, the playwright-satirist Josef Richter (1749–1813), similarly claimed that his *A. B. C. Buch für Kinder* was 'a philosophical dictionary aimed at the man in the coffee house'.[6] During the 1780s there was, indeed, an efflorescence of public coffee houses in Vienna: some 70 by 1790 in a city of around 215,000 inhabitants.[7] A historian of the Viennese coffee house has written that the coffee house was to become during this period a virtual substitute for parliament in a country that had no official forums for political debate.[8] 'One doesn't just drink coffee here', Johann Pezzl (1756–1823) tells us in his *Skizze von Wien* (*Sketches of Vienna*), published in 1789, 'one studies, plays, applauds, sleeps, negotiates, haggles, advertises, intrigues, reads papers and journals'.[9] As in London, certain coffee houses became identified with particular circles of Viennese society: Kramer's on the Graben was well known to be the best place to get hold of foreign journals; the Café Stierbock in the Leopoldstadt suburb was a popular masonic haunt, where in 1785 a reception was held for Lafayette, the French hero of the American Revolution.[10]

The model of the English weekly journal also spread throughout Europe, and by the 1760s weeklies were appearing in Vienna. The longest-lived and most influential of these was the journal *Der Mann ohne Vorurtheil*, produced by the prominent Enlightenment jurist Joseph von Sonnenfels, which first appeared in 1767. The journal's title (*The Man without Prejudice*), and Sonnenfels' description of himself in the journal as the 'Beobachter' (spectator) pay obvious homage to Addison. Sonnenfels recognized that 'Laws can only achieve so much. An enlightened people obeys because it wants to; one led by prejudice because it must'.[11] Unable to find a suitable phrase to convey his idea in German, he adopts an English phrase: 'This "Spirit Public"'.[12] Sonnenfels considered the creation of this enlightened 'Spirit Public' to be the most important task facing the modern legislator, educator and artist. His articles from the journal were republished in 1784 in an edition of his complete works, of which the first four volumes (in which the *Mann ohne Vorurtheil* articles reappear) were owned by Wolfgang Amadeus Mozart (pl.88).

Joseph's relaxation of literary and press censorship unleashed a further torrent of publications that fed the new appetite for information and opinion. In 1780 there were only six book publishers in Vienna, but by 1787 there were 21. As in London at the beginning of the century, booksellers and lending libraries sprang up in response to the new industry, creating additional forums for intellectual discussion. The most successful of the Viennese publishers, the millionaire property developer Joseph Trattner, was himself forced to open a reading-room of his own, where readers could peruse the Trattner titles without having to buy them, to counter the success of the other public reading-rooms in Vienna. Mozart was for a while a tenant in the Trattnerhof near the Graben, and hired a hall in the complex for one of his subscription concerts.

These developments were an indication of the new liveliness of Viennese intellectual and literary life in the early years of Joseph II's reign, prompting the poet Aloys Blumauer (1755–98), collaborator and friend of Mozart, to exclaim in 1782: 'Is not Vienna now the sun around which Germany's smaller and lesser planets orbit? Is it not the focus for the whole of Europe? Have philosophy and science themselves ever had such a wide influence?'[13] And this intellectual liveliness was complemented by the deliberately egalitarian openness of Joseph II's own social vision. The imperial gardens, the Prater and the Augarten (in the grounds of which Joseph himself lived quite modestly) were thrown open to the Viennese public, and there, sections of society, from the emperor down, intermingled. Mozart himself promoted a successful series of

87
Bust of Voltaire
Jean Claude François
Joseph Rosset (1706–86)
Carved marble, 1768
V&A: A.4-1919

88
Wolfgang Amadeus Mozart
Joseph Lange (1751–1831)
Oil on canvas, 1789
Mozarteum, Salzburg

88

VIENNA

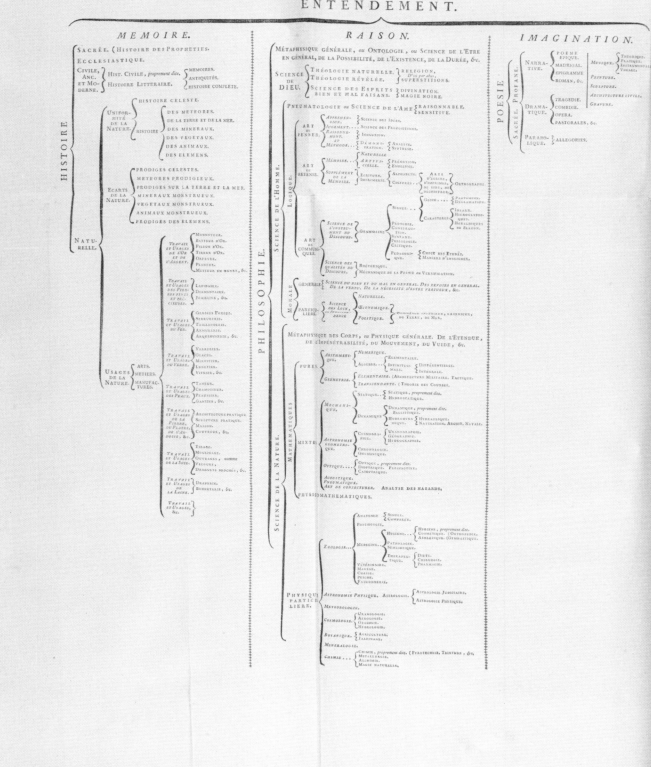

*SYSTÊME FIGURÉ
DES CONNOISSANCES HUMAINES.

ENTENDEMENT.

89

concerts in the Augarten. The great ballroom, the Redoutensaal, formerly the preserve of the aristocracy, was made available to all classes at carnival time, and Joseph himself sometimes admitted the public to imperial balls, on one such occasion in December 1781, according to a report by Mozart, being jostled by the mob of 'friseurs and housemaids' that had been permitted entrance.[14]

MOZART AND THE ENLIGHTENMENT

Among the 50 or so books to be found in Mozart's small personal library, there was only one novel, *Faustin, oder das philosophische Jahrhundert* (*Faustin, or the Philosophical Century*), first published in 1783 by Johann Pezzl (pl.90), Mozart's exact contemporary from his home city of Salzburg. The novel's young hero Faustin travels throughout Europe in search of Enlightenment, everywhere meeting with disappointment, until he finally reaches the Vienna of Joseph II, where he proclaims: 'Here ... under the rule of Joseph, will be the complete victory of reason and humanity. Will be the philosophical century. This long-desired, long-awaited epoch, which will raise up all Germany, began in the year 1780'.[15]

There is in Faustin's joyous arrival in Vienna a parallel with the turning-point in Mozart's life: his own arrival in Vienna, which was to be his home for the last ten years of his life, early in 1781. Like Faustin, Mozart had left Salzburg, a small, ecclesiastical backwater, in search of a congenial base, travelling throughout Europe and meeting everywhere with rebuffs, until at last he found his way to Vienna at exactly the moment when it seemed to promise everything. Like Faustin, and indeed Joseph II, Mozart had spent time in Paris, where he encountered some of the most prominent figures of the French Enlightenment. During the Mozart family's first visit to Paris in 1763, they had been taken up by the German Baron Melchior Grimm, a close associate of the Enlightenment philosophers and writers Denis Diderot (1713–84) and Jean-Jacques Rousseau (1712–78). When Mozart returned to Paris as a young adult in 1778, his father provided him with letters of introduction to 'Diderot, d'Alembert and the rest', naming the two distinguished editors of the crowning achievement of the French Enlightenment, the *Encyclopédie* (pl.89).[16] During his stay, Mozart and his mother lodged with Baron Grimm's partner Madame d'Épinay, a writer and prominent intellectual salon hostess. The visit to Paris ended in disaster professionally, as well as personally when Mozart's mother died. But it planted the seeds of Enlightenment thinking in Mozart's mind, and enabled him to recognize the importance of Joseph II's reforms.

MOZART IN VIENNA

The news of Joseph's accession reached Mozart in Munich, where, he was deep in work on his grand *opera seria Idomeneo*. In March 1781, he was summoned from Munich to attend his employer Archbishop Colloredo, who was travelling to Vienna to pay his respects to the new Emperor. Mozart's response to the city was instantaneous and joyous. Here at last was a forum in which his talents could find both worthy expression and proper reward. For a single concert, playing in the palace of a nobleman, he could earn 50 florins – half his miserable annual salary in Salzburg.[17] The burgeoning economy had led to a newly established public concert life that soon embraced the young virtuoso. Within a few weeks Mozart had clearly persuaded himself that Vienna was the place for him, and was preparing his anxious father for the imminent shock of rupture from Salzburg by describing the rich rewards he could expect in the city: Vienna was 'a splendid place – and for my metier the best one in the world. Everyone will tell you the same'.[18]

90

89
Système Figuré des Connaissances Humaine (*Figurative System of Human Knowledge*)
Denis Diderot (1713–84) and Jean-Baptiste le Rond d'Alembert (1717–83)
Encyclopédie, ou Dictionnaire raisonné des Sciences, des Arts et des Métiers, 1751, vol.1
V&A: National Art Library

90
Faustin, oder das philosophische Jahrhundert (*Faustin, or the Philosophical Century*)
Johann Pezzl (1756–1823)
Zürich, 1783
Vienna City Library

91

92

Before long he had engineered his dismissal from his restricting post with the Archbishop and had launched himself upon the dynamic musical free market of Vienna, at the same time plunging into the whirlwind of social and intellectual activity that had been whipped up by Joseph's reforms. And for the first time in his life, Mozart found himself being accorded the respect that he and his father had so long sought for him. 'All possible honour is shown me', he informed Leopold.[19]

Mozart's entrance into Viennese social and intellectual life was via the salon of the Countess Wilhelmine Thun (pl.91). The Thun-Hohenstein family belonged to the greater Austrian aristocracy, and Franz-Joseph and his wife were intimate friends of the Emperor. But as supporters of the Viennese Enlightenment they extended their largesse regardless of class or status, welcoming statesmen, intellectuals, artists and freemasons alike into their home, confirming Pezzl's observation in the *Skizze von Wien*, that the greater aristocracy 'estimated bourgeois intellectuals, artists and businessmen incomparably more than the unproductive minor nobility'.[20] The Mozart family had made the acquaintance of the Thuns on previous visits to Vienna, and Wolfgang made speedy contact when he arrived in 1781. Within a week of setting foot in Vienna he was able to write to his father that he had already lunched twice with the Countess, and that he was visiting her house almost every day.[21]

The salon, an institution imported to Vienna from France (pl.92), was the preserve of the society hostess. Pezzl tells us that the Viennese salon hostess was an educator and muse, and that a salon evening was as 'educative and tasteful as it is charming'.[22] The Countess Thun's salon was evidently the most important informal meeting place

91
Portrait of Maria Wilhelmine,
Countess Thun-Hohenstein
Heinrich Friedrich Füger (1751–1818)
Watercolour on ivory in an ormolu frame, c.1790
The Cleveland Museum of Art,
Edward B. Greene Collection, 1942.1142

92
The Party — at the Concert
François Dequevauviller (1745–1807), after
Nicolas Lafrensen (1737–1807)
Etching, 1783–4
V&A: E.364-2013

93

94

for adherents of Enlightenment thought in Vienna, and there Mozart met and engaged with some prominent Josephine statesmen. In April 1781 Mozart wrote that he had met the great Sonnenfels at the Countess' salon, and in December of the same year he was intimate enough with Sonnenfels to suggest to his anxious father that if Leopold had any doubts about the esteem that Wolfgang enjoyed in Vienna, he should write to Sonnenfels.[23] Sonnenfels' name is also to be found on a list of Mozart's concert subscribers in 1784. It was at the Thun household, too, that Mozart met Gottfried van Swieten (pl.93), one of Joseph's most trusted ministers as Director of the State Education Commission from 1781, and one of the most vigorous promoters of musical activity in Vienna. By April 1782, Mozart was attending Van Swieten's Sunday musical evenings weekly.

Acquaintance with the Thuns promised to allow Mozart access to the Emperor himself, for Joseph used to attend private parties there. A mere three weeks after his arrival in Vienna, Mozart missed meeting Joseph at a private concert given by the Thuns because of the domestic demands of Archbishop Colloredo. This frustration almost certainly decided him to seize the earliest opportunity to provoke an argument with his employer and to hand in his notice of resignation. Two months after arriving in Vienna he had at last liberated himself from the company of the Archbishop's kitchen staff, with whom he was forced to dine, and from his musician colleagues – the 'coarse and dirty' violinist Brunetti, and the bloated and ignorant castrato Ceccarelli – with whom he was required to linger in the Archbishop's anterooms in anticipation of Colloredos' sudden wish for some music to distract him.[24] Mozart now launched himself as a freelance musician–entrepreneur, offering his services for private soirées, teaching piano to the daughters of the old and new aristocracy, as well as the aspirant middle classes, and promoting a series of public subscription concerts for which he wrote a sequence of dazzling piano concertos to show off his talents as both composer and player. The Mozarthaus museum in Vienna, the spacious and elegant apartment where Mozart lived with his family between 1784–87, speaks of the prosperous bourgeois status that Mozart achieved in his heyday in Vienna.

FREEMASONRY

In 1784 Sonnenfels, who was vice-master of the masonic lodge 'Zur wahren Eintracht', wrote a masonic essay in which he claimed that freemasonry had been the chief vehicle for the propagation and dissemination of the ideals of the Enlightenment in Austria. Writing about Viennese masonry, the Austrian literary historian Leslie Bodi adds: 'It is certain that virtually all representatives of the Austrian Enlightenment, whether writers or civil servants, aristocrats or bourgeois … belonged to one or another of the Lodges'.[25] It has been estimated that some 80 per cent of the Austrian higher bureaucracy were masons during the 1780s.[26] And Freemasonry was to play an important role in Mozart's life in Vienna.

Modern freemasonry was founded in England in the second decade of the eighteenth century as a vehicle for the dissemination of progressive ideas based on reason and science. During the 1720s it spread to the rest of Europe, and reached Vienna in the 1740s, Joseph II's father having already been initiated by Sir Robert Walpole at Houghton Hall in Norfolk in 1731. In late 1781, the distinguished metallurgist Ignaz von Born (pl.94) took over the mastership of the small Viennese lodge known as 'Zur Wahren Eintracht' (At True Harmony) and rapidly turned it into the main forum for the Viennese Enlightenment (pl.95). His aim was to fulfil a long-held dream to create in Vienna an academy of intellectual and scientific enquiry to match the famous Royal Society in London. By 1785 'Zur wahren Eintracht' had 197 members made up of the intellectual, scientific and literary elite of Vienna. The lodge produced a serious scientific journal,

95

96

DER MICHAELERPLATZ, DIE KIRCHE, DIE K.K. REITSCHULE   LA PLACE ET L' EGLISE S. MICHEL, LE MANÈGE I. ET R.

UND DAS K.K. NATIONAL THEATER   ET LE THEATRE NATIONNAL, À VIENNE.

Vienne chez Artaria et Comp.

97

with contributors from all over Europe, and the more general *Journal für Freymaurer*. It also had a significant library. The important role that 'Zur wahren Eintracht' played in Vienna is testified by a series of visitors to the city, such as the Danish clergyman and freemason Friedrich Münter, who visited Vienna in 1784, and wrote that 'The whole Bornian (lodge) is a sort of Academy of Science'.[27] Another northern visitor confirmed this impression in the same year: 'The best Viennese heads amongst scholars, and the best writers, are members'.[28] The Born circle was a close, tight-knit group, most of them, like Mozart, in their twenties at the dawning of the Josephine era (Born himself was only 38 in 1780). They considered themselves to be the revolutionary vanguard of the Josephine Enlightenment, and in time became its revolutionary conscience.

Mozart's initial contacts with the Viennese Enlightenment were with establishment Josephine figures like Sonnenfels and Van Swieten. But he soon came into contact with the Born group, for socially the circles of Born and Countess Thun were interchangeable. Evidence of his close acquaintance with Born is extensive: Born's name appears in Mozart's visiting book, and Mozart's name appears in Born's lodge minutes a number of times in 1785, the year in which Mozart wrote the music for *Die Maurerfreude*, a masonic cantata in honour of Born's scientific achievements. Mozart himself had joined a lodge in 1784, although he joined a smaller lodge, 'Zur Wohltätigkeit' (At Beneficence) which was the main focus for a group of churchmen and intellectuals who believed specifically in the possibility of a Catholic Enlightenment. Mozart's extensive engagement with Viennese freemasonry was the clearest indication of his wider engagement with the progressive aims of the Viennese Enlightenment.

OPERA IN VIENNA

For all Mozart's facility in public forms of music such as the symphony or concerto, or in more intimate forms of chamber music, writing operas was always his foremost goal, and by the time he came to Vienna (pl.96) he was already an experienced opera composer with some 12 works under his belt (depending on how you count unfinished or quasi-operatic works). Most of these were in the genre of Italian *opera seria* (serious opera) or *opera buffa* (comic opera), which were the gold standard for opera throughout Europe. But Mozart had also expressed his desire on a number of occasions to contribute to the development of opera in German, a form known as *Singspiel* since it combined speech and song.

Theatre played an important part in the reform programme of Maria Theresa, who sought to 'improve' Austrian theatre by bringing plays from France to create a theatre that would be, in Sonnenfels' words, a 'school for morals'.[29] Joseph also saw theatre as a means of modelling public opinion, and involved himself closely in the running of the two court theatres in Vienna, the Burgtheater (pl.97), in a square immediately adjacent to the Hofburg, the royal palace, and the Kärntnertortheater. Wanting to appeal to a wider audience than the aristocratic patrons who attended plays in French, he established a German-speaking theatre in 1776, an act that was applauded throughout Germany.

Opera played an even more important role in the life of the Habsburg court than spoken theatre. The Italian poet and librettist Pietro Metastasio (1698–1782), whose opera texts, set to music over 600 times in the eighteenth century, set the standard for opera throughout Europe for most of the century, had settled in Vienna in 1730, where he was accorded the title of Caesarean Poet. His heroic dramas of love and duty, usually extolling the virtues of the wise and beneficent ruler, were carefully crafted to give the virtuoso singers of the age the opportunity to shine. Maria Theresa's taste in opera was less lavish than that of her father Charles VI, and by the 1760s, Metastasian operas were increasingly being seen as dry and formulaic, with preference being given to the simpler, more affective style of opera being developed by Christoph Willibald Gluck (1714–87) in

96
Vienna viewed from the Belvedere Palace
Bernardo Bellotto (1721–80),
also called Canaletto
Oil on canvas, 1759–60
Kunsthistorisches Museum, Vienna

97
Michaelerplatz and the old Burgtheater
Carl Schütz (1745–1800)
Coloured engraving on paper, 1783
Theater Museum, Vienna

Vienna. These were often associated with the spread of the middle-class taste for less formal, more natural modes of expression. Joseph II disliked *opera seria* altogether, and in 1777 he followed his founding of a German theatre by decreeing that a German company should be established as the official court opera.

Mozart's first opera in Vienna, *Die Entführung aus dem Serail* of 1782, was therefore written for the German opera company that Joseph II had installed in the court theatre. It was an explicitly political work, written to re-enforce stereotypes of the barbaric nature of the Turks in support of Joseph's negotiations with Catherine the Great of Russia for an opportunistic war against the already crumbling Ottoman Empire. The opera, which tells the tale of the rescue of a captive European woman from the hands of some cruel and lascivious Turks, was hastily prepared for the anticipated visit to Vienna of the Grand Duke Paul of Russia to conduct the negotiations. The musical ambition of *Die Entführung* was recognized by many of Mozart's contemporaries, but it did not conform to the general expectation that German *Singspiel* should be simple and direct. The bland, moralizing fare offered by most creators of *Singspiel* soon lost the support of the more sophisticated court audience, and by 1783 an aristocratic faction was planning to re-instate an Italian company in the Burgtheater. German opera would henceforth be banished to the new, popular theatres in the suburbs, for which Mozart would write his last opera, *Die Zauberflöte*, in 1791.

When he became aware that plans were afoot for an Italian opera company, Mozart immediately set about identifying a suitable libretto for an *opera buffa* with enthusiasm, claiming to have read a hundred possible candidates. After a couple of false starts, he alighted upon the perfect subject, for which he also found the perfect librettist, the Italian Lorenzo da Ponte. Thus it was Mozart, finger on the pulse of his times, who suggested turning a play by the French watchmaker, musician, fortune-hunter, diplomat, spy and gun-runner Pierre-Augustin Caron de Beaumarchais, that had recently caused an uproar in Paris, into an Italian opera for the court theatre in Vienna. Originally accepted for production at the Comédie-Française in 1781, the play – *Le Mariage de Figaro* – did not actually reach the stage until 27 April 1784 due to its politically provocative subject matter: the play is an outspoken attack on the feudal privileges of the aristocracy, conveyed in the conflict between the aristocratic Count Almaviva and his servant Figaro (pl.98) over the Count's attentions to Figaro's bride-to-be Susanna (pl.99). The battle between masters and servants had long been a staple of comic drama, but Beaumarchais brought to his archetypal story a topical twist that made it much more dangerous – for Count Almaviva claims the feudal right of the lord of the manor to enjoy the favours of any newlywed on his estate on her bridal night. Lurking beneath the age-old plot is a devastating critique of the social structures of late eighteenth-century Europe, and of the continued dominance of the aristocracy, which erupts in a great tirade by Figaro against the injustices of wealth and power that still resonates today. Napoleon considered that the play had been the first step towards the French Revolution, which began only five years later.

Mozart knew about the indignities of class all too well. In 1777 he wrote to his father to convey his own resentment that, for all his talent as a musician, he was treated as no better than a servant. After a humiliating encounter with some young aristocrats in his father's home city of Augsburg he resolved from that moment, he told his father: 'to let the whole company of patricians lick my arse'.[30] The play spoke directly of his own experience, and Mozart was politically astute enough to know that the play's message was also in accord with Joseph II's own attempts to dismantle the power of the feudal aristocracy. Despite having banned German translations of the play, Joseph let Mozart go ahead, for presented as an *opera buffa* sung in Italian at the court theatre the drama would speak directly to the aristocratic audience that Joseph was hoping to educate. Indeed, support for people freely to marry whom they liked had been one of Joseph II's

98

most distinctive policies, enshrined in his *Ehepatent* (Marriage Law) of 1783, and in his Serfdom Patent, which placed great emphasis upon the freedom of marriage for servants. As such, the opera endorses the modern, middle-class ideal of affective marriage, an ideal that Mozart himself clearly espoused. In a letter to his father of 1778, Mozart asks Leopold to send his congratulations to an aristocratic Salzburg acquaintance who had recently been married. But he cannot refrain from expressing reservations:

> I wish him joy with my whole heart; but his, I daresay, is again one of those money matches and nothing else. I should not like to marry in this way... People of noble birth must never marry from inclination or love, but only from interest and all kinds of secondary considerations... But we poor humble people can not only choose a wife whom we love and who loves us, but we may, can and do take such a one.[31]

Beaumarchais' play is a fast-moving intrigue with ingenious twists and turns, plots and subplots. Da Ponte had to shape this into an opera, substituting, in his own words: 'canzonettas, arias, choruses and other forms, and words susceptible to music'.[32] And he had to tone down some of the more confrontational political content – Figaro's great tirade does not appear. Nonetheless, social criticism is inherent in both the plot and the music as Figaro and Susanna express their anger at their predicament. When Figaro realises what his master the Count is up to, he declares war in an aria of scarcely controlled rage. 'Se vuol ballare': 'If you want to dance, little mister Count, I'll play the tune'. The aria starts with a mockingly formal minuet, the dance of the aristocracy, and then explodes into a series of unseemly middle-class hopping dances as Figaro imagines the indignities to which he will subject the Count. Mozart drew on his audience's knowledge of the class associations of the dances of his day to make the point.

    Opera buffa was a vehicle that allowed Mozart to tackle these kinds of social issues in a way that wasn't possible in *opera seria*. As a form derived from Italian *commedia dell'arte*, *opera buffa* had social satire at its core. Yet during the course of the eighteenth century it had increasingly introduced the more humanizing elements that allowed Mozart to give his comic characters, and in particular the middle-class and working-class characters, greater depth of feeling and seriousness. Throughout the opera Mozart carefully deploys the various musical languages of the opera of his day (comic, serious, sentimental, parodic) to depict the different characters according to their class and status. He then brings them together in the equalizing ensembles and finales.

    And the opera is not just about social issues. The theme of loss, of both happiness and innocence, is prevalent throughout: the Countess Almaviva remembering happier times; Cherubino, the adolescent page boy hopelessly in love with every woman he sees (pl.100), who must be cast out of Eden into the adult world of strife, which Figaro characterizes as a battlefield in his martial aria 'Non più andrai'; Susanna's heartfelt invocation of the recovery of Eden in her noctural garden aria 'Deh vieni'; even the gardener's daughter Barbarina who, in a wistful little song with the banal words 'I have lost it', ostensibly laments a lost pin. Nudge-nudgingly we know that the song refers to the loss of her sexual innocence; but in truth it mourns a whole fallen world of regret for lost innocence, which Mozart conveys tenderly in his uniquely bitter-sweet music.

    People living in societies undergoing the fundamental transition from closed, customary and religious patterns of organization to more open, individualistic, relativistic and secular systems experience with special intensity humankind's otherwise universal (since we must all abandon infancy) sense of a lost past in which order, wholeness and certainly prevailed. During the reigns of Maria Theresa and Joseph II between 1740 and 1790, the Habsburg Empire, hidebound and backward, was dragged breathlessly and traumatically from the medieval into the modern age, a process that had taken place

99

98
Francesco Benucci (interpreter of Figaro)
Johann Hieronymus Löschenkohl (1753–1807)
Ink and gouache on paper
Theater Museum, Vienna

99
Anna Storace (interpreter of Susanna, also known as Nancy Storace)
Johann Hieronymus Löschenkohl (1753–1807)
Ink and gouache on paper
Theater Museum, Vienna

100

101

over three centuries in England, and over two centuries in France. No great artist has been more acutely aware of the nature of that transition than Mozart, nor lived through it so intensely, nor conveyed it so poignantly.

THE END OF THE ENLIGHTENMENT IN VIENNA

Le nozze di Figaro opened in Vienna in 1786 (pl.101), and was revived at the court opera a few years later. Although we know that it was well-received, and that several numbers had to be encored, the critical praise all refers to the music and singing. We do not know whether its social message was understood. But its faith in human perfectibility was already out of step with its times, for by the mid-point of the decade, Joseph II's programme of reforms had begun to come under attack. People complained both that he was dictatorial, and that his reforms had led to a breakdown of social order and discipline. Public opinion, which had worked in his favour at the beginning of the decade, now turned against him, as did the aristocracy that he had so alienated. To make things worse, the economic boom of the beginning of the decade, that had served Mozart so well as a freelance musician, slowed and turned into a recession that was compounded by Joseph's pursuit of his futile war against the Turks from 1787 to 1791. Demand for music, now seen as a luxury, dried up, and so did Mozart's main sources of income, given that he never managed to secure anything but a very minor court position in 1787, composing dances for the court balls. His last attempt to mount a concert series in 1789 failed to attract subscribers other than the always loyal Van Swieten, who was himself politically discredited by his association with Joseph by this date. When the French Revolution broke out in 1789 many people in Austria saw it not as the fulfilment of the Enlightenment project, but as its nemesis. Joseph II would die in 1790, a disappointed and embittered man, followed by Mozart in 1791.

100
Draft of part of Cherubino's Act I
aria 'Non so più cosa son' (K492, no. 6)
Wolfgang Amadeus Mozart (1756–91)
Autograph score, 1786
British Library, London, Zweig MS 57

101
Poster for the premiere of *Le nozze di Figaro*
at the Burgtheater, Vienna, 1 May 1786
Theater Museum, Vienna

102

VIENNA

103

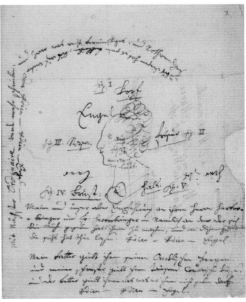

104

102

*Leopold Mozart, Maria Anna Mozart
and Wolfgang Amadeus Mozart*
Louis de Carmontelle (1717–1806)
Hand-coloured lithograph, 1764
V&A: S.2928-2009

As a child, Mozart travelled extensively to the
different courts of Europe. His father organized
concerts in cities such as Munich, Prague, London
and Paris, in order to show off the talent of both
his children, Wolfgang and Maria Anna (Nannerl).
Louis de Carmontelle, an employee of the French
Court, was known for his aquarelle portrayals of
his contemporaries, including important figures
of the Enlightenment in art, literature and music.

103

Piano played by Wolfgang Amadeus Mozart
in Prague in 1787
Franz Xaver Christoph (1733–93)
Mahogany, c.1785
Czech Museum of Music, Prague

This piano was played by Mozart during his stay
in Prague in 1787. After the success of *Le nozze
di Figaro* in late 1786, the impresario Pasquale
Bondini commissioned Mozart to write a new
opera, leading to the premiere of *Don Giovanni*
in Prague on 29 October 1787.

104

Letter to Maria Anna Thekla Mozart
(1758–1841)
Wolfgang Amadeus Mozart (1756–91)
Ink on paper, 10 May 1779
British Library, London, Zweig MS 67

During a stay in Augsburg in 1777, Mozart got
to know his cousin Maria Anna and they became
lovers. Several letters survive and reveal Mozart
to be a playful, infatuated young man. This letter
starts: 'Dearest, most beloved, most beautiful,
most amiable, most charming little bass, or little
cello, whom a worthless cousin has enraged!'
Mozart later fell in love with Aloysia Weber, a
trained singer, before finally marrying the latter's
sister Constanze in 1782.

105

106

105
Pedal harp
Jean-Henri Nadermann (c.1734—99)
Carved giltwood with painted soundboard,
metal strings and crochettes
France, c.1780
V&A: 4087-1857

The harp was a popular instrument in
eighteenth-century Vienna. The sister of Joseph
II, Marie Antoinette, brought the fashion to France
when she became the Dauphine. This object may
have been made by Jean-Henri Nadermann, a
popular harp maker in Paris, although some of the
features differ from his usual style.

106
Furnishing fabric with Apollo and the Muses
Printed cotton
France, 1750—99
V&A: T.412-1919

This type of toile was first created in
Jouy-en-Josas, France, in the second half
of the eighteenth century, and became popular
across Europe as wall furnishing fabric. The
theme depicted here shows Apollo, God of Sun
and Music, accompanied by the nine Muses.
The Muse of Music, Euterpe, is in the centre
playing an ancient form of flute.

107
The Young Musician
Michel Garnier (1753—1829)
Oil on canvas, 1788
Olivier Berggruen Collection

The genre painting was a style highly popular
at the end of the eighteenth century, inspired by
the earlier works of Jean-Antoine Watteau
(1684—1721) and Jean-Honoré Fragonard
(1732—1806). Here a young woman is perfecting
her skills at the harp. The practice and
understanding of music was integral to the
everyday life of an aristocratic woman in the age
of the Enlightenment.

107

VIENNA

109

108

Woman's *robe à la piedmontaise* and petticoat
Silk brocaded with silk and silver threads
France, 1775–80
V&A: 750&A-1898

The *robe à la piedmontaise* was a short-lived trend
in the late 1770s. According to the *Galerie des
Modes et des Costumes Français*, the style was first
worn by Madame Clothilde de France, Princess of
Piedmont to the theatre in Lyon in 1775.

109 (and detail)

Coat, waistcoat and breeches
Cream figured silk velvet
France, 1770s
V&A: T.129-1921&A,B

This ensemble is made from expensive fine silk
velvet and is an example of fashionable men's
dress from the 1770s. Such a style was suitable
for formal afternoon or evening occasions.

110

111

The brilliant Nymph from the Palais Royal offering to the public eyes the charms of her figure and the elegance of her waist, which bring upon her the most merited praises; Her hair is styled 'à la Suzanne' and she is wearing a bodice 'à la Figaro'
François Louis Joseph Watteau (1758–1823)
Hand coloured engraving
Cahiers de Costumes Francais, 1785
Museum of London, 2002.139/749

This engraving was published in a French fashion magazine in 1785, after Pierre-Augustin Caron de Beaumarchais' play *Le Mariage de Figaro* was finally performed at the Théâtre Français in 1784. The play had previously been banned for five years by the censor, due to its politically sensitive content. It became a huge success and inspired several fashion trends, such as here the hair *à la Suzanne* and bodice *à la Figaro*.

111
Coat
Pale blue velvet, imitation fur motif
France, 1785–90
V&A: T.17-1950

112
Sack-back dress
Blue ribbed silk, blue and white floral embroidering
France, 1750s (altered 1780s)
V&A: CIRC.157&A-1920

The sack-back gown was a style that originated in France and became fashionable throughout Europe from the 1740s to the 1780s. It has loose pleats from shoulder to hem at the back, and the front is open to reveal the petticoat underneath, which is embroidered with flower motifs.

112

113

113
Fan, with central scene showing a marriage
Gouache on silk and paper with tortoiseshell sticks
France, c.1780
V&A: 97-1864

The central scene of this fan, inspired by the 1761
painting *L'Accordée de Village* by Jean-Baptiste
Greuze (1725–1805), shows a father accepting
a gentleman's offer of marriage for his daughter.
Romantic marriage was a popular subject in
eighteenth-century Salons, seen as a way of
correcting society evils by philosophers such as
Denis Diderot (1713–84). This subject was echoed
in *Le nozze di Figaro*, where Figaro marries for
love rather than status.

114
Figure group symbolizing winter
Imperial Vienna Porcelain factory
Hard-paste porcelain, c.1760
V&A: C.17-1912

Under the patronage of Empress Maria Theresa
and afterwards her son Emperor Joseph II,
the Imperial Vienna Porcelain factory became a
successful producer of hard-paste porcelain
and was the second oldest factory in Europe after
Meissen. Allegorical and pastoral designs
depicting love and courtship, as seen here, were
popular during the end of the Rococo period.

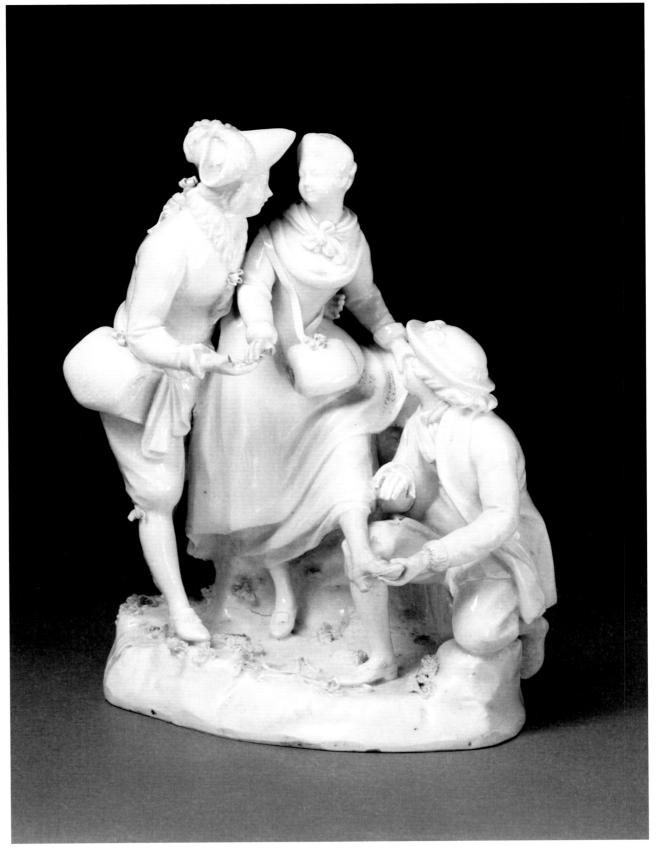

114

VIENNA

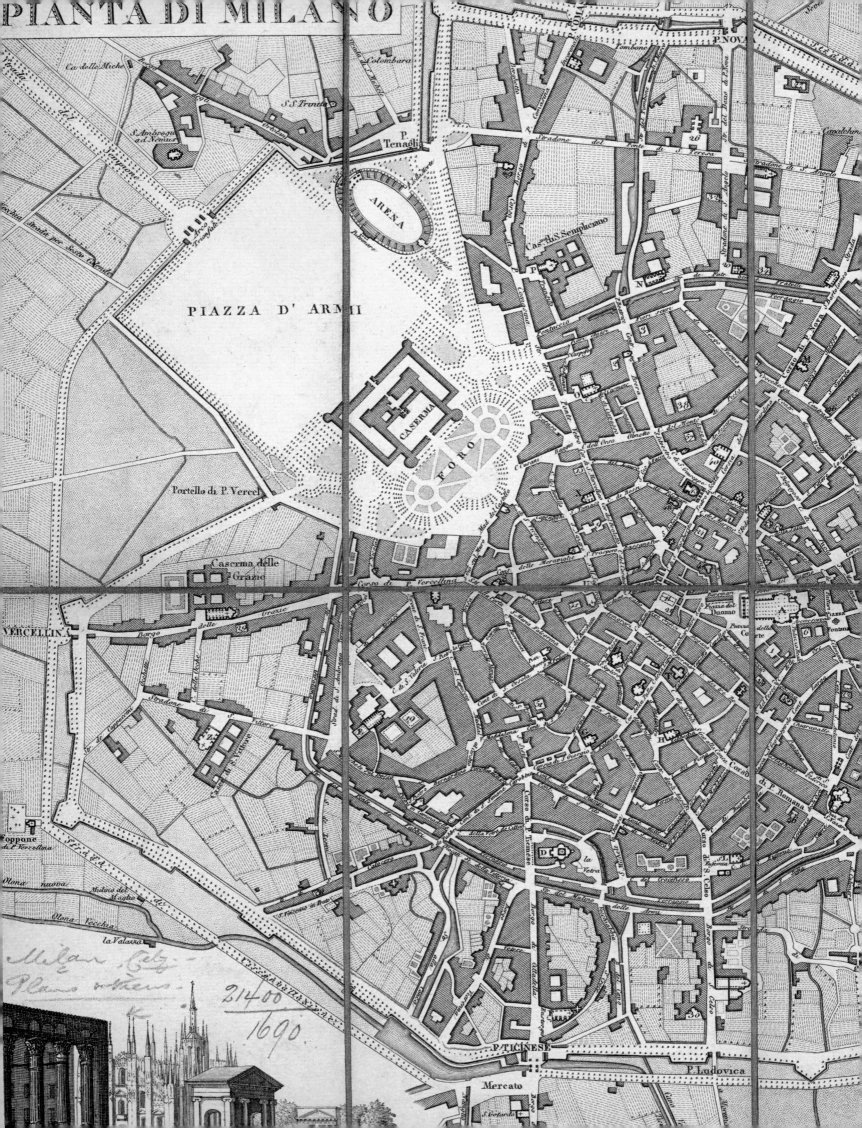

PIANTA DI MILANO

PIAZZA D' ARMI

ARENA

CASERMA

FORO

Portello di P. Vercel

Caserma delle Grazie

P. Tenaglia

P. NOVA

Cas.ma S. Semplieiano

P. Ticinese

VERCELLINA

P. Ticinese

Mercato

P. Lodovica

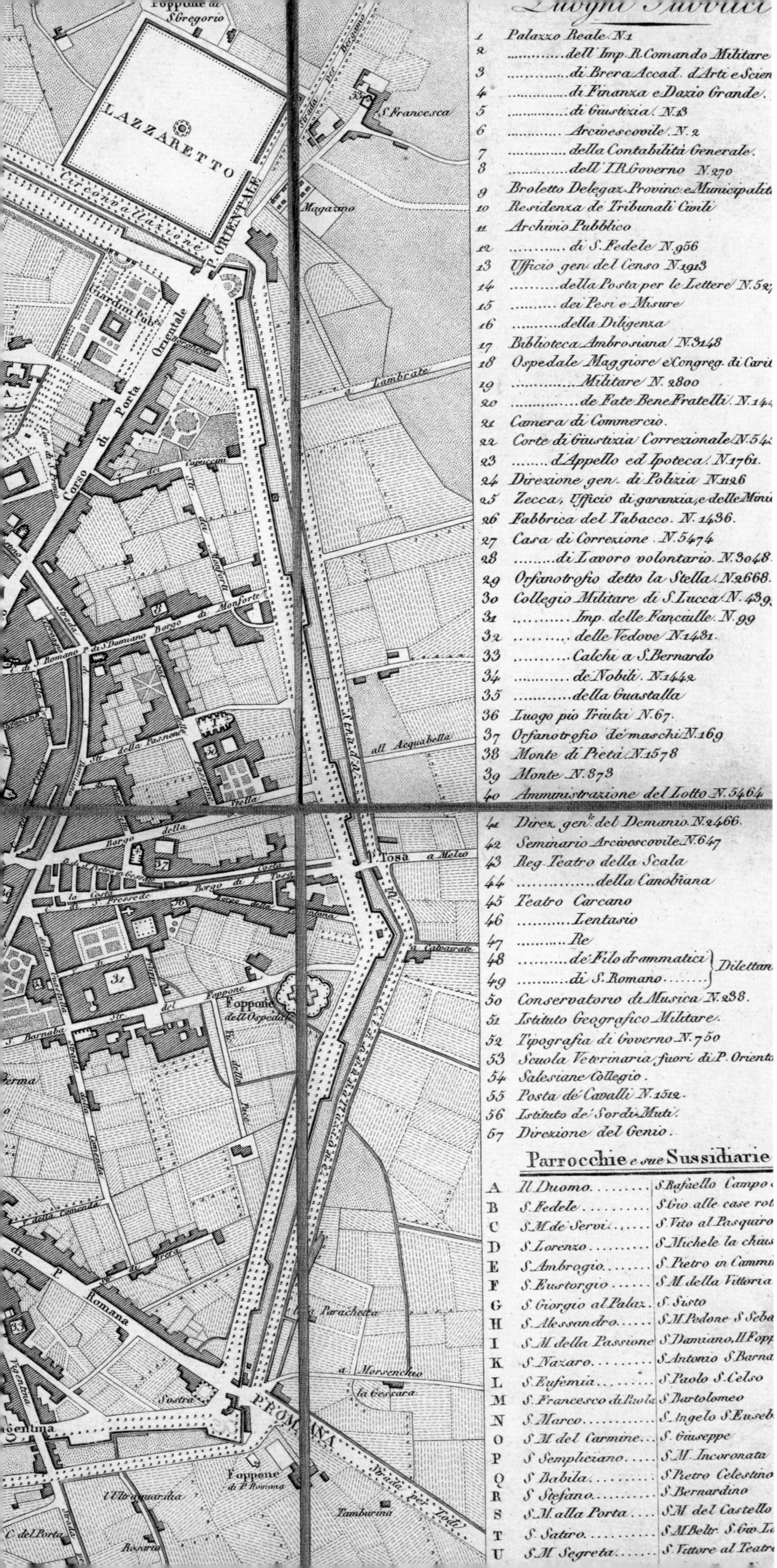

Luoghi Pubblici

1 Palazzo Reale N.1
2 .... dell'Imp.R.Comando Militare
3 .... di Brera Accad. d'Arti e Scien
4 .... di Finanza e Dazio Grande
5 .... di Giustizia. N.13
6 .... Arcivescovile. N.2
7 .... della Contabilità Generale
8 .... dell'I.R.Governo N.270
9 Broletto Delegaz.Provinc.e Municipalit
10 Residenza de Tribunali Civili
11 Archivio Pubblico
12 .... di S. Fedele N.956
13 Ufficio gen.del Censo N.1913
14 .... della Posta per le Lettere N.52
15 .... dei Pesi e Misure
16 .... della Diligenza
17 Biblioteca Ambrosiana N.3148
18 Ospedale Maggiore e Congreg. di Carit
19 .... Militare N.2800
20 .... de Fate BeneFratelli N.144
21 Camera di Commercio
22 Corte di Giustizia Correzionale N.54
23 .... d'Appello ed Ipoteca N.1761
24 Direzione gen. di Polizia N.1126
25 Zecca, Ufficio di garanzia, e delle Min
26 Fabbrica del Tabacco. N.1436
27 Casa di Correzione N.5474
28 .... di Lavoro volontario N.3048
29 Orfanotrofio detto la Stella N.2668
30 Collegio Militare di S.Lucca N.439
31 .... Imp. delle Fanciulle N.99
32 .... delle Vedove N.1431
33 .... Calchi a S.Bernardo
34 .... de Nobili N.1442
35 .... della Guastalla
36 Luogo pio Triulzi N.67
37 Orfanotrofio de'maschi N.169
38 Monte di Pietà N.1578
39 Monte N.373
40 Amministrazione del Lotto N.5464
41 Direz. gen.le del Demanio N.2466
42 Seminario Arcivescovile N.647
43 Reg.Teatro della Scala
44 .... della Canobiana
45 Teatro Carcano
46 .... Lentasio
47 .... Re
48 .... de'Filo drammatici } Dilettan
49 .... di S. Romano
50 Conservatorio di Musica N.238
51 Istituto Geografico Militare
52 Tipografia di Governo N.750
53 Scuola Veterinaria fuori di P. Orient
54 Salesiane Collegio
55 Posta de'Cavalli N.1512
56 Istituto de'Sordi-Muti
57 Direzione del Genio

Parrocchie e sue Sussidiarie

A Il Duomo .... S.Rafaello Campo
B S. Fedele .... S.Gio alle case rot
C S.M de'Servi .... S.Vito al Pasquiro
D S.Lorenzo .... S.Michele la chiu
E S.Ambrogio .... S.Pietro in Cammi
F S.Eustorgio .... S.M. della Vittoria
G S.Giorgio al Palaz. S.Sisto
H S.Alessandro .... S.M.Pedone S.Seba
I S.M. della Passione S.Damiano, Il Fopp
K S.Nazaro .... S.Antonio S.Barna
L S.Eufemia .... S.Paolo S.Celso
M S.Francesco di Paola S.Bartolomeo
N S.Marco .... S.Angelo S.Euseb
O S.M del Carmine .... S.Giuseppe
P S.Sempliciano .... S.M.Incoronata
Q S.Babila .... S.Pietro Celestino
R S.Stefano .... S.Bernardino
S S.M. alla Porta .... S.M del Castello
T S.Satiro .... S.M.Beltr. S.Gio.la
U S.M. Segreta .... S.Vittore al Teatro

4

GIUSEPPE VERDI
1813–1901

Nabucco

Nabucco, the King of Babylon, leads the invasion of Jerusalem. His daughter Fenena, held hostage by the Israelites, falls in love with the Israelite Ismaele. Fenena's half-sister Abigaille also loves Ismaele, who rejects her. After discovering that she is not Nabucco's real daughter, Abigaille swears vengeance against Nabucco, Fenena and all the Israelites. Nabucco, who has been struck mad in punishment after claiming to be divine, prays to the God of the Israelites. He recovers his sanity, defeats Abigaille and liberates Jerusalem.

INTRODUCTION

PLÁCIDO DOMINGO

The life of a performing artist is full of surprises. During my long career as a tenor, I never thought that I would eventually add a substantial number of baritone parts to my repertoire. Although I had sung some high baritone roles in my parents' zarzuela company in Mexico, when I was still in my teens, I had never sung baritone roles on the opera stage. Much later, when I was in my sixties, the idea of singing the title baritone role in Verdi's *Simon Boccanegra* occurred to me; I particularly loved that part for its combination of high drama and deep humanity, and I thought I might try it if my voice developed in the right way. But the thought of singing the title role in *Nabucco* never entered my mind in those years.

I first saw and heard *Nabucco* during my 'apprentice years' with the Israel National Opera, when I was in my early twenties — and how appropriate it was to be introduced to an opera about the sufferings and survival of the Jewish people during my three seasons in Israel! But I did not perform in that *Nabucco* production or in any later ones. In the early 1980s I sang the tenor role of Ismaele in conductor Giuseppe Sinopoli's recording of the complete opera, but I never performed the role in the theatre. In that recording, Nabucco was sung beautifully by Piero Cappuccilli, and I remember attending performances of the opera in which Carlo Guelfi and Juan Pons brought the part off magnificently.

Over the last few years, as my voice has darkened and as I have been adding more baritone roles to my repertoire, I have focused mostly, although not entirely, on characters who are fathers. They seem to me more appropriate to a man in his seventies than the 'young lover' tenor parts that I used to sing, or even than the jealous, rejected lover baritone parts that would also fit my voice today. Simon Boccanegra, Giorgio Germont in *La traviata*, Francesco Foscari in *I due Foscari* — these are human beings whose stories are dominated in both positive and negative ways by their paternal feelings.

Nabucco, too, is partly a fatherly character. Of course, we don't know what sort of father the real Babylonian king Nebuchadnezzar II was — he was a military man, a conqueror who certainly does not have the reputation of

having been a tender soul. As far as I've been able to discover, the names of only two of his children have been preserved: there was a son, Amel-Marduk, who succeeded him, and a daughter, Nitocris. Fenena, his daughter in Verdi's opera, and Abigaille, who initially believes that she is Nabucco's daughter, and all the other characters except the king himself, were invented either by Temistocle Solera, the librettist, or by the authors of the stories on which Solera based his text.

But historical fact doesn't matter very much in opera or in the theatre in general: just think of Shakespeare's kings and Schiller's heroes! What matters is the intensity of the living emotions conveyed by the text, by the stage action and, above all, by the music. In *Nabucco*, the king is a real father who loves his real daughter, does everything in his power to save her — and really does manage to save her. In fact, *Nabucco* can be seen as an anomaly: it certainly is not a comedy, but it isn't a tragedy either, because in the end the 'good guys' triumph. Or rather, Nabucco, who begins as a bad guy, turns into a good guy after he has been punished and then pardoned by the all-powerful God of the Israelites.

For all of these reasons, the role of Nabucco requires tremendous emotional range. Through most of the first two acts, the king is arrogant, aggressive, threatening — a bully, in short — but at the end of Part II he is stricken with insanity. Through the third act and in the beginning of the fourth, any singer who interprets this part has to try to demonstrate fragility, confusion, regret and many other emotions. But then, after God restores Nabucco's sanity, the king becomes a good, just, dignified ruler. As performers, it is our duty and our privilege to attempt to make these changes convincing.

From the vocal point of view, too, singing the part of Nabucco is a demanding task — not as taxing, perhaps, as the terrifying soprano role of Abigaille, but still very difficult. It is interesting, though, that according to most contemporary observers, Giorgio Ronconi, the 31-year-old baritone who sang the title part at the premiere at La Scala in 1842, did not have either a beautiful voice or a wide vocal range — and this was at a time when composers often adapted roles to fit specific voices. Ronconi was described as a convincing figure on the stage, but I can't help wondering how he coped with this part, if the descriptions of his voice are correct. We do know that Giuseppina Strepponi, the first Abigaille, had great success in the role, but singing it too many times during the following seasons probably contributed to her vocal decline. She was only 26 at the time of the premiere, and she had to retire at the age of 30. Later, she became Verdi's second wife.

Thinking about *Nabucco*'s premiere brings to mind this strange Wagner-Verdi coincidence: each composer enjoyed his first major success with his third opera — Verdi with *Nabucco*, Wagner with *Rienzi* — and both of those operas were first performed in 1842. Wagner was 29 at the time; Verdi would turn 29 a few months later. These two men were so different, both personally and artistically, that this convergence is all the more noteworthy.

If we think of the 15 or 16 operas (depending on how you count them) that Verdi wrote before the great, popular trilogy of *Rigoletto*, *Il trovatore* and *La traviata*, only four of them — *Nabucco, Ernani, Macbeth* and *Luisa Miller* — are still performed relatively frequently today, and *Nabucco* is the oldest of the four. Its energetic overture, its great 'Va, pensiero' chorus, and the beauty and intensity of its arias and ensemble scenes have kept it before the public for 175 years. I feel sure that it will continue to attract audiences for many years to come.

115 (pp.126–7; detail)
Tourist map of Milan
Printed paper on canvas, 1842
British Library, London,
Maps 12.a.2

116 (p.130)
Plácido Domingo as Nabucco
in *Nabucco*
Directed by Daniele Abbado
with designs by Alison Chitty
Royal Opera House, London, 2013

117
Chorus in *Nabucco*
Directed by Daniele Abbado
with designs by Alison Chitty
Royal Opera House, London, 2013

118
Scene from *Nabucco*
Directed by Daniele Abbado
with designs by Alison Chitty
Royal Opera House, London, 2013

117

118

VERDI AND MILAN:
FROM *NABUCCO* TO *NABUCCO*

ROGER PARKER

120

In June 1832, 18-year-old Giuseppe Verdi moved from Busseto (near Parma) to Milan to complete his musical training privately with teacher and composer Vincenzo Lavigna (1776–1836). He must have felt keenly the change in cultural climate: from a provincial town in which his reputation had been largely that of a church musician, he transferred to one of Italy's major capital cities, an international operatic centre with a rich tradition of intellectual and cultural achievement (pl.120). At the heart of this culture, at least from a musical point of view, stood the Teatro alla Scala, one of the four or five major theatres in Italy (only La Fenice in Venice, the Pergola in Florence, the Argentina in Rome and the San Carlo in Naples could claim equal status). But it is important to recall that Milan, then a flourishing part of the Austro-Hungarian empire, was also the centre of Italy's publishing trade and in general regarded as one of the most forward-looking intellectual centres on the peninsula. It was hardly an accident that, when Italy's so-called Risorgimento came to a climax with nationalist uprisings in the mid-nineteenth century, Milan was a prominent site of revolutionary activity.[1]

Much later in life, Verdi (pl.121) recalled in a letter his training with Lavigna as being extremely restricted, with no reference to the music of the day.[2] But this latter-day emphasis (the letter was written in 1871, some 40 years after the events described) tells us more about Verdi's reactions in the 1870s to an Italy increasingly influenced by foreign opera composers – in particular Giacomo Meyerbeer (1791–1864) and Richard Wagner (1813–83) – than it does about the reality of his own student experiences. Written statements by Lavigna are clear that Verdi also received instruction in free composition (what the Italians called *composizione ideale*).[3] Perhaps even more significant is that Lavigna instructed Verdi to attend La Scala every single night of the season (pl.122 and 123).[4] Even though the cost was substantial, it was clearly an important part of Verdi's education. Lavigna had been a noted *maestro al cembalo* at La Scala, and knew well that to excel in *composizione ideale* the young student had to study contemporary scores and, above all, witness directly in the theatre the successes and failures of the period's best opera composers.

We can, then, be fairly sure that Verdi began attending La Scala regularly when it opened for the autumn season of 1832: in the years that followed (Verdi the student was resident in the city until June 1834, and again during the first half of 1835) there were many events in the theatre that must have left a lasting impression. *Norma* by Vincenzo Bellini (1801–35) and *Otello* by Gioachino Rossini (1792–1868) – both in 1834 and both starring Maria Malibran – must have been formative. Yet if we had to identify one key event in this student period, it might be the world premiere on 26 December 1833 of *Lucrezia Borgia* by Gaetano Donizetti (1797–1848). Although *Lucrezia* was a considerable success with the public, enjoying 33 performances, all the major reviewers decried the unfortunate influence of the source play, Victor Hugo's *Lucrèce Borgia*. It is easy to imagine that this early dispute over 'Romantic' subject matter had a profound effect on Verdi, in particular when, somewhat later in his career, he too confronted Hugolian drama in the operas *Ernani* and *Rigoletto*.

In the middle of 1835, Verdi returned home to Busseto, and in March of the following year was appointed *maestro di musica* there. However, during his student years in Milan he had made contact with Pietro Massini, director of the Società Filarmonica, whom he assisted in various amateur performances in the city, notably of *The Creation* by Joseph Haydn (1732–1809) in April 1834 and of Rossini's *La Cenerentola* in April–May 1835. Even in the isolation of Busseto, he managed to keep in contact by providing Massini and his Società with a Cantata in honour of the Austrian Emperor, Ferdinand I, a piece that one reviewer described as 'full of warm and respectful affection for the August Sovereign to whom it is addressed'.[5] However embarrassing such an encomium

119 (pp.134–5)
Teatro alla Scala, Milan
Originally built in 1776–8, the opera house has undergone several renovations in the 20th and 21st centuries.

120
The Duomo Square and the Rebecchino area
Amanzia Guerillot Inganni (1828–1905)
Oil on canvas, 1850
Palazzo Morando, Milan

121
Portrait of Giuseppe Verdi
Francesco Torriani
Oil on canvas, c.1840s
Museo Teatrale alla Scala, Milan

122

123

might later have been to the future 'bard of the Risorgimento', Verdi's contact with Massini was of enormous value. In a series of letters to Massini over the next few years, we learn that Verdi soon produced an opera, originally entitled *Rocester*. It was refused by the impresario at the Teatro Ducale in Parma in late 1837, but – in part through Massini's advocacy – was accepted at no less a venue than La Scala for the autumn season of 1839. In late 1838 Verdi resigned his post in Busseto and moved to Milan.

1839–43: FIRST SUCCESSES

The fact that Verdi's first opera, retitled *Oberto, conte di San Bonifacio*, was first performed at La Scala needs some explanation. Massini may have been of some help, but the key figure in the decision was the La Scala impresario Bartolomeo Merelli. The reception of *Oberto*, premiered on 17 November 1839, can be summed up as what the Italians call a *successo discreto*. This was partly because Verdi had taken considerable care to fashion the *prima donna's* role (Leonora) to a particularly unusual voice, that of Antonietta Ranieri-Marini, evidence of whose impressive range and powerful lower register are clear in many parts of the score. The success of the opera encouraged the Milanese publisher Giovanni Ricordi to acquire the rights to the opera, thus forming a relationship between composer and publishing house that would endure to the end of Verdi's long life.

After the unfortunate fiasco of Verdi's next opera at La Scala, *Un giorno di regno* (1840), there came in 1842 his first triumphant success: *Nabucco* (see pl.137 and 139). Although various documents exist that chart the opera's first published forms (pl.138), the story of its creation is reliant to a large extent on the composer's own memories, recounted long after the event. From these it is clear that, at least in Verdi's later life, *Nabucco* was, quintessentially, imagined as one moment – one lyrical inspiration that stood for the whole. This is the famous Part III chorus 'Va, pensiero sull'ali dorate', in which exiled Hebrew slaves lament the loss of their homeland (pl.124). And there is no doubt that his concentration on the piece reflected the meanings that gradually accumulated around it during the nineteenth century – meanings that have remained in robust currency until the present. Almost as often as 'Va, pensiero' is evoked, we are patiently schooled as to its meaning. The biblical setting of *Nabucco*, the story of Nebuchadnezzar and his taking of the Jews into captivity, was and is, we are told, diaphanous. Time and again the metaphor is rehearsed: Verdi and his librettist may overtly have given voice to 'Hebrew slaves' lamenting their exile from Israel, but they were in fact in covert dialogue with their audience. Everyone at La Scala is supposed to have known that the Hebrew slaves were merely a fiction, mere stock operatic motley. The real purpose of the chorus was as an expression of poignantly contemporary Italian feeling, at the loss of their homeland, then under the yoke of foreign domination.

There is no doubt that *Nabucco*, first performed on 9 March 1842, was a huge success, and that it decisively launched Verdi's national and international career. During that first spring season it was performed only eight times, as the season ended on 19 March; but when the opera was revived in autumn 1842, it achieved a record number of 57 performances, and in the 21 months that followed (up to the end of 1844) it was played in nearly 60 theatres, in Italy and elsewhere in Europe. On the other hand, there is no evidence that 'Va, pensiero' was greeted with particular enthusiasm, in spite of the attempts of some to invent such evidence. An egregious example of the latter involves the premiere at La Scala. Franco Abbiati's 1959 exhaustive biography of the composer (the standard biography in Italian) quotes a newspaper review of this premiere, in which it is reported that the audience demanded an encore of 'Va, pensiero' despite an Austrian proclamation forbidding such public manifestations. The story is repeated by biographer

122
The façade of the Teatro alla Scala
Angelo Inganni (1807–80)
Oil on canvas, 1852
Museo Teatrale alla Scala, Milan

123
Interior view of Teatro alla Scala in Milan, newly restored in 1830
Unknown artist
Hand-coloured drawing or etching, ink and paint on paper, c.1830
V&A: S.3882-2009

124 (pp.140–1)
Va, pensiero sull'ali dorate, Part III
Giuseppe Verdi (1813–1901)
Autograph score
Archivio Storico Ricordi, Milan

Julian Budden and many others, and is indeed a commonplace of Verdian reception history.[6] But in fact Abbiati's 'quotation' simply doesn't appear in the review from which he purports to quote: he made it up, or rather (in an interesting example of scholarly etiquette), he took it from a completely different review, referring to an entirely different chorus.[7]

Nabucco, though, *was* a watershed, and undoubtedly caught the Milanese imagination (pl.125). Although we have hardly any evidence about the circumstances of its creation, it seems clear that *I Lombardi alla prima crociata*, first performed at La Scala on 11 February 1843, was from the start intended as nothing less than *Nabucco* 2. Another grand, scenically splendid work; another religious subject; lots of impressive choruses: what could go wrong? Popular rumour has it that, after *Nabucco*, Merelli left to Verdi's discretion the fee for his new opera: further achievements on that scale seems to have been well nigh beyond price, and the first night was again a clamorous success with the public. Verdi was firmly established as a 'Milanese' composer, with La Scala as his home.

126

1843-68: DELUSIONS, INTERREGNUM

In this context it is something of a surprise that, after the triumphant reception of *I Lombardi*, there ensued a period of sharp decline in the relationship between Verdi and La Scala, one seemingly brought about by a decline in the artistic standards and financial stability of the theatre. Of course, this was only a part of a more complex story. It was inevitable that, as Verdi's reputation grew, he would receive offers from other prestigious theatres within Italy: the premiere of his next opera, *Ernani*, went to La Fenice in Venice, while others then went to Rome and Naples. There was also, though, a continuing undercurrent of mistrust and exasperation on the part of Verdi, a good deal of it aimed personally at Merelli. Even knowing this, it is difficult to understand Verdi's decision to break with Merelli and La Scala. Whatever the general standards of the theatre, Verdi's operas were being received with increasing rapture by an adoring public. His personal relationship with Merelli, the man who had been so instrumental in his earliest successes, must have had a good deal to do with it. By 1846 there seemed to be a state of open war between composer and impresario, with both money and artistic standards at stake. Even though Verdi's threats of a total ban on his operas at the theatre were hardly realistic, it would be many years before he set foot again in the city's greatest theatre.

The importance of Milan to Italy's struggle for independence in the mid-nineteenth century has been mentioned already (pl.126). When reading through Milanese theatrical correspondence from 1844 to 1848, it is striking to see that from late 1846, even the theatrical news becomes invaded by political issues. And the nearer we get to the revolutions of 1848, the clearer it becomes that operatic performances became a focal point of civil unrest: in early 1847, the young conductor Angelo Mariani was reprimanded by the Milanese commissioner of police for his performances of *Nabucco* at the Teatro Carcano, 'for having given to Verdi's music an expression that is too obviously revolutionary and hostile to the Imperial government'.[8] By the beginning of 1848, any event seemed capable of generating a riot. At La Scala the Austrian ballerina Fanny Elssler, who had been greeted with enormous enthusiasm in previous seasons, met with a hostile reception in the months immediately preceding the 1848 revolution. On 12 February 1848 she was whistled and booed at La Scala, fainted onstage, and retired immediately to Vienna.[9] As if to confirm the opera house as an increasingly dangerous place to perform, on 22 February the *Gazzetta privilegiata di Milano*, the only newspaper permitted to report political events, carried a notice from the Governor of Milan threatening harsh penalties for demonstrators and mentioning in particular:

125
Poster for the autumn 1842 revival
of *Nabucco* at the Teatro alla Scala, Milan
Single sheet, 1842
Museo Teatrale alla Scala, Milan

126
*Political and route map of Italy
showing all the states*
L. Vivien (1802–96)
Printed paper on canvas, 1837
British Library, London, 20570 (70)

127

The wearing of certain colours, or otherwise making them evident, the wearing of certain symbols or signs, the singing or declaming of certain songs or poems, the applauding or whistling of certain passages from a theatrical performance.[10]

All this was of course to no avail: all sorts of revolutionary styles came into sartorial vogue (pl.127). And then, on 18 March, the barricades went up. In five days of hard street fighting, the Milanese drove the Austrians from the city, remaining in control until the middle of August, when military defeats led to the capitulation of the northern Italian armies and the retaking of the city by the Austrians (pl.128).

During these turbulent months the theatres, as was hardly surprising, mostly closed their doors. When the Teatro Carcano tried to interest the public even in such a 'revolutionary' work as Auber's *La muta di Portici (La Muette de Portici)*, it was largely ignored. As the critic of Ricordi's house journal, the *Gazzetta musicale*, put it on 3 May 1848: 'The Carcano opened with Auber's materpiece *La muta di Portici*. The theatre was not crowded because the populace is now occupied with things more serious than music'.[11]

However, on 19 April another Milanese theatrical journal, *Il pirata* (which naturally enough had a strong vested interest in theatrical activity), ran a long article entitled 'Prossima Primavera' (The Coming Spring), mostly concerned with the future of La Scala. As well as supplying information about administrative conditions before the revolution (during which Merelli had frequently been accused of both bad management and pro-Austrian sympathies), it suggests some of the many problems to be faced by any new government administration, including how to maintain appropriate audience behaviour and so avoid a descent into anarchy.[12] It was an ambitious programme, and although on 22 April *Il pirata* carried an announcement by the new management of the proudly renamed 'Teatro Nazionale della Scala', Milan's main theatre did not in fact open for opera during the months of the uprising.

In the midst of this activity, Verdi made a brief journey from Paris to Milan, arriving on 5 April. The experience of seeing the city at its revolutionary peak encouraged him finally to write an overtly 'patriotic' opera (which eventually became *La battaglia di Legnano*). However, what musical activity *did* take place (there were various concerts in aid of the wounded, and other ceremonial events) did not include him or his music, an omission that alone might cause us to reconsider Verdi's reputation as a 'patriotic' composer during this period.[13] After settling some business affairs, Verdi returned to Paris, and by the middle of August the military battles had been lost and thousands of Milanese (including most of Verdi's revolutionary friends) had fled the city. The bass Carlo Cambaggio, in letters to the impresario Alessandro Lanari, offers us a doleful picture of life in Milan immediately after the return of the Austrians. Control was far harsher than it had been before the revolution:

Milan is crowded with soldiery. All the houses and *palazzi* are full of them. Soldiers cook their rations in magnificent apartments and gilded *salons*. The famous Casino de' nobili, the Archbishop's Palace and many churches are crowded with Croats and other insects…. Meanwhile the theatre does well, Merelli laughs and the military carouse.[14]

In the midst of this extreme clamp down on any expression that could lead to further civil unrest, when censorship and police control was at its height, the 1848–49 carnival season staged revivals of *Ernani* (3 January), *I due Foscari* (8 January) and *Macbeth* (24 February).[15] *Attila*, *Ernani* and *Nabucco* (complete with 'Va, pensiero'!) followed in the next full season. It seems inconceivable in the circumstances that any of these operas had been actively associated with the failed revolution.

128

129

Verdi did not return to Milan, or have any dealings with La Scala, over the next decade.[16] The theatre continued to feature his operas at the centre of its repertory (pl.130-3), but although Merelli ceased to be impresario in 1850 (albeit with a brief return to the post from 1861 to 1863), Verdi kept alive his antagonism to the theatre (and perhaps also to the city). What is more surprising is that his attitude continued through most of the 1860s. This period, the second major military phase of the Risorgimento after 1848, saw the formation of the Italian state in 1861, with the former King of Piedmont, Victor Emmanuel, becoming the first King of Italy (pl.129). All parts of the peninsula apart from the Veneto (still under Austrian control until 1866) and the Papal States (which did not capitulate until 1870) were precariously united under an Italian parliament and his titular control. Not surprisingly, a very different political atmosphere surrounded the city, not least a new sense of financial constraint brought about by the dissolution of old sites of privilege. And by that time, other enemies were making themselves felt: alongside Verdi's new works, the repertoire of La Scala began to include an increasing number of foreign operas, first and foremost those of Meyerbeer, but also Fromental Halévy (1799-1862), Charles Gounod (1818-93) and others. This international vogue came with the enthusiastic support from a younger generation of Italian composers – men like Franco Faccio (1840-91) and Arrigo Boito (1842-1918), the latter of whom made a celebrated attack on Verdi and his reliance on *formula* rather than *form*.

Verdi's extreme distrust of this new fashion gradually moved him into a staunchly conservative position, something of an irony as, at same time, he was increasingly being cast as the musical saint of the Risorgimento, with 'Va, pensiero' as his principal signature tune. When consulted about the proper courses of study in the reformed Italian conservatories, he recommended little but strict counterpoint and ancient Italian music. Students should submit to constant, daily doses of fugue, enlivened only by music by ancient Italian composers Palestrina (c.1525-94) and Marcello (1686-1739). In some ways this resembled the training he himself had received in Milan at the hands of Lavigna in the 1830s. However, as we saw earlier, Lavigna also taught Verdi *composizione ideale*, and required him to take out a season ticket at the opera to learn at first hand the modern style. According to Verdi, nothing so liberal should happen now. From such a position, the way back to newly cosmopolitan Milan and to a forward-looking La Scala was difficult and complex.

The fact that a rapprochement was forged in the late 1860s is due for the most part to the tact and generosity of Verdi's second wife Giuseppina Strepponi (1815-97) (pl.134). In May 1867 she took it upon herself to visit Milan alone, and called on Clara Maffei (pl.135), one of Verdi's oldest friends in the city but someone he had not seen for more than 20 years. On her return to Sant'Agata she wrote to Maffei in great detail of the moving effect her visit had had on Verdi.[17] The wheels were in motion, but it was not until a year later, and after a preliminary visit from Maffei to Sant'Agata, that on 30 June 1868 Verdi again entered the city of his first triumphs, to meet the famed novelist Alessandro Manzoni and marvel at a changed urban landscape.

1868-79: RAPPROCHEMENT

While Strepponi was working on the home front, Verdi's publisher Giulio Ricordi (grandson of Giovanni) was also trying to lure Verdi back to Milan and La Scala. The project for him had an eminently practical side. Ricordi was based in Milan, and so it was inevitable that La Scala would be his focus of attention: small wonder that he was anxious to reunite the theatre with the composer who was his most lucrative asset. At first the enticement was a production of *Don Carlo*, scheduled for March 1868: the composer refused to participate, claiming that the complexity of the opera would be quite

Abigaille abito 1°

130

Daniele

131

Baldassare

132

Sacerdoti

133

134

beyond La Scala's means.[18] However, Verdi finally agreed to supervise a revised version of *La forza del destino*, first heard in St Petersburg in 1862. It was a decision that would enormously influence the rest of his career.

So far as we know, the first time since 1848 that Verdi re-entered La Scala was to attend a performance of *Don Carlos* in mid-January 1869, and – typically cautious – he insisted that the visit be cloaked in secrecy.[19] But soon after he was back in the theatre for rehearsals of the revised *La forza*, which was first performed on 27 February 1869. The public's enthusiasm was in no doubt; it was clear that some kind of reconciliation had taken place. The next La Scala project followed hard on the heels of *La forza*. Verdi had accepted the project of writing *Aida* for the opening of the Cairo Opera House by the middle of 1870, but even in these first negotiations it was clear that he had little intention of travelling to Egypt for the premiere, and in his contract he reserved the right to stage the work in Europe at a theatre of his choosing. Given the circumstances of the revised *La forza* premiere, it now needed little persuasion to assure him that La Scala was the fitting venue for this event. *Aida* duly appeared in Cairo on 24 December 1871, but in many ways the true premiere took place at La Scala, only a few weeks later on 8 February 1872, and under the composer's every-exigent supervision.

Throughout the last 30 years of his long career, one senses that the disastrous period in the mid-1840s was forever stamped on the composer's mind in his dealings with La Scala – that, even though its personnel had now changed completely, the theatre would remain a place that could potentially damage his work. In a word, La Scala brought out a vein of insecurity that would be one of the least attractive sides of Verdi's personality in his later years. It is in this sense revealing that, notwithstanding the fact that the Milan premiere of *Aida* was a huge success, Verdi's later memories of the event were clouded by the few negative reactions that appeared among the storms of applause. In particular, he was distressed by the fact that some critics had dared to suggest Verdi had been influenced by foreign composers such as Gounod, Meyerbeer and Wagner. It was an accusation that had already been made against his works, more forcefully and repeatedly, by the first French critics of *Don Carlos*; but when applied by Italians to an opera of his at La Scala, the wound somehow seemed deeper. As he wrote to Giulio Ricordi, some three years after the event: 'A fine result after a 35-year career – to finish as an *imitator*!!!'[20]

1879-1901: FINAL TRIUMPHS

The pattern that was established with the Milanese premiere of *Aida* would hold for the subsequent Verdi premieres in the last 30 years of his life, all of which occurred at La Scala: first came two major revisions of past works, *Simon Boccanegra* (24 March 1881) and *Don Carlos* (10 January 1884); and then the two late Shakespearean operas, *Otello* (5 February 1887) and *Falstaff* (9 February 1893). The huge logistical complexities of modern opera were ever present, indeed ever increasing, as was Verdi's desire to control all aspects of the theatrical message. What also intensified was the disjunction between massive public acclamation and an awareness on Verdi's part that he was in cultural terms an increasingly isolated figure, a single barrier against the dangerous tide of cosmopolitanism sweeping through Italian culture. In this sense, the reception of *Otello* and, in particular, *Falstaff* is highly significant. Critical plaudits came from every conceivable side, many of them openly celebrating Verdi's status in later life as a kind of one-man *festa nazionale*; but it is plain that both critics and public were perplexed by Verdi's last manner.

In the face of these momentous cultural and political developments, and despite periodic bursts of professional and social activity, Verdi chose strategic withdrawal: physically behind the walls of his villa in Sant'Agata; mentally into an image of himself

135

134
Portrait of Giuseppina Strepponi
Unknown artist
Oil on canvas, c.1840s
Museo Teatrale alla Scala, Milan

135
Portrait of Clara Maffei
Francesco Hayez (1791–1881)
Oil on canvas, c.1845
Museo Civico, Riva del Garda (Trento)

as a rough, untutored man of the soil, the peasant from Roncole, the self-made man, an 'authentic' Italian willing to set himself against the tide of cosmopolitan sophistication he saw washing around him. It was overwhelmingly this image that he offered to interviewers who now began to pester him for his views on cultural matters and for biographical tid-bits. The resulting self-portrait was one he sedulously cultivated (along with his farm lands) for the rest of his long life. Hence his support for the canonization of 'Va, pensiero' as a kind of alternative national anthem, and his passive acceptance of the fact that, in effect, he had become a living national monument (pl.136).

During the final two decades of Verdi's life, and in spite of the triumphs he enjoyed there, the composer rarely spent much time in Milan. Dividing his time mostly between Genoa and his farmlands near Busseto, with a summer break at Montecatini Terme, he would appear only occasionally in Milan, settling in to the Hotel Milan and going about his business: supervising rehearsals at La Scala, ever his exigent self about all manner of small details, musical or otherwise; meeting Boito and other friends; arranging for the construction of the Casa di Riposo (a Milanese home for retired musicians) and other charitable works; consulting lawyers or doctors. Once his business was over, he would leave. In other words, Milan never claimed him back after those first successes of the early 1840s. Or – perhaps better – it did so only at the last. In mid-December 1900, a year in which La Scala had produced Wagner's *Lohengrin* and *Siegfried*, Verdi journeyed one final time to the Hotel Milan, ostensibly to visit his dentist. But this time he remained there until his death on 27 January 1901. According to the dictates of his will, his funeral was simple in the extreme. But a month later, a solemn procession through Milan, accompanied by hundreds of thousands of mourners, assisted the transfer of his remains to their final resting place at the Casa di Riposo. The procession was sent on its way, famously, by an orchestral and choral rendition of 'Va, pensiero', conducted by a young Arturo Toscanini. And so, in that sense at least, the story came full circle: that first success at La Scala, a *Nabucco* now nearly 60 years old, sounded forth in Milan's streets as a final farewell.

CONCLUSION

As we have seen, the story of Verdi, Milan and La Scala presents a very uneven picture of the composer's development, mostly because it involves in detail only the extremes of his career. It is a story in which the entire corpus of middle-period masterpieces, from *Rigoletto* to *Un ballo in maschera*, have gone entirely unmentioned. In one sense, though, the manner of Verdi's connection to what became Italy's greatest nineteenth-century theatre is indicative of a crucial larger aspect of his life. The fact that his first and last successes occurred at La Scala emphasizes the sense of connectedness and continuity Verdi achieved in his career, the sense of remaining rooted in one ambience, ultimately the ambience of Italian opera. But this perception is important only if we also understand the struggle entailed in maintaining such continuity. In that sense, the fact that Verdi started and ended his career at La Scala is a symbol of the connections within his life's work; but equally important is to contemplate the huge rift that emerged between him and the theatre in his middle years. Such continuity as Verdi achieved was, in other words, anything but a sign of passivity on his part: it was struggled for and often struggled against. To return to Milan and La Scala after so many years meant to measure the immense distance he had travelled since leaving his operatic 'home'; it was a homecoming in which the buildings might have been the same, but the surrounding landscape was utterly changed.

136
Bust of Giuseppe Verdi
Raffaello Romanello (1856–1928)
Bronze mounted on marble, c.1890
V&A: S.1694-2014

MILAN

Numero di Protocollo	DATA della cessione	AUTORE	CEDENTE	TITOLO DELL'OPERA	CONDIZIONI	Estensione della proprietà	Scadenza quote al cedente	OSSERVAZIONI
1354	1° Sett. 1856	Villanis	autore	Giuditta di Kent	L 1500 in contanti, altre il 30 % in note e il 40 % nelle vendite per cinque anni principiando dal 1ª nota che si farà.	Tutti i paesi	5 anni dopo il primo nota che si farà.	Autore morto.
167 1408	30 Giu 1859	Verdi	autore	Oberto Conte di S. Bonifacio	Spartito L 2000.— Ricordi era già proprietario della riduzione in forza del contratto coll'Impresa della Scala. N 140.	Tutti i paesi	— —	
481 1408	20 Maggio 1845	Verdi	Merelli	Un giorno di regno ossia Il finto Stanislao	Spartito.— Ricordi era già proprietario della riduzione in forza del contratto coll'Impresa della Scala. N 140.	Tutti i paesi	— —	
225 1408	19 Marzo 1842	Verdi	Merelli	Nabucco	Metà Spartito e tutto il Libretto £ 3000 L'altra metà dello Spartito appartiene al Lucca. Ricordi era già proprietario della riduzione in forza del contratto coll'Impresa della Scala, N 140.	Tutti i paesi	Spartito in società col Lucca	
283 1408	11 Febb. 1843	Verdi	Merelli	I Lombardi	Spartito e Libretto £ 8000 Ricordi era già proprietario della riduzione in forza del contratto coll'Impresa della Scala, N 160.	Tutti i paesi	— —	

137

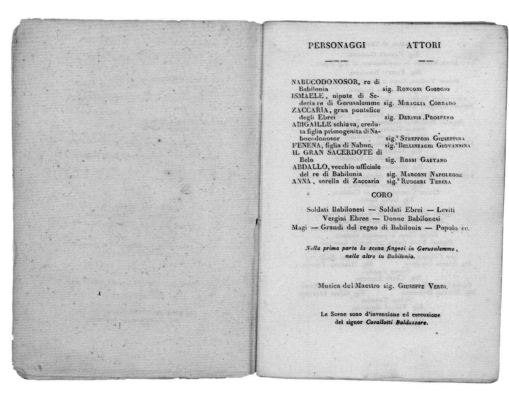

138

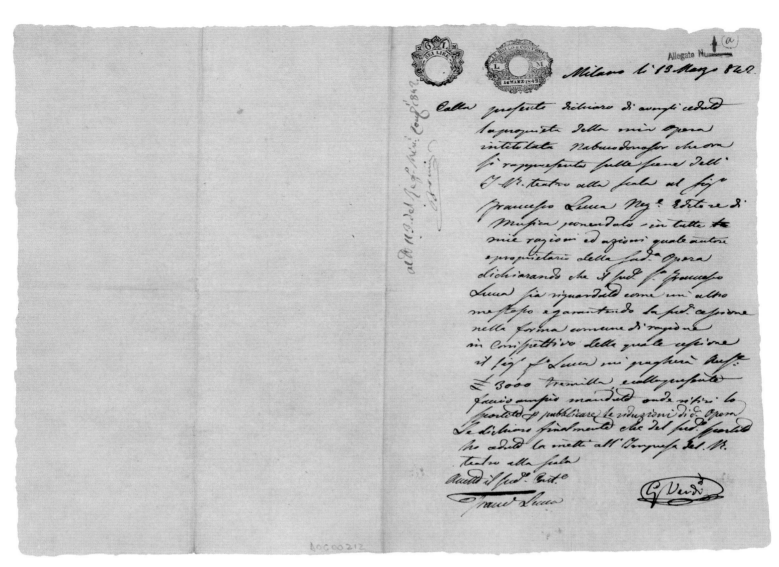

139

137
Ricordi, Summary of Purchase Agreement,
19 March 1842
Archivio Storico Ricordi, Milan

This document from the Archivio Ricordi
summarizes all the operas for which the publisher
acquired the rights. Here it shows the first three
operas that Verdi created for Teatro alla Scala:
Oberto, *Un giorno di regno* and *Nabucco*. Ricordi
still owns the rights to these operas today.

138
First page of the libretto of *Nabucco*
Teatro alla Scala, Milan, 9 March 1842
Archivio Storico Ricordi, Milan

Nabucco premiered at La Scala on 9 March 1842,
during the carnival season. Giuseppina Strepponi
and Giorgio Ronconi, who played Abigaille and
Nabucco respectively, were established opera
singers at Teatro alla Scala and endorsed Verdi's
talent by agreeing to perform in his new work.
The opera was performed over 60 times in its
first year.

139
Agreement between Giuseppe Verdi, Teatro
alla Scala Impresario Bartolomeo Merelli and
Music editor Francesco Lucca, 13 March 1842
Archivio Storico Ricordi, Milan

Nabucco was commissioned by the impresario
and manager of Teatro alla Scala, Bartolomeo
Merelli, as part of the 1842 carnival season.
This contract, which bound Verdi, Teatro alla
Scala and Francesco Lucca, demonstrates
the income a composer could receive from
the performance of a new work and future
performances. Lucca later merged his business
with Giovanni Ricordi to establish one of Europe's
largest music publishing houses.

140

140
A Scene from the Risorgimento
Gerolamo Induno (1825–90)
Oil on canvas, 1865
Buckinghamshire County Museum

Gerolamo Induno was a painter from Northern
Italy who specialized in domestic scenes, depicting
various aspects of contemporary everyday life.
This painting shows two women making an Italian
flag, while a third looks out the window in case
the police arrive.

141
Giuseppe Garibaldi (1807–82)
Unknown artist
Photograph, 19th century
V&A: 584-1956

Giuseppe Garibaldi was part of Giuseppe Mazzini's
political group Giovane Italia, which advocated
a reunited and republican Italy. He took part in
the 1848 uprising of the Italian states and is best
known for campaigns where his supporters wore
red shirts between 1859 and 1861. His actions in
regaining the south of Italy led to Italian unification
(except for the Papal State and the Veneto) under
the rule of the Piedmontese King Victor-
Emmanuel II in 1861.

142
The Kiss
Francesco Hayez (1791–1881)
Oil on canvas, 1859
Pinacoteca di Brera, Milan

The Kiss was first exhibited in 1859, after Victor
Emmanuel II's triumphant entrance into Milan
when it had been liberated from Austrian rule.
The colours of the clothes worn by the lovers
represent both the Italian and French tricolour,
as Napoleon III had been instrumental in the
liberation of Lombardy. The embrace of the
couple has been interpreted as an illustration
of European collaboration and optimism for
a new independent state.

141

142

MILAN

143

The Refugees of Parga (the inhabitants of Parga abandon their homeland)
Francesco Hayez (1791–1881)
Oil on canvas, 1826–31
Musei Civici, Brescia

This painting was inspired by the handover of the city of Parga from the British to the Ottoman Sultan Ali Pacha at the beginning of the nineteenth century. It addresses the themes of exiled patriots and loss of the homeland, subjects that resonate with the story of *Nabucco* — and, arguably, with the feelings of many Milanese living under Austrian rule after the Vienna treaties of 1815.

PLAN DE PARIS

Indiquant le tracé
des voies nouvelles dont
S.M. L'EMPEREUR NAPOLÉON III
a pris l'initiative.

PARIS

RICHARD WAGNER
1813–83

Tannhäuser

In the mythological realm of Venusberg, the singer Tannhäuser tires of Venus' love and decides to return to his home in the Wartburg. When Tannhäuser reveals during a song contest that he has been in the Venusberg, the people are horrified. His former beloved Elisabeth intervenes to save his life, and Tannhäuser is ordered to make a pilgrimage to Rome. The Pope refuses to absolve him, but Elisabeth sacrifices her life for his sake and Tannhäuser's soul is saved.

145

INTRODUCTION

MICHAEL LEVINE

DESIGNING *TANNHÄUSER*

For me personally, designing for the theatre is a collaborative art. The design springs from the alchemy of everything and everyone involved. I think of my role as someone who gathers information — the text, the music, the physical requirements of the story, the technical limitations. Only after I have gathered this information can I start to form the design. I find the parameters set by these realities are what shape the end result. The artistry for me comes from a distillation of the ideas circling around the production.

In Wagner there are always two levels at play. Firstly, there is the larger picture informed by the music and wider themes that Wagner tackles again and again: redemption, salvation, greed. Secondly, there are the more intimate stories and relationships of the characters: father and daughter, father and son, siblings … these sit within and at the centre of these broader themes. With *Tannhäuser* you have the exploration of the balance between flesh and spirit, salvation and damnation and the act of creativity that comes from the struggle between the two. Inside this you have the intimacy of Tannhäuser's relationship with Elisabeth and Elisabeth's relationship with her family. Then there is the unrequited love of Wolfram for Elisabeth.

At the centre of the opera is the song contest where all the themes of the opera meet. This particular contest has a history within the community of the Wartburg, where the values of art are scrutinized and held up for all to see. The contest has lapsed since its most famous competitor, Tannhäuser, left the community. The Wartburg has suffered in his absence.

When Tim Albery and I began to look at the opera we wanted to understand the nature of the song competition. What was the context in which it was taking place? What kind of community has music at its heart? Is this is a place where there is a pursuit of a 'pure' form of music that is connected to spirit? We wanted to find a parallel in our time where music is something that is held in such high regard that the community is willing to defend it.

The first world that the audience discovers is the Venusberg — the very opposite of the Wartburg. It is a mythological realm where excess and decadence reign. Venus embodies physical love. Elisabeth is spiritual love. So, with these two worlds at play, you have the body and the soul in battle expressed through poetry and song. This is Tannhäuser's struggle.

How do you begin to represent this in form on stage? We were determined to give the production relevance. We agreed that the song contest should take place somewhere that the audience would immediately relate to and recognize. As we explored this idea it became clear that the setting should be a place of high art. And so it made sense to us to begin exactly where the audience found themselves — the Royal Opera House, London, where our production of *Tannhäuser* was taking place. What better place for a song contest then an opera house? The Venusberg — a mythological place — becomes a production on the stage of the opera house. Our theatre becomes a mythological place. Venus is an opera singer eternally playing a character. The singers may change but the character plays on, year after year. We spent a lot of time talking about the excess and decadence of the Venusberg. We wanted to make our theatre a place of constant indulgence. When we began working with choreographer Jasmin Vardimon, we searched for ways to express the insatiable atmosphere of the Venusberg. In our early conversations we thought we wanted an outrageous banquet with endless food and drink. But once we were in rehearsal Jasmin found a movement vocabulary to express this orgiastic world. It wasn't necessary to be so literal with food and wine. Instead I designed a spinning banquet table that became the place where the dancers could act out their rituals. They used it as a table, a bed, a game.

The Wartburg then becomes the opposite of this decadent world: a place where song and music-making is precious, careful and possibly covert. It is also a place where the flesh and the spirit are in battle. Some kind of conflict has taken place here, where song has been forbidden. We began to look towards contemporary places of conflict where to sing publicly was thought to be a crime; where theatres, monuments and cultural centres were being destroyed. I then began to explore how we could destroy what the audience had just experienced: the death of the self-indulgent, hedonistic world of the Venusberg. This then became our setting for the song contest, the ruined stage of an opera house. It is a place governed by the conflict of religious war. As the opera progresses, the conflict between the excesses of the flesh and the purity of the spirit is slowly destroying the place of art. As a result, the lifeblood of the community is being drained and the physical representation of the community is fading. The opera house, our home for the song contest, begins to disintegrate and return to nature. In Act III the opera house begins to disappear and we are left with an artistic wasteland.

There is something poignant in *Tannhäuser* that is particular to our time. It is the story of the conflict between body and soul that is so central to contemporary religious conflicts around the world.

144 (pp.158–9; detail)
Map of Paris showing the new avenues initiated by H.M. the Emperor Napoleon III
Erhard (1821–80)
Engraving, 1874
Bibliothèque Nationale de France, Paris, Ge D 15286

145 (p.162)
Christian Gerhaher as Wolfram von Eschinbach in *Tannhäuser*
Directed by Tim Albery with set designs by Michael Levine
Royal Opera House, London, 2016

146
Peter Seiffert as Tannhäuser in Act II of *Tannhäuser*
Directed by Tim Albery with set designs by Michael Levine
Royal Opera House, London, 2016

147
The Venusberg scene in Act I of *Tannhäuser*
Directed by Tim Albery with choreography by Jasmin Vardimon and set designs by Michael Levine
Royal Opera House, London, 2010

146

147

WAGNER AMONG THE BOULEVARDS: *TANNHÄUSER* IN PARIS

FLORA WILLSON

149

The Paris premiere of Richard Wagner's *Tannhäuser* is one of the more scandalous episodes in opera's long and colourful history. The story unfolds in 1861 in the capital of the French Second Empire (1852–70): Offenbach's operettas were all the rage; crinolines were huge, waists tightly cinched; leading politicians courted financial ruin by day and the era's most glamorous socialites by night. Looking back on the period from 1925, the composer Reynaldo Hahn (1874–1947) described it as 'essentially anti-musical ... its music resembled its furniture: it was ill-assorted, mediocre, and heavy'.[1] Yet Paris was also a metropolis that proudly asserted itself as the centre not just of France but of the nineteenth century as a whole. It was unrivalled as a cosmopolitan hub, a place where European nations met and mingled, and as a purveyor of a fashionably Gallic-tinged brand of cultural internationalism.

When Wagner – self-proclaimed musical revolutionary and sometime political exile – arrived in the city in 1859, it was his second bid to have one of his works staged there. His first attempt had failed almost 20 years earlier. By 1859, however, his operas had achieved considerable success elsewhere in Europe and the composer himself was preceded by a headline-grabbing reputation for radical pronouncements and his supposed penchant for producing 'the music of the future'.

Tannhäuser – first performed in Dresden in 1845 – was accepted for performance at the Paris Opéra, then arguably the most prestigious opera house in the world. But difficulties soon arose, above all when Wagner (not given to compromise) was told that he would have to insert a ballet into his opera to conform with Parisian conventions. Ballets were usually performed at the end of an opera's second act, in time for the arrival of the influential group of young, aristocratic male audience members known as the Jockey Club (pl.150). Instead, Wagner decided to expand the first act of his work, inserting a short ballet into the scene set in Venus' bacchanalian realm. This failed to satisfy the Jockey Club, who responded to the opera with dog whistles and booing. After three disrupted performances, the opera was pulled from the stage. Wagner left Paris, never to return.

Told thus, the story's appeal is clear: one of today's unassailably Great Composers is mistreated by an audience behaving badly; the troubled genius struggles against the conventions of his time. But there is much more to this moment in music history than the collision of artistic conviction and reactionary hooliganism. The Paris of the *Tannhäuser* incident was a city literally in flux – in the midst of the largest programme of urban renovations ever known (pl.149) – and its cultural climate was no more 'anti-musical' than its audiences were unilaterally anti-Wagnerian. To understand more fully what happened on those three nights at the Opéra in March 1861, we need to look much further afield than *Tannhäuser* itself. We need to consider the place of *Tannhäuser* in Wagner's career, the composer's own complicated relationship with the French capital, and, most revealing of all, the role of opera in Paris' rapidly changing urban fabric in 1861.

PARIS, CAPITAL OF NINETEENTH-CENTURY OPERA

Richard Wagner first arrived in Paris in September 1839. Twenty-six years old, he had already completed two operas (*Die Feen* and *Das Liebesverbot*) and had begun work on another, *Rienzi*. He had escaped to France in secret from Riga, where he had been employed as the theatre's musical director. While there – and not for the last time in his financially chaotic life – he had run up ferocious debts and his passport had consequently been impounded. Smuggled with his wife Minna onto a merchant vessel bound for London, he would later claim that the dreadful first stage of the journey by sea was the inspiration for his opera *Der fliegende Holländer*. The Wagners then crossed the Channel between Gravesend and Boulogne, where they were met by Giacomo Meyerbeer (1791–1864), a Prussian composer then based in Paris, who had become one of the most

150

148 (pp.166–7)
Paris Opéra Garnier auditorium
Originally built in 1861–75,
the ceiling of the auditorium
was painted by Marc Chagall in 1964

149 (detail)
*Paris Panorama as seen from the
St Jacques Tower, looking West*
Paul Augustin Gueuvin (b.1809)
Albumen print, c.1864
V&A: E.1380-2000

150 (detail)
A ballet class
Frank Teichel, printed by J. & E. Bettanier
Print, mid-19th century
V&A: E.5077-1968

THÉATRE IMPÉRIAL DE L'OPÉRA.

151

151
Bill for 2000 francs for an annual
box at the Théatre Impérial de l'Opéra
Ink on paper, 1861
The Bowes Museum, Barnard Castle

152
A Box at the Théatre des Italiens
Eva Gonzalès (1849–83)
Oil on canvas, c.1874
Musée d'Orsay, Paris, gift of
Jean Guérard, 1927

153
*The Ballet Scene from
Meyerbeer's Opera 'Robert le diable'*
Edgar Degas (1834–1917)
Oil on canvas, 1876
V&A: CAI.19

powerful figures on its operatic scene. Meyerbeer offered to equip Wagner with letters of introduction to the director and conductor of the Paris Opéra, and sent the couple on the final leg of their journey.

Fast-forward to April 1842, and they were on the move again: this time to Dresden, where *Rienzi* had at last been accepted for performance at the Hoftheater. Wagner was bitter and disillusioned with the French capital. Despite Meyerbeer's assistance – and the established composer was, Wagner wrote in 1840, 'untiringly loyal' – he had failed to get his operas staged there and had lived an impoverished existence as a frustrated, acerbic columnist for the *Revue et gazette musicale* and (still worse) making arrangements of other people's operatic hits for the music publisher Schlesinger. Nothing seemed to work out as Wagner had hoped: *Das Liebesverbot* was actually accepted for performance at the Théâtre de la Renaissance in 1840 – only for the theatre to declare itself bankrupt two months later.

There is little question that Wagner did not experience the best of Paris' operatic culture during his two and a half years there from 1839. But the city's attraction to any ambitious nineteenth-century composer remains absolutely clear. Perhaps most important, it boasted no fewer than three major opera houses, each generously subsidized by the State. At the Théâtre Italien (pl.152), only Italian opera was performed – sometimes works imported in the wake of success in Italy, sometimes new operas tailor-made for Paris – and productions often starred the most celebrated Italian singers of their day. The Opéra-Comique, meanwhile, served up an essentially French brand of lighter, family-friendly operas with spoken dialogue and guaranteed happy endings. But neither could compete with the Paris Opéra for sheer global cachet. Since the premiere of Gioachino Rossini's (1792–1868) *Guillaume Tell* in 1829, the Opéra (or Académie Royale de Musique, as it was more properly known) had specialized in a type of vast operatic work boasting five weighty acts, an in-built ballet, high-tech scenic spectacle, grandiose historical settings and a musical construction that showed off what could be achieved by the best-rehearsed orchestra in the world, a chorus trained by the Paris Conservatoire, and an international roster of vocal stars drawn to Paris by the promise of high fees and extensive exposure in the city's vibrant musical press (pl.151).

Not for nothing was the genre called grand opera. From the 1830s onwards, its figurehead was Meyerbeer, the same composer who tried to help Wagner gain a foothold in the French capital in 1839. Wagner's attitude towards the older man would gradually sour, his bitterness about his own lack of success inflected by a particularly anti-Semitic take on the continued popularity (and profitability) of Meyerbeer's works, above all the apparently unassailable trio of *Robert le diable* (1831), *Les Huguenots* (1836) and *Le Prophète* (1849) (see pl.153, which shows the famous ballet from the opera that launched Meyerbeer's Parisian career).

Even before fleeing from Riga, Wagner – ever-ambitious – had hoped to get a work staged at the Paris Opéra. As early as 1837, he had sent a scenario for a new work to Eugène Scribe, the most prolific producer of opera librettos in mid-nineteenth-century Paris. Nothing came of the enquiry. Wagner's next attempt, this time made in Paris, saw him offer Scribe (again) a prose scenario for *Der fliegende Holländer* in 1840. Scribe didn't want it, but Meyerbeer suggested showing it to the new director of the Opéra, who subsequently bought it for 500 francs as a subject perhaps worth elaborating and passing on to one of his stable of composers. (As it turned out, *Le Vaisseau fantôme*, a shortlived opera by Pierre-Louis Dietsch that premiered at the Opéra in 1842, was based on a similar story; but its librettists did not make use of Wagner's scenario.)

Although Wagner would have to wait until 1861 to see one of his works staged at the Opéra, his years in Paris nonetheless had a huge impact on him and on the music he would write next. While there, he completed *Rienzi* and *Der fliegende Holländer* – both of which show the influence of the city's local operatic climate. The former in particular

152

153

PARIS

154

was clearly conceived in part as a grand opera in the Meyerbeerian vein. *Rienzi* was a great success at its premiere in Dresden in October 1842; *Der fliegende Holländer* went down there slightly less well in January 1843. By this time he had also begun work on *Tannhäuser*, which would be premiered – again in Dresden – in October 1845. What we must recognize is that this opera, too, already showed the unequivocal traces of his years in Paris, long before he returned to the work at the end of the 1850s to tailor it more precisely to the demands of the Parisian audiences.

The intervening years would see Wagner's career take important new directions – directions that would, at least in the first instance, lead him away from Paris. He was once again on the run: this time to escape arrest in the wake of his participation in the Dresden uprising in 1848. Exiled from Germany, he next settled in Switzerland, where he produced his so-called 'Zürich essays' – the immense, philosophy-drenched reflections on musical aesthetics for which he would soon gain notoriety across Europe. Musically, it was at this time that he sketched out plans for a vast operatic tetralogy and gradually produced the text and music for the *Ring* cycle. And, from a personal perspective, it was while living in Switzerland that Wagner fell in love with the wife of his friend and financial supporter Otto Wesendonck. His affair with Mathilde supposedly inspired him to break off work on *Siegfried* (the *Ring*'s third opera) in 1857 to write *Tristan und Isolde*. Each of these developments would have an impact on Wagner's second major visit to Paris: he was a significantly more experienced, significantly more mature, and – above all – significantly more famous a composer than the young man who had arrived in the French capital from Riga in 1839 (pl.155).

A CITY TRANSFORMED

It was not only Wagner who had altered in the intervening decades, however. Between the composer's first, dismal trip to Paris at the end of the 1830s and his return two decades later, the city itself had also changed enormously – indeed some claimed that their city had become unrecognizable. In a century characterized by political upheaval in France, one particular regime-change had an extraordinary impact on the urban landscape of Paris itself – and it would also play a major role both in Wagner's relationship with the city, and in its world-famous operatic life. On 2 December 1852, the Second Empire was declared by Napoleon III (pl.154) – previously Louis-Napoleon, elected president of the Second Republic – following a coup d'état exactly a year earlier.

The two decades that followed were among the most politically stable that France had seen since the French Revolution – and, at least early on, the new regime was also popular. That popularity rested partly on the Emperor's claims to legitimate succession as the nephew of the legendary Napoleon Bonaparte. But another important factor was that the Emperor's apparently progressive attitudes to social and political reform appealed to a society in transition: mid-century France was split between a continuing economic reliance on agriculture and new signs of industrialization. As the Emperor reportedly enthused: 'March at the head of the ideas of your century, and those ideas will strengthen and sustain you; march behind them and they will drag you after them; march against them and they will overthrow you'.

A crucial figure in the era's simultaneous reliance on the past and on the notion of progress was the prefect of the Seine, Baron Georges-Eugène Haussmann (1809–91). His plans for the transformation and modernization of Paris, carried out during the Second Empire, provide us with some of the most clearly visible manifestations of the regime's twin obsessions: with safeguarding and driving a path into the future; and with preserving (perhaps even reviving) the past. The process of what became known as 'Haussmannization' saw the demolition of much of medieval Paris and the construction

155

PARIS

156

157

of a new network of wide boulevards linking the city centre to its ever-expanding outskirts. The biggest single concern driving the project was to ensure that in the new, modern Paris, it would be possible to mobilize troops rapidly across the city. The renovated capital was, above all, to be revolution-proof – an aim in which the extension of the rue de Rivoli, running from the centre to the traditionally unruly *quartiers* of the Marais and Saint-Antoine, played a crucial role.

This radical reorganization of urban space also presented an opportunity to showcase the new regime. The city's grandeur was to be a reflection of Napoleon III's own status, its modernity a by-product of his belief in progress and innovation. But there were also less obvious side-effects of Haussmann's works: alongside his programme of modernizing initiatives, the prefect attempted to catalogue what was being lost of the old city. 'Vieux Paris' – old Paris – came into being at the very moment of its destruction, marked by the founding of heritage-focused institutions such as the Bibliothèque Historique de la Ville de Paris. Meanwhile the renowned photographer Charles Marville (1813–79) was employed expressly to record the changes in the urban landscape.

Amidst the large-scale renovations across the city, one particular building project stood out. *Paris for the English*, a popular British guidebook to the city, advised new arrivals in 1867:

> Let the visitor make his first walk in New Paris from the Northern Station,
> straight as an arrow to the New Opera which faces the rue de la Paix
> and the Great Boulevards, and he will get almost at every step astonishing
> glimpses of the capital of the Second Empire.[2]

The tourist is assumed to have arrived by rail (guidebook in hand), delivered into the heart of the city by that recent and fastest mode of long-distance travel. His journey retains its momentum as he leaves the Gare du Nord on foot. This ideal pedestrian is no ambling, idling *flâneur* – Walter Benjamin's characteristic figure of the nineteenth-century city – but is instead efficient, purposeful, taking full advantage of Paris' new, long, straight, wide boulevards.[3] The entire sentence-length journey is imagined in specifically modern terms: so rapid is his traversal of the city that the traveller moves – 'straight as an arrow' – as if still on board his train. He catches only fleeting glimpses of the renovated urban environment through which he passes. His destination is the Opéra: not the current, venerable home of the Académie Impériale de Musique in the rue Le Peletier, but the 'New Opera' designed by Charles Garnier and still under construction at the end of the similarly rubble-strewn Avenue de l'Opéra (pl.156 and 157).

Louis-Emile Durandelle's photograph of the eastern side of the 'Palais Garnier', as it would become known, was taken in the same year that *Paris for the English* was published. Had the Englishman in Paris made his way through the boulevards, as instructed, to the New Opera, this is the scene he might have found. It is not the magnificent vista he had been led to expect: the structure itself is still clad in scaffolding (its interior is far from completed) and the grand Place de l'Opéra around it has yet to emerge from a building site scattered with heaps of rubble. In this photograph the ruins of the city's past still need to be carted away; the blurry huddle of half-captured workmen is a ghostly reminder of the hard labour on which Haussmann's radical transformations relied in the Second Empire present. The opera house remained years away from functioning as a venue for performance.

156
General view as seen from the walls of the stage
Louis-Emile Durandelle (1838–1917)
Albumen print, May 1864
V&A: E.2341-1990

157
The new Paris Opéra, east side façade
Louis-Emile Durandelle (1838–1917)
Albumen print, 1867
V&A: E.2351-1990

'THE MUSIC OF THE FUTURE'

When Wagner arrived back in Paris in September 1859, then, he found himself in a city whose past and future were simultaneously present. Although work on Charles Garnier's

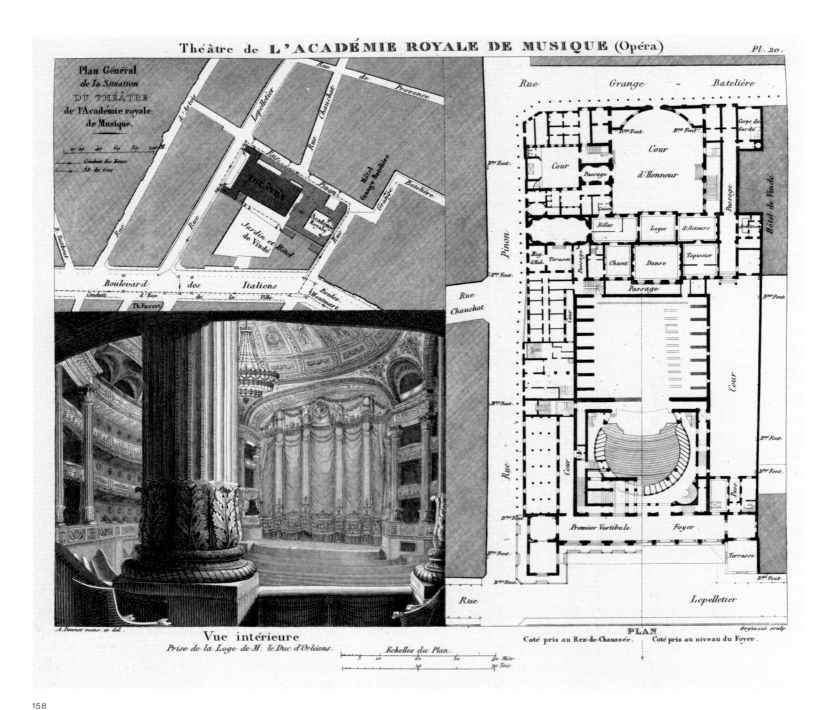

Théâtre de **L'ACADÉMIE ROYALE DE MUSIQUE** (Opéra)

Pl. 20.

Plan Général
de la Situation
DU THÉÂTRE
*de l'Académie royale
de Musique.*

Rue de Provence

Rue Grange — Batelière

Cour d'Honneur

Cour

Cour

Rôles — Loges — d'Acteurs

Chant — Danse — Tapissier

Passage

Cour

Cour

Premier Vestibule — Foyer

Vue intérieure
Prise de la Loge de M. le Duc d'Orléans.

Echelles du Plan.

PLAN

Coté pris au Rez-de-Chaussée.   *Coté pris au niveau du Foyer.*

158

new Opéra began during Wagner's sojourn, the composer would never see the completed building. The Opéra he was trying to conquer was still the Salle Le Peletier, just a few streets away across the boulevards, which had housed the Académie Impériale (or Royale) de Musique since 1821 (pl.158). Located on the rue Le Peletier, tucked away behind the boulevard des Italiens and with the modest colonnaded façade typical of European opera houses of its age, the venue could hardly have been more different to the bombastic, centrally placed, attention-grabbing institution planned as the new opera house of the modernized city.

This is not to say that Haussmann's programme of works did not touch Wagner's own experience of Paris. On the contrary, the composer's home there would turn out to have an unfortunate minor role in the transformation of the city. Wagner's initial accommodation in Paris was unsustainably deluxe (and thus temporary), but a useful base from which to begin cultivating sources of institutional support. By the end of October, he had moved into what he hoped was a more permanent home: cheaper, less sumptuous, but in urgent need of expenditure on decoration and restoration. It was only with this work duly paid for that he discovered the house was due to be demolished as part of Haussmann's renovations.[4]

It was not all bad luck, however. Even during his decades of absence from the city, Wagner's name had appeared with relative regularity in the Parisian press: in 1843, the composer and prominent critic Hector Berlioz reported back from Dresden with considerable enthusiasm for *Der fliegende Holländer*.[5] In the 1850s, Wagner's theoretical writings were the subject of a series of long and critical articles by the still-more eminent French critic François-Joseph Fétis.[6] As the cliché goes, there's no such thing as bad publicity: this sustained attack from a member of Paris' musical old guard, combined with Wagner's new reputation as a political revolutionary following the 1848 Dresden uprising, attracted the attention of Paris' self-consciously radical cultural figures – writers, artists and musicians who wanted to break with tradition and who sensed a fellow-traveller in this exiled musical maverick. Wagner's writings and music were increasingly discussed in the city's press during the 1850s. In 1858, for instance, one critic used his regular column in the republican paper *Le Siècle* to examine Wagner's status in Germany, in terms that would become ever-more widespread: the composer, he reported 'has his fanatics and his detractors. His fanatics claim that his music is a revelation of the future. His detractors, no less impassioned, maintain that he is, on the contrary, a composer of the past, redoing what has been done'.[7] Like contemporary Paris, that is, Wagner's music seemed to gesture both towards the past and to the future.

Despite the surge in interest in Wagner during the 1850s, public experience of his music in Paris was limited to two performances of his *Tannhäuser* overture. The composer seems to have first thought seriously about arranging a Parisian production of the entire opera in 1857, when he authorized a colleague to negotiate on his behalf in the French capital. Around the same time, an enthusiastic (if, as it would turn out, underqualified) young French writer approached Wagner to propose a French translation of *Tannhäuser*'s libretto.[8] Promising as these developments were, the crucial step forward came in August 1859, when Napoleon III issued a decree of clemency to those involved in the 1848 revolutions. This liberalizing gesture meant that Wagner was not only free to enter France; he had also been offered a nod of approval by the Second Empire's ruling establishment.

When the composer arrived in Paris a month later, he was determined to see *Tannhäuser* on stage at the Opéra. He began work accordingly on a French translation of the libretto with the first of a sequence of collaborators – each of whom were found wanting. (A prose translation would be published in November 1860 as part of a French edition of four of Wagner's librettos, accompanied by an essay explaining his theories of music drama for a French audience – see pl.159.) As work progressed, Wagner reflected

158
Floor plan and interior view of Le Peletier theatre
Alexis Donnet (1782–1867) and
Jacques-Auguste Kaufmann
Architectonographie des Théâtres de Paris, 1837
V&A: National Art Library

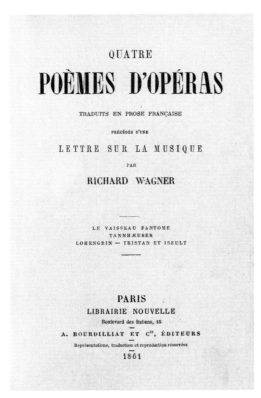

159

159
*Quatre Poèmes d'Opéras et Lettre sur la Musique
(Four Opera Poems and a Letter about Music)*
Richard Wagner (1813–83)
Printed book, 1861
Bibliothèque Nationale de France, Paris, Res 935

160
Richard Wagner
Cover page of the journal *l'Eclipse*, 18 April 1869
Louis-Alexandre Gosset de Guignes,
known as André Gill (1840–85)
Bibliothèque Nationale de France, Paris,
Est. Portr. Richard Wagner 1

161 (p.180)
Princess Pauline of Metternich
Franz Xaver Winterhalter (1805–73)
Oil on canvas, 1859
Private collection

162 (p.181)
Princess Pauline of Metternich
Edgar Degas (1834–1917)
Oil on canvas, c.1865
National Gallery, London, NG3337

in a letter to Mathilde Wesendonck on how he might modify his now almost twenty-year old opera:

> Here and there I'm giving the orchestra, especially, more expressive
> and elaborate passages. The only scene I mean to rework totally is the Venus
> scene. I found the Lady Venus a bit stiff: a few good points but no real life.
> Here, I have added quite a series of verses: the Goddess of Beauty has,
> herself, become genuinely moving, and Tannhäuser's pain has become real,
> so that his cry to the Virgin breaks out of his soul like a powerful cry of fear.[9]

But there was more to work on in Paris besides his score and translation – particularly when a production hadn't yet been arranged. By the late 1850s, however, Wagner was well aware of the power of publicity. In a bid to generate financial and political support for his proposed *Tannhäuser* staging, the composer organized and conducted three concerts of his music in the Salle Ventadour of the city's Théâtre Italien in January and February 1860.[10] The programme (repeated on each occasion) comprised extracts from *Der fliegende Holländer*, *Tannhäuser* and *Lohengrin*, as well as the prelude from his recently completed *Tristan und Isolde*. Financially, the concerts were an unequivocal disaster. But as publicity material, they could hardly have been bettered. They were attended by most of Paris' musical luminaries and, almost more important, by virtually all of the city's high-profile critics – and this despite the fact that Wagner (never quite in step with Parisian conventions) had failed to issue the press with official invitations. The debates about Wagner and his theories had finally found a musical focus: these concerts were understood to mark, for better or worse, the arrival in Paris of what had already become known as 'la musique de l'avenir'. (pl.160 is one of the many contemporary caricatures depicting the damage that Wagner's music of the future could supposedly inflict on its listeners of the present.)

Responses of the Parisian critics were often extreme: from the anti-Wagnerians who, for instance, described his music as 'a series of piercing chords, of high-pitched whistling, of the screeching of enraged brass', to the fanatics' assurances that his futuristic music could transport the listener 'to unknown worlds'.[11] This rhetoric is full of hyperbole and references to a 'music of the future' from which Wagner had failed to distance himself quickly enough (his 1849 book title *The Artwork of the Future* had proved to be a good headline). But the critical discourse generated by Wagner's promotional concerts nevertheless established the frame of reference for *Tannhäuser*'s Paris premiere the following year.

Seizing on his sudden celebrity in the wake of these concerts, the composer established a weekly salon at his home – on Wednesday evenings to avoid clashing with those held by Offenbach (on Fridays), Rossini (on Saturdays) and Princesse Mathilde Bonaparte (on Sundays). His regular guests were a mixed crowd of politicians, artists, administrators and writers – individuals all largely associated with the republican opposition to the Second Empire regime. But it was official favour that would prove to be both Wagner's salvation in the short term, and his opera's downfall shortly thereafter. In March 1860, Napoleon III issued an official decree instructing that *Tannhäuser* was to be staged at the Opéra, following the personal intervention of Princess Pauline von Metternich, the wife of the Austrian ambassador – see plates 161 and 162, in which she is portrayed first by Franz Winterhalter (1805-73), one-time court painter to the July Monarchy, and later by the more obviously avant-garde Edgar Degas (1834-1917). The Emperor was apparently keen to appease the Austrians after his recent military support of the Italian nationalist cause against Habsburg rule and to continue to make overtures to the liberal left closer to home. Promoting Wagner's opera appeared to be a convenient means by which to do both.

Deuxième année. — N° 65   Un numéro : 10 centimes   18 Avril 1869.

RÉDACTEUR EN CHEF
F. POLO

ABONNEMENTS
PARIS
Un an............. 5 fr. »
Six mois ..... 3 »
Trois mois. 1 50

Rue du Croissant, 16.

DIRECTEUR
F. POLO

ABONNEMENTS
DÉPARTEMENTS
Un an............. 6 fr. »
Six mois........ 3 50
Trois mois...... 2 »

Rue du Croissant, 16.

L'ECLIPSE

JOURNAL HEBDOMADAIRE

RICHARD WAGNER, par GILL.

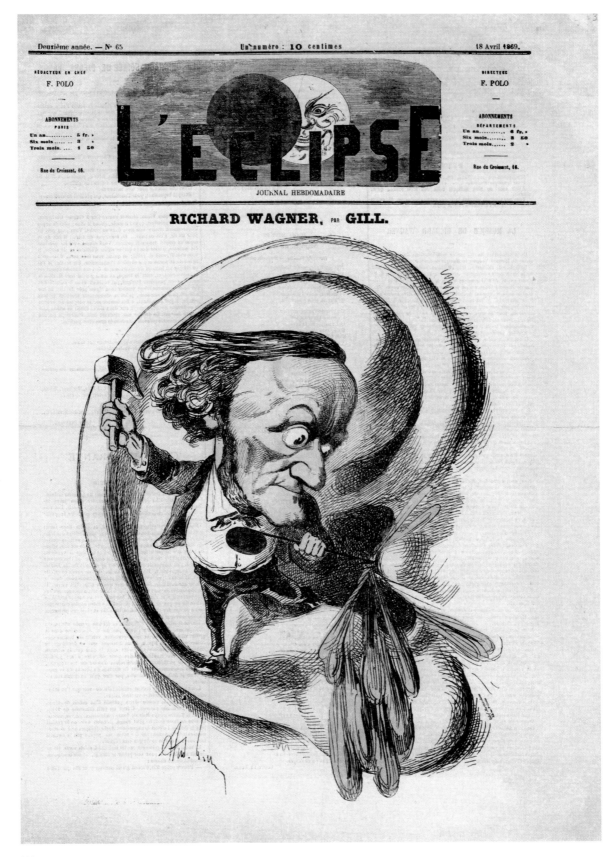

160

161

162

PARIS

163

With the work accepted for performance, Wagner was immediately informed by Alphonse Royer, the Opéra's director, that he would need to add a ballet scene. Royer himself suggested inserting it into Act II, following the opera's famous March (incidentally one of the excerpts performed in the 1860 concerts); but Wagner decided instead to extend the Venusberg music in Act I to incorporate dance music where he felt it would also help to develop his depiction of Venus' realm (pl.163 and 164). What is clear is that, as he had suggested to Mathilde Wesendonck in the letter quoted above, Wagner was not simply 'trapped' by Parisian operatic conventions in 1861, but rather stimulated by their requirements to expand on and modernize parts of his opera. (*Tannhäuser* is actually unique in Wagner's entire body of work in that its post-Paris versions contain music first written to a French libretto and only subsequently adapted for German text.)

But what of the opera's reception – the famously raucous audience behaviour and the piece's abandonment after only three performances? The problem stemmed partly from Napoleon's intervention: on the one hand, Wagner's opera had, with the Emperor's assistance, been fast-tracked for production at the Opéra over new works by influential local composers including Hector Berlioz (1803-69) and Charles Gounod (1818-93). And, on the other, Wagner's existing supporters among Paris' political and artistic radical 'opposition' felt to some extent betrayed by his sudden absorption into the political and cultural establishment. Nor had Wagner helped himself towards success with PR gaffes such as his failure to issue the press with official invitations to the premiere. But a more important factor in *Tannhäuser*'s reception in 1861 was the sheer level of expectation and prejudice that had accumulated around the composer's music in its *absence* from the

163
Tannhäuser on the Venusberg
Henri Fantin-Latour (1836–1904)
Oil on canvas, 1864
Los Angeles County Museum of Art

164
Costume design for Venus
Alfred Albert (1814–79)
Drawing, 1861
Bibliothèque Nationale de France,
Paris, D216-20 (11)

Parisian stage. Hence the descriptions from anti-Wagnerian critics in 1861 of *Tannhäuser* as, for instance, 'symphonic devilry, quite painful to hear, and all too capable of clouding an idea – if there were one'.[12] It is difficult to imagine how the music of *Tannhäuser*, not so far removed from the idiom of Meyerbeer, after all, could have been genuinely 'painful to hear' in 1861. But these critics and audiences were listening to Wagner's music, often for the first time, through years of heated discussion of his theories – theories that were felt to put the very future of music in jeopardy.

There was, though, one final aspect of *Tannhäuser*'s 1861 outing at the Paris Opéra that might, with hindsight, have made its failure more or less inevitable. The fact that Wagner appeared to be advertising himself as no less than the purveyor of 'the music of the future' both appealed and appalled in a city undergoing its own, aggressively future-facing transformation. But his loudly proclaimed musical progressiveness sat uneasily, at best, in the broader tendencies in Parisian operatic culture in this period. At the Opéra and elsewhere, audiences and critics alike seemed drawn increasingly not to new works, but to revivals of already-established, already acclaimed operas of the past. Just as Haussmann's renovations simultaneously precipitated an interest in the city's past – in the idea of *history* itself – so too was operatic culture looking backwards ever more regularly, rediscovering the operas of Gluck and of Mozart, and judging all new works against a gradually emerging yardstick of universal greatness that would eventually become known as the operatic canon.

164

It was in this Paris, a Paris with a new consciousness of its own past, that Garnier's new Opéra belonged. It rose up vast and monumental amid the new *grands boulevards*, as a symbol of, and focal point for, the modern city. Yet it would only be inaugurated on 5 January 1875 – five years to the day since the prefect had been dismissed from his post, and over four years since the Second Empire itself had fallen after Napoleon III's military surrender at Sedan. The finished building was adorned with the names (and busts) of the great and the good of the city's operatic past: Auber, Rossini, Meyerbeer, Halévy. The generous spaces originally allocated to be the Emperor's private pavilion had been converted, tellingly, into a library housing the institution's precious scores and manuscripts. Now a relic of another era's dreams of the future, the opera house finally opened in the Third Republic with a gala performance of excerpts from the ancient pillars of the grand operatic repertoire: *La Muette de Portici*, *Guillaume Tell*, *La Juive* and *Les Huguenots*.

Wagner was not among the names commemorated on the building's façade; nor did *Tannhäuser* or any other of his works appear on its stage for some years to come. What's more, the composer never returned to Paris after the failure of *Tannhäuser* in 1861. But shortly before his death, Wagner supposedly remarked that 'I still owe the world *Tannhäuser*': the opera's Parisian outing had left him with a sense of unfinished business.[13] What he couldn't have known was that his own mortality would ultimately provide the turning point for his music's Parisian fortunes. In the later 1880s, so-called 'Wagnerism' had taken hold as a significant movement in Parisian culture; eminent figures in music and the other arts made pilgrimages to Wagner's own specially designed theatre at Bayreuth, a venue by then felt to be the spiritual home of his works; and, in 1895, *Tannhäuser* was finally re-staged at the Opéra. What had changed in the meantime was crucial: Wagner's opera no longer seemed to destabilize the present in its apparent invocation of a musical future. On the contrary, the composer had effectively joined the ranks of those ensconced in the symbolic operatic pantheon of the Opéra's façade. The actual music of the future had turned out to be precisely the music of the past – a past into which Wagner, by the final decades of the nineteenth century, had finally been ushered.

165
Music in the Tuileries Gardens
Edouard Manet (1832–83)
Oil on canvas, 1861–2
National Gallery, London, NG3260

Like Wagner, Edouard Manet faced scorn from his contemporaries, in his case for his realistic portrayals of contemporary society. This painting focuses on the place of music in Parisian society, showing intellectual figures of the day such as the popular composer Jacques Offenbach, the writer Charles Baudelaire and the painter Henri Fantin-Latour. The latter two would later defend Wagner's *Tannhäuser* from critics.

THE IMPERIAL VISIT.—THE STATE BOX AT THE ROYAL ITALIAN OPERA.

167

166

'The Imperial Visit — The State Box
at the Royal Italian Opera'
The Illustrated London News
Print, 28 April 1855
V&A: S.17-2009

A visit to the opera was not uncommon for royalty
during diplomatic visits. Here Empress Eugénie
can be seen sitting on the right next to Prince
Albert at the Royal Opera House in London,
wearing a similar dress to the one in plate 167.

167
Evening bodice from Empress Eugénie's
wardrobe and reconstructed skirt
Silk, chiné (warp-printed) and trimmed
with silk blonde lace
Skirt by Luca Costagliolo, print design
by Leon Maurice
c.1855 and 2017
The Bowes Museum, Barnard Castle, 1959.47

The bodice of this dress was made for Empress
Eugénie, and would have been worn on grand
occasions such as attending an opera. The
Empress in fact attended the *Tannhäuser* premiere,
which had been staged with the encouragement of
her close friend Princess Pauline von Metternich,
wife of the Austrian Ambassador (pl.161—2).

168

168
Opera hat and box
Gibus
Black silk with grey silk lining
France and England, 1850–9
V&A: T.25-1946

It is this type of elegant hat that a gentleman might
have worn to the opera. An interior mechanism
allowed the hat to collapse, so that it could
be stored safely in a small box during the show.

169
Fan
Chantilly bobbin and tortoiseshell sticks
France, 1850–70
V&A: T.5-1916

The creation of lace became increasingly
mechanized by the middle of the nineteenth
century, leading to a greater number of accessories
created in Chantilly bobbin, as seen here. Fans
were popular fashion accessories during this
period, as can be seen in plate 166 (p.186).

170
Opera glasses
Steel and brass
France or England, late 19th century
V&A: S.320-1981

A similar pair of opera glasses can be seen in
the left hand of the lady depicted in Eva Gonzales'
A Box at the Théâtre des Italiens (pl.152). Not only
could the owner follow the singers on stage with
these glasses, but also look into the auditorium for
famous faces or sources of gossip.

169

170

PARIS

171

171
Costume design for a Lord (chorus)
Alfred Albert (1814—79)
Drawing, 1860—1
Bibliothèque Nationale de France, Paris,
216-20 (4)

This costume design was for a member of the
chorus, who would have sung the role of a citizen
of the Wartburg watching Tannhäuser's singing
contest in Act II. A representation of the chorus
in the relevant scene can be seen in the press
illustration in plate 172.

172
Tannhäuser: The Singing Contest
Print with 4 illustrations in the corners
Press illustration, 1861
Bibliothèque Nationale de France, Paris,
4-ICO THE-2827

Tannhäuser provoked outrage and heated
debate in Paris in 1861, in addition to inspiring a
number of contemporary artists. The opera was
cancelled after the third performance, and this
press engraving is the only representation of the
Venusberg scene (top left-hand corner) as seen
by artists including Fantin-Latour, who created
Tannhäuser on the Venusberg (pl.163) and Paul
Cézanne, who created *l'Idylle* (now at the Musée
d'Orsay), both inspired by the opera.

173
Model for Act II of *Tannhäuser*
Philippe Chaperon (1823—1906)
Set model, 1861
Bibliothèque Nationale de France, Paris

Philippe Chaperon was an in-house painter
and set designer for the Paris Opéra between
1864 and 1900. This set model shows that the
Tannhäuser premiere made use of traditional
theatre techniques such as painted cloths displayed
in several layers to suggest perspective. The
deliberate medieval look was inspired by
Wagner's libretto, which was in turn based
on medieval German legends.

THÉATRE IMPÉRIAL DE L'OPÉRA. — LE *TANNHAUSER*, 2e acte : *Le tournoi des ménestrels*. — Page 114. *1861.*

172

173

PARIS

DRESDEN

Mit gesetzl. Musterschutz.

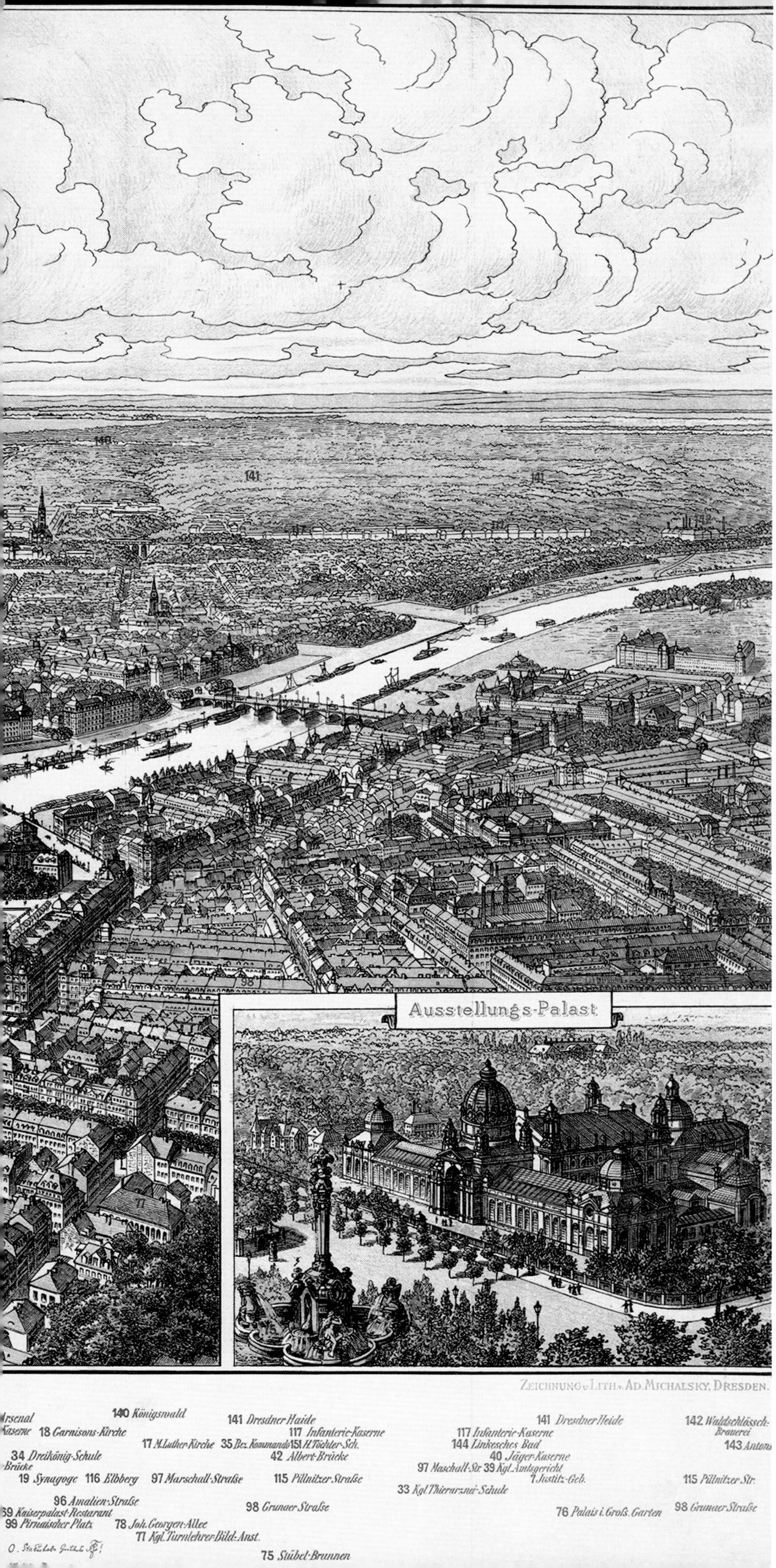

Ausstellungs-Palast
Zeichnung u. Lith. v. Ad. Michalsky, Dresden.
140 Königswald
141 Dresdner Haide
18 Garnisons-Kirche
117 Infanterie-Kaserne
17 M.Luther-Kirche
35 Bez. Kommando
151 H.Töchter-Sch.
34 Dreikönig-Schule
42 Albert-Brücke
19 Synagoge
116 Elbberg
97 Marschall-Straße
115 Pillnitzer Straße
96 Amalien-Straße
98 Grunaer Straße
99 Pirnaischer Platz
78 Joh. Georgen-Allee
71 Kgl. Turnlehrer-Bild.-Anst.
75 Stübel-Brunnen
141 Dresdner Heide
142 Waldschlössch.-Brauerei
117 Infanterie-Kaserne
144 Linkesches Bad
40 Jäger-Kaserne
97 Maschall-Str.
39 Kgl. Amtsgericht
7 Justitz-Geb.
115 Pillnitzer Str.
33 Kgl. Thierarznei-Schule
76 Palais i. Groß. Garten
98 Grunaer Straße

DRESDEN

6

RICHARD STRAUSS
1864–1949

Salome

Salome is the stepdaughter of Herod, King of Judea, and the daughter of his wife Herodias. Salome becomes infatuated with John the Baptist, who has been imprisoned for condemning Herod's incestuous marriage to her mother. But he rejects Salome. Herod lustfully asks Salome to dance for him, and as a reward she asks for the severed head of John the Baptist. When it is brought to her, she kisses it passionately. Disgusted, Herod has Salome killed.

175

INTRODUCTION

SIMONE YOUNG

Salome is, I believe, the perfect opera. There is not one note, not one word that is superfluous. The synthesis of the text and its melodic and rhythmic setting is not only complete but extremely subtle, with nuanced meaning and emotional interpretation already built into its phrases. The orchestration is sumptuous, extravagant and deeply sensual and it is an opera of which I never tire, be it as conductor or audience member.

Growing up in Sydney, in a family where endeavour was encouraged but means were slim, my access to operatic performance was very limited. The New York Metropolitan Opera broadcasts were an essential accompaniment to my school homework, and as a teenager, after my Saturday morning job in a newsagency was complete, I would rush in to the Sydney Opera House to try to bag a standing-room or student rush ticket to that day's performances.

So it came that I saw my first *Salome* performance in the Concert Hall of the Sydney Opera House when I was about 14. I was blissfully ignorant of all things German, other than the Beethoven and Bach that I practised assiduously at the piano. Fascinated equally by literature, I had read just about anything I could lay my hands on that was written by Oscar Wilde, and on discovering his play *Salomé*, was intrigued to see it as an opera.

The experience was nothing short of shattering — I was hurled into a world of musical and linguistic decadence that my teenage brain was incapable of understanding; I was hooked. The visceral power of this music, the spectacle of the exoticism of the staging and the fascinating but almost nauseatingly compelling final scene simply blew me away. It was the beginning of a life-long obsession with this masterpiece.

Over the next decade, my fascination with the German language, and with librettist Hugo von Hofmannsthal and composer Richard Strauss in particular, drew me closer to the decadent opulence of Strauss' opus and then to *Salome*. After years of playing the piano reduction, coaching and assisting with the preparation of the work, I finally conducted my first *Salome* in 1995, at the Vienna State Opera. In the house where Mahler had hoped to premiere the work, and had been defeated by the censors, I was surrounded by the sound of the silken Vienna strings and rejoiced in all the luscious eroticism of this beautiful score. Twenty-two years on and numerous *Salome* productions and performances later, I am just as overwhelmed by this score as I was as a teenager!

Strauss had an extraordinary ability to set the complexity of women's emotions and sexuality into musical thought. The languid, almost morbidly nostalgic world of the Marschallin, later transformed into her generosity and fortitude in Act III of *Der Rosenkavalier*, the animal-like viciousness and the paranoia of the gorged Klytemnästra, the naiveté and maternal longings of Chrysothemis, the coquettish and rebellious Sophie, dreamy Arabella, virginal Daphne — all these characters and more find in Strauss' melodies and rhythms a direct and almost physical relationship with the audience member. He achieves this sometimes within a single phrase — the Marschallin's 'Ach ja!' in Act III of *Der Rosenkavalier* contains within two notes a whole world of nostalgia, resignation, courage and compassion. At other times it takes an entire scene — from Klytemnästra's 'Ich habe keine gute Nächte' until her maniacal laughter when she hears the news of Orestes' purported death, her greed, paranoia, sloth, blood-lust and lasciviousness build into a complete portrait.

Salome presented Strauss, and therefore her interpreters and conductors, with a complex challenge. Here was a character who, while she well appreciated the effect of her beauty on the men around her, was as yet unaware of her own sexual desires and saw the appetites of her mother as disgusting and alienating. Dramaturgically, she is presented to us as the projection of various men's fantasies — in the first scene, Narraboth sees her as a delicate light creature of beauty and innocence, but the Page recognizes the moral vacuum at her core. Each compares her with the moon — one as magical and one as dead. Both are correct.

John the Baptist does not see her at all — for him she is merely the embodiment of the evil that is her mother, a classic, Old Testament 'sins of the father' (or in this case, the mother) judgement — and ignores, perhaps does not even hear the beauty of the poetry that Salome creates in

176

177

order to express her desire for him — a desire of which she is still not fully cognisant and the consequences of which are to her immaterial. The ambiguity of the situation of this indulged child-woman draws sympathy from no-one — other than from Strauss himself. The entire score is pervaded by waltz-rhythms and he accompanies her manipulative flirtation with Narraboth with flutes, harps, solo-violin and celesta — fragile and transparent. Her worshipping of John the Baptist — his skin, his hair and finally his mouth — is bathed in gorgeous harmonies of major tonalities and joyous cadences, and her enraged responses to each of his rejections is chromatic, spiky, fitful and exaggerated — the complex and extremely uncomfortable world of the adolescent.

A sinuous phrase on the solo clarinet presents us with Salome's theme right at the start of the opera and specifically, the five-note turn which is later extended, augmented and extravagantly orchestrated with tutti strings or horns, or whispered in shadowy woodwinds and almost inaudibly on the celesta, should be paid careful attention.

Through this figure, Strauss engages us with Salome and her descent into the darkly sensual morass that is the final scene. But to suggest that it parallels a development or decay of morality in the title figure would be to incorrectly ascribe a morality to the 'innocent' Salome, who is amoral from the beginning. Her world is defined by her narcissism, and therefore cannot admit a morality or purpose that is not the response to her own desires and needs.

Strauss allows us, her observers and audience, to find a beauty in her decay: Strauss clothes her manipulation of Narraboth in waltz-rhythms that charm us as well as Narraboth, and gives her phrase after glorious phrase of melody as she becomes increasingly desperate at John the Baptist's refusals. An orchestral interlude of exaggerated and violent climaxes precedes her smouldering brooding under Herod's eyes. We watch and listen, fascinated and appalled at the same time, as her obsession with the object of her desire overwhelms her repugnance of Herod and he too falls victim to her persuasion. Salome's cold and vocally ever more demonic 'Ich will den Kopf des Jochanaan' punctuates the scene like stab wounds.

As Salome is presented the head of John the Baptist, after an unbearable suspense (was the stifled repeated scream of the solo double bass an inspiration for Hitchcock's *Psycho*?), the orchestra explodes into an extravagant and sickly triumphant celebration of the achievement of her desires and the horns soar over the massed forces with her theme.

The decadent triumph finally gives way to an uneasy calm and an organ, almost imperceptible in the pianissimo sustained strings, plays a chord of dissonance which is almost physically nauseating, and which provides an abstract acoustic picture of the distortion of love which Salome has embodied. There is no other way for all this to end, than that Salome and we ourselves are crushed beneath the weight of the final violent rhythms.

I have not tried to offer you a dramaturgical study of the score, but rather my own personal response to this extraordinary work. I am often asked whether the fact that I am a woman makes me more aware of such central female characters as Salome (or Elektra, or Tosca, or Butterfly, or …) and whether I therefore more directly and emotionally resonate with the opera than a man would. This is nonsense. The role was written by one man — Oscar Wilde — and given the most extraordinary musical expression by another — Richard Strauss.

Whether the conductor is a man or a woman is completely irrelevant; a conductor must find his/her way into the protagonist's head, and the only route is through a thorough and analytical study of the text — both words and music. Only then can one honestly claim to be attempting to serve the work and unlike Salome, not one's own egotistical needs.

VISIONS OF WOMEN:
SALOME AND DRESDEN

KATE BAILEY

179

Once, in Berlin, I went to Max Reinhardt's 'Little Theatre' in order to see Gertrud Eysoldt in Oscar Wilde's *Salome*. After the performance I met Heinrich Grünfeld who said to me 'My dear Strauss, surely you could make an opera of this!' I replied: 'I am already busy composing it'.[1]

From the seemingly simple, if horrific, story of Salome emerges a uniquely complicated character. Outlined in a few short verses the biblical narrative (Matthew 14:1–12) tells of Salome, daughter of Herod's wife, dancing for Herod on his birthday at the request of her mother Herodias (married previously to Herod's brother). His stepdaughter 'pleased Herod so much that he promised with an oath to give her whatever she asked', whereupon Salome requested, and duly received, the head of John the Baptist – brought to her on a platter.

This basic outline is the foundation for an operatic super-star and seductive anti-heroine. Salome had fascinated artists for centuries, as different generations attempted to address her ambiguous motivation and the emotional consequences of her actions – but at the end of the nineteenth century she became a potent symbol of hedonism, decadence and the embodiment of the *femme fatale*. The interpretation and reinterpretation of the story of a teenage girl who demanded to be in charge, but struggled to control her own destiny and desires, was a *fin-de-siècle* obsession, taking Europe by storm.[2]

180

WILDE IN BERLIN

Salomé, the one-act play by Oscar Wilde (1854–1900) – published in French in 1893 and English in 1894, illustrated by Aubrey Beardsley (1872–98) – represents the culmination of the late nineteenth-century European obsession with the biblical subject, and is one of the best examples of human engagement with the story (pl.180). The play's underlying themes of sexuality, power, madness, sadism and orientalism resonated particularly strongly during this period. As described by American musicologist and composer Laurence Kramer (b.1946): 'Salome, in her heyday, was in short a kind of all-purpose cultural symptom, and treated as a focal point for a bundle of instabilities in and around the *fin-de-siècle* gender system'.[3]

Known for his feminist sympathies and admiration of strong women, it is perhaps unsurprising that Wilde was drawn to Salome as a subject. He originally intended for Sarah Bernhardt (1844–1923) to play the lead and for the play to premiere in London. However, the Lord Chamberlain refused to license the work for performance: under blasphemy laws it was illegal to present biblical characters on stage (Wilde was so outraged that he threatened to renounce his British citizenship and leave for France). In fact, Wilde had developed a narrative that was even more shocking than the biblical text. It also raised controversial questions of sexual equality and female sexuality at a time when the perception and status of women was changing rapidly across Europe. In the story, he consciously moved the narrative away from John the Baptist and gave Salome, the girl, centre stage. His Salome is violently aroused by Jochanaan (Wilde restores John the Baptist's Hebrew name) and demands his death after he has rejected her advances. Salome then makes passionate love to his head, kissing the dead lips of the man who in life treated her with contempt.[4]

The play was staged in Paris in 1896, shortly after Wilde was convicted of sodomy and during his subsequent incarceration. Even as Wilde was imprisoned in Reading Gaol, his controversial play was being given freedom in Europe, and was particularly popular in Germany. During the 1903–4 season there were 248 performances of Wilde's plays in the country, including 111 performances of *Salomé*. Wilde's work became 'a litmus test between the right, which condemned him as representative of the decay

178 (pp.200–1)
Semperoper auditorium, Dresden
Main building rebuilt post-war in 1985,
following the design of the 1878 building

179
Street, Dresden
Ernst Ludwig Kirchner (1880–1938)
Oil on canvas, 1908; reworked 1919
The Museum of Modern Art, New York

180
Gertrud Eysoldt as Salome in Max Reinhardt's
staging of Oscar Wilde's *Salomé* at the
Little Theatre in Berlin
Unknown artist
Postcard, 1903
Theater Museum, Vienna

of the British, and the left, which saw the persecution of homosexuality as a sign of the inherent hypocrisy of the Germans'.⁵

STRAUSS AND *SALOME*

Even before Richard Strauss (pl.181) saw Wilde's play he was fascinated by the text and its subject. The Viennese poet Anton Lindtner began to turn Wilde's play into a libretto for an opera in 1902, and Strauss was inspired to set the drama to music, in the end using not Lindtner's versified version but Hedwig Lachmann's German translation of Wilde's original text (pl.182). Strauss described the opening song 'Wie schön ist die Prinzessin Salome heute nacht...' ('How beautiful is the princess Salome tonight'), the dance and the final scene as 'simply calling for music'.⁶

Born in Munich in 1864, Strauss received a strong musical education, with both his parents nurturing his talent. Aged six, Strauss was already composing his first pieces; by his eighteenth birthday, he had composed 140 works and premiered his first symphony in Dresden; at the age of 21 he was the musical director in Meinengen. In 1874 Strauss had discovered Richard Wagner's operas *Lohengrin* and *Tannhäuser*, but his opinionated musical father prevented him from studying them in detail. However, the defiant, ambitious and innovative Strauss was greatly influenced by Wagner as he boldly created a new direction for classical music in the twentieth century. In 1882, Strauss entered the Ludwig Maximilian University of Munich where he studied art history and psychology – alongside his music education.⁷ In Salome, he was to discover a subject that could combine a nuanced artistic heritage with the influential ideas of psychoanalyst Sigmund Freud (1856–1939).

Strauss embraced Wagner's belief in the *Gesamtkunstwerk* – the idea of creating a total work of art. Yet he was also seeking to create something new, something modern in subject and form. By selecting Salome as a subject for his opera, Strauss was engaging both with its success in various other art forms whilst also consciously harnessing Wilde's popularity in Germany. Furthermore, the subject identified him with the avant-garde, the progressive generation, and also with the Jewish artistic community which in itself connected with the biblical narrative. In his attempt to become the new Wagner, Strauss was making a statement as he pushed against traditions in opera.

In 1907, Strauss wrote an essay entitled 'Is there an avant garde in music?' in which he described the reaction of audiences to Wagner's music and the constant challenge of captivating the masses: 'I cannot bear those who demand that Biblical subjects should be taboo because Richard Wagner took his subjects from Teutonic legends'.⁸ Many of Wagner's operas, including *Tannhäuser*, were based on popular German legends; Strauss considered himself a radical and defied this convention as he looked to the Bible as a source for inspiration. With the choice of *Salome* he broke with any previous attempts to write mock-Wagnerian operas, identifying instead with modernists and the avant-garde.⁹

> I had long been criticising the fact that operas based on oriental and Jewish subjects lacked true oriental colour and scorching sun. The needs of the moment inspired me with truly exotic harmonies, which sparkled like taffeta particularly in the strange cadences. The wish to characterise the *dramatis personae* as clearly as possible led me to bitonality, since the purely rhythmic characterisation Mozart uses so ingeniously did not appear to me sufficient to express the antithesis between Herod and the Nazarene.¹⁰

Strauss' extraordinary ability to react immediately and holistically to the cultural landscape around him, and to translate it imaginatively into new musical forms meant that he was able to take advantage of a swirling maelstrom of cultural expression. *Salome*

181

Eine grosse Terrasse im Palast des Herodes, die an den Bankettsaal stösst. Einige Soldaten lehnen sich über die Brüstung.
Rechts eine mächtige Treppe, links im Hintergrund eine alte
Cisterne mit einer Einfassung aus grüner Bronze. Der Mond
scheint sehr hell.

DER JUNGE SYRIER: Wie schön ist die Prinzessin
Salome heute Nacht!

DER PAGE DER HERODIAS: Sieh die Mond-
scheibe! Wie seltsam sie aussieht! Wie eine Frau,
die aus dem Grab aufsteigt. Wie eine tote Frau.
Man könnte meinen, sie blickt nach toten Dingen
aus.

DER JUNGE SYRIER: Sie ist sehr seltsam. Wie
eine kleine Prinzessin, die einen gelben Schleier
trägt und deren Füsse von Silber sind. Wie eine
kleine Prinzessin, deren Füsse weisse Tauben sind.
Man könnte meinen, sie tanzt.

DER PAGE DER HERODIAS: Wie eine Frau, die
tot ist. Sie gleitet langsam dahin.

Lärm im Bankettsaal.

ERSTER SOLDAT: Was für ein Aufruhr! Was
sind das für wilde Thiere, die da heulen?

ZWEITER SOLDAT: Die Juden. Sie sind immer
so. Sie streiten über ihre Religion.

ERSTER SOLDAT: Warum streiten sie über ihre
Religion?

182

183

is perhaps the most influential score Strauss wrote.[11] It is recognized for changing the nature of opera and pushing the boundaries of expressionism, evoking personal visions and inner emotions. Like Wilde, Strauss ensured that Salome was the main protagonist in his opera, confirming her central position as a subject of the male gaze, a performer and as a character in control of her own femininity and sexuality.

THE PREMIERE IN DRESDEN

By 1905 Strauss' music was growing in popularity across Germany, and he was working in many of its cities, including Munich, Berlin and Dresden. In the capital of the Kingdom of Saxony, Dresden's opera house, the Semperoper, was central to the city's identity.[12] Built by architect Gottfried Semper (1803–79) and first opened in 1841, it staged several Wagner premieres – including his 1845 *Tannhäuser*. It was considered as one of the most beautiful opera houses in Europe, reflecting three different architectural styles – Early Renaissance, Baroque and Classical. Unfortunately, the Semperoper burnt down in 1869 and was later rebuilt in 1878 by Manfred Semper (1838–1913), Gottfried's son. In political exile after supporting the 1848–89 uprisings in the city, Gottfried was able to oversee his son's building of the new opera house in a Neo-Renaissance style, reimagining yet retaining much of the characteristics of the previous building (pl.183). This magnificent opera house, which was rebuilt again in 1985 after Dresden was bombed during the Second World War, is regarded as one of the finest examples of Dresden Baroque architecture. The impressive curved façade and opulent, rich architecture reflects its status and significance in the city. Interestingly, detailed letters written by Gottfried Semper while in exile provided important references and specifications for the rebuilding in 1985.

Before the Second World War, Dresden was often called 'the Florence of the Elbe' and was home to romanticists including the painter Caspar David Friedrich. In architectural terms it was regarded as one of the world's most beautiful cities, with numerous Baroque and Rococo buildings, palaces, museums and cathedrals. At the turn of the century it was well connected by trains and waterways to other German cities, as well other European centres. Today the city has been largely restored and the cobbled streets lead to the striking architecture of the Semperoper, which is situated at the heart of the city.[13]

At the beginning of the twentieth century, German cities and universities were making great scientific and technological progress. Germany was home to leading researchers working in physics, mathematics, chemistry and engineering and by 1945 it had been awarded more Nobel Laureates than any other nation. Dresden and its university had strong links with many great inventors including Wilhem von Siemens (1855–1919), one of the Siemens family of engineers who was awarded an Honorary Doctorate from the University in 1905[14]. In 1903, Dresden hosted the First German Municipal Exhibition, which promoted the progress of German municipalities at the beginning of the twentieth century and showcased the work of industrial firms working in cities. Dresden had made significant progress in the use of gas street lighting and was pioneering in the field of electrical engineering and the use of electrical power to transform the modern city (pl.184).[15] Dresden was one of the four most important German-speaking cultural metropolises, alongside Vienna, Berlin and Munich. As a city, it was turning its back on its aristocratic and courtly roots, and attracting instead a diverse mix of artists and musicians, with the influential city bourgeoisie often supporting this new wave of artists.

In 1905, the city was relatively small, with only 520,000 inhabitants in its centre and a further 180,000[16] living in the suburbs. The population included a considerable number of overseas visitors who came to the city for the Sanatorium and for education. The Königlich-Sächsischen Technischen Hochschule Dresden technical university (now the Technische Universität Dresden, founded in 1828) and the Hochschule für Bildende Künste Dresden (the Dresden Academy of Fine Arts, founded in 1764) were highly regarded internationally, along with the music school – the Dresden Royal Conservatory.[17] The city's urban planning was conducted sensitively, with industrial developments taking place outside the historic city centre. Heavy industry was discouraged, but businesses that used precision engineering, or those that manufactured goods including electronic equipment, cosmetics, tobacco and chocolate, were all thriving.[18]

Photography and the production of cameras were also key to the development of the city. In 1887 Richard Hüttig moved his company from Berlin to Dresden, and by 1900 several other manufacturers of cameras or other photographic equipment were also based there. The proliferation of printing techniques and greater access to cameras led to a far greater amateur adoption of photography – as well as to a European-wide *fin-de-siècle* pornography boom. In 1903, the enterprising Ernemann Camera Company, which was based in Dresden, began developing film projectors for cinema.[19] The city was also host to several theatres and, like many cities, had an industry devoted to erotic entertainment. The citizens of Dresden could watch a diverse mix of theatre, including performances by the Japanese Theatre Company at the Dresden Albert Theatre, which was depicted by the expressionist painter Ernst Ludwig Kirchner (1880–1938). In 1911 Karl Schmidt had founded the Festspielhaus, a progressive theatre that attracted revolutionary directors, including Max Reinhardt (1873–1943) and Konstantin Stanislavsky (1863–1938).

The citizens of Dresden in the first decades of the twentieth century were educated, cultured and sensitive to the city's history and beauty. Many supported the cultural reform movement initiated by Ferdinand Avenarius in his journal *Der Kunstwart*. And Dresden had strong links with the Arts and Craft and Design movements associated with Schmidt and Wolf Dohrn (1878–1914), who established the *Deutschen Werkstätten für Handwerkskunst* (German workshops for Craftmanship). These reform movements

184

183
The Second Semperoper (The New King's and Court-Theatre) on Theatre Square in Dresden, main façade
Collotype print, 1880
Staatliche Kunstsammlungen Dresden,
A 1995–3322

184
Electrical Works, Dresden
Photomechanical print from *Die Architektur des XX^{te} Jarhunderts*, 1903, vol.3, pl.25
Royal Institute of British Architects, London

DRESDEN

185
Poster of the world premiere of *Salome* by
Richard Strauss at the Semperoper, Dresden
9 December 1905
Saxon State and University Library, Dresden

186
*Portrait of the Director of
Music Ernst Elder von Schuch*
Robert Sterl (1867–1932)
Oil on canvas, 1914
Staatliche Kunstsammlungen Dresden, 2334 C

187 (pp. 210–11)
Particell of Salome op. 54 TrV 215
Richard Strauss (1864–1949)
26 September 1904 / 10 August 1905
Richard Strauss Institute,
Garmisch-Partenkirchen

aimed to move away from historicism, and look at new forms of art, craft and design, and easier production. Interestingly, although overall Dresden's tastes were more conservative and traditional than other metropolises, the city was receptive to cultural change and provided the setting and the context for some of the greatest artistic and musical expression of the time. Strauss was able to premiere some of his greatest progressive works in the city, and in 1905, the year of the *Salome* premiere, Dresden was also the birthplace of the radical German expressionist movement. Strauss said of Dresden:

> In my opinion, cities like Berlin and Vienna are quite unsuited to pronounce the judgment on untried new works. The fact that the composition of the audience is left entirely to chance and the enormous influence wielded by metropolitan criticism alone would make it appear inadvisable to entrust the vicissitudes of such a metropolitan first performance a work only too likely to make abnormal demands on receptivity....
>
> Dresden, which, under the inspired leadership of Schuch, was in position to satisfy my artistic requirements ... had the advantage that two-thirds of the audience consisted of friends and patrons from elsewhere, and the critics who came to Dresden were in a better frame of mind to appreciate the opera undisturbed....[20]

Despite these recollections and his strong connections with Dresden, it was not just a matter of personal preference to stage *Salome* in the city (pl.185); Strauss had run into issues with the censors in Berlin and Vienna. His good friend Gustav Mahler (1860–1911), who was the Director of the Vienna State Opera, tried to persuade the court censors that Vienna should premiere *Salome*. However, the censor acted both on moral and religious grounds: 'Irrespective that the representation of actions from the New Testament raises considerations to the court theatre, the presentation of the perverted sensuality, as incorporated in the figure of Salome is morally repugnant'.[21] *Salome* was not performed in Vienna until 1918.

Hence the first production, and the risk, ultimately fell to Ernst von Schuch (1846–1914) at the Semperoper in Dresden. Von Schuch was an Austrian conductor who had already worked with Strauss on the premiere of *Feuersnot* in 1901. An ambitious and progressive presence, von Schuch had the courage needed to produce *Salome*. Perhaps his legal background gave him the confidence and business acumen required by the first producer of Strauss' demanding, epic production (pl.186). Yet no sooner had the rehearsals started than difficulties with staging the production arose.

The first rehearsals started with a strike from many of the musicians and singers because the score was too difficult to learn by heart. Detailed correspondence between von Schuch and Strauss reveals the slow progress of rehearsing the opera. One famous anecdote describes how Marie Wittich, the soprano who would play Salome at the premiere, refused to dance the 'Dance of the Seven Veils'. As an honest and respectable woman, Wittich was not prepared to perform Salome's suggestive dance. In the end Sidonie Korb, a dancer from the corps de ballet, took the role for the sequence. This helpfully reinforced the duality of Salome's character – a respectable virgin combined with a seductive temptress.[22] This is an approach which would be favoured by directors staging this opera in the twentieth century; Robert Wilson, for example, divided Salome's psyche into several bodies on stage in his production at La Scala in 1987.[23]

Von Schuch also had to prepare the Semperoper for the other dramatic developments in Strauss' opera. The 'Dance of the Seven Veils', for example, required an orchestra numbering over 100, compared to an average of 70 to 80 members for a Wagner opera. Even before the premiere, a critic challenged the theme of the opera,

186

DRESDEN

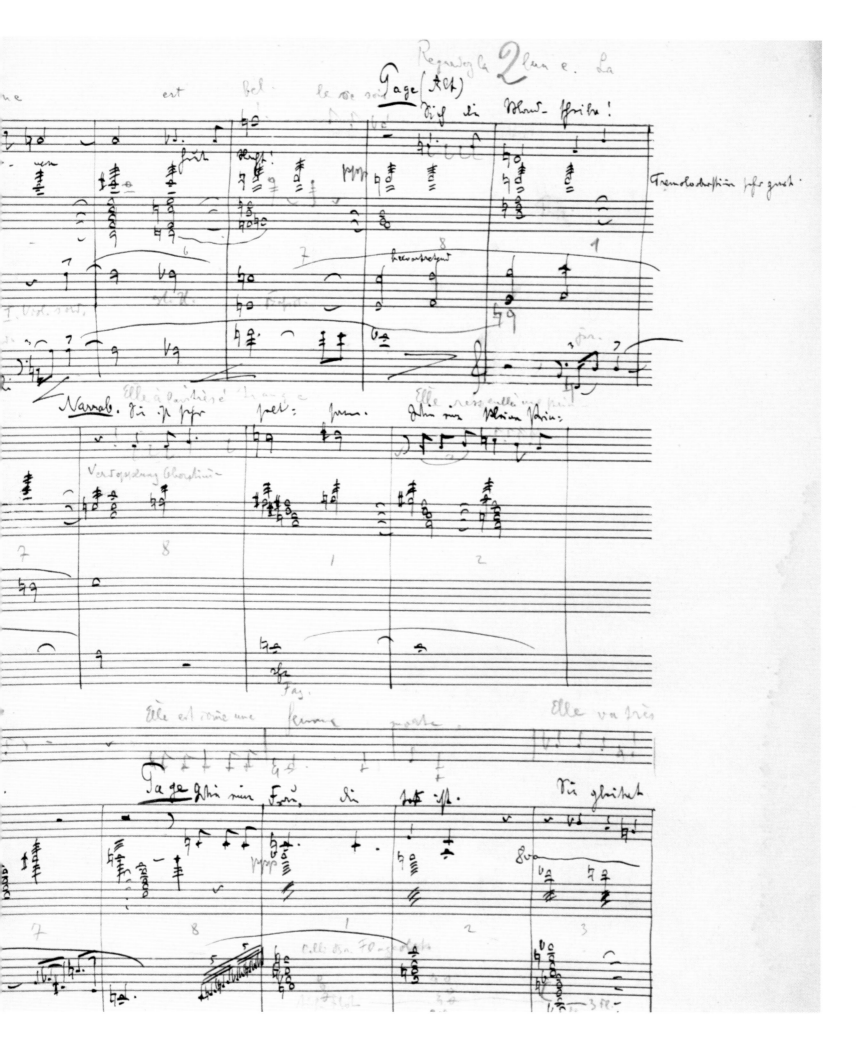

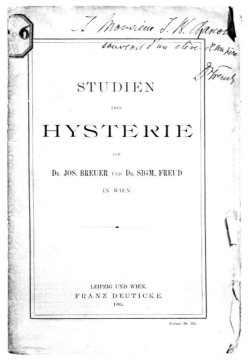

188

writing: 'This is not a drama, nor a poetry advisable or necessary for the soul, nor a libretto. It is a vicious, bloodthirsty event on a Terrace(!), an act of sensation in the sphere of pure perversion, an act of horrible lust to the taste of the all modern'.[24]

Despite the troubled preparations, the premiere fulfilled the ambitions of both Strauss and von Schuch. The audience loved it – requiring 38 curtain calls. Von Schuch's carefully chosen audience, made up of fellow musicians and journalists, applauded Strauss' opera and immediately recognized its significance as an opera of its time. Interestingly, in the week of the premiere, which took place on Saturday night, the Semperoper also staged classic operas from their repertoire, including Wagner's *Die Meistersinger von Nürnberg*, Mozart's *Die Zauberflöte* and Bizet's *Carmen*. This suggests that the opera connoisseurs in Dresden immediately recognized the importance of this new masterpiece. One passionate critique from the premiere said:

> No one can claim that they were bored. You could feel angry of hurt but not bored. Strauss keeps you in constant tension. He is an ambitious, experienced and clever man who understands how to make his compositions relevant to today and who understands how to follow the spirit of the age....[25]

Another viewer stated: 'our opera house has not seen a sensation with such an important impact since Wagner's last works. You must go and see it, if you want to be part of today's discussions about the latest music and the highest artistic performance'.[26]

Within two years of the Dresden premiere, the opera had been performed in 50 cities. Its success was such that the royalties from *Salome* alone enabled Strauss to build his villa at Garmisch-Partenkirchen in Bavaria, where he lived until his death in 1949. In reaction to criticism from Kaiser Wilhelm II (1859–1941) that with this opera he would 'do himself terrible damage', Strauss replied that 'It was from this damage that I built my villa in Garmisch!'[27] Strauss is often described as an opportunist, and was unquestionably a composer who could sense the zeitgeist of the time.

SALOME AND STRAUSS' VISIONS OF WOMEN

An intensely secretive man, Strauss was able to express his emotions and his passion through music (pl.187). The enduring power of the opera derives from his ability to empathize with the extremes of Salome's character – the juxtaposition of her feelings with the monstrosity of her actions. Revealed through musical leitmotifs, Salome is represented through a range of deep emotions from fear, to love, to jealousy and lust. He continued his fascination with strong female characters in his subsequent opera *Elektra*, loosely based on Sophocles' tragedy, which also premiered in Dresden in 1909.

Strauss married the soprano Pauline de Ahna (1863–1950) in 1894. Her multi-faceted character is often seen as the inspiration for the female roles in his operas – her *femme fatale* in Salome, or her sharp edges in Herodias. Pauline had a *prima donna* temper and although not a feminist she believed that being a woman did not mean that she should automatically take second place. Strauss described his wife to French novelist Romain Rolland in a letter dated 1900: 'She's very complex, very much a woman, a little depraved, something of a flirt, never twice alike, every minute different to what she was the minute before'.[28]

Beyond his personal relationships, Strauss was also tapping into the modern obsessions with psychology, gender, sexuality, hysteria and philosophy. Strauss was fascinated by the works of Friedrich Nietzsche and wrote a tone poem called *Also sprach Zarathustra* in 1896, inspired by the author's book of the same name. Dresden was only a short train ride from Vienna, home to Freud, the Austrian neurologist and founder of psychoanalysis. At the beginning of his career, Freud studied hysteria and nervous

188
Studien über Hysterie (Studies on Hysteria)
Joseph Breuer (1842–1925) and
Sigmund Freud (1856–1939)
Leipzig und Wien: Franz Deuticke
Published 1895 (first edition)
Pitié-Salpêtrière Hospital, Paris

189
Clara Zetkin (1857–1933) with socialist women's movement activists Lore Agnes and Mathilde Wurm
Unknown artist
c.1920

190
Poster for 'Internationaler Frauentag' (International Women's Day)
Mihály Biró (1886–1949)
Ink on paper, c.1925
V&A: E.1354-1931

disorders, publishing his *Studies on Hysteria* in 1895 (pl.188). By 1896, after initial experiments using hypnosis on patients, Freud began to use psychoanalysis in his treatments, believing that symptoms could be cured if patients talked freely and without inhibitions. As a result of his research, Freud developed theories relating to the unconscious, dreams, personality, femininity and female sexuality.[29] The character traits and backstory of Salome echo the subjects that informed Freud's studies – the mad, teenage girl who is the subject of her stepfather's obsession, and who is expressing her own sexual desires. Like the subjects explored in Strauss' opera, Freud's studies respond to the changing attitudes towards women and the shifting role of women in society.

Arguably, in the Western world, the *fin-de-siècle* obsession with Salome, as a powerful young woman, was partly a result of a masculine fear of the new woman fighting for independence and equality. In contrast to the mid-nineteenth century, where women were seen as wives and mothers or as 'consumer goods' on the marriage market, by the end of the century, women were fighting for greater emancipation. The international feminist movement was gathering ground and primarily focused on women's suffrage, the right to education and the right to own property. In Germany, women were granted the right to enter university in 1904, although they were not given the right to vote until 1919.

The biblical story of *Salome* has become shrouded in these contemporary layers of psychological theories, juxtaposed with the growth of women's independence. Salome's character and the narrative of the drama presented feminine power and sexuality to a predominantly male intellectual and artistic society who were both fearful and curious about the twentieth-century woman. The opera defies and at once reveals the dichotomy of women as goddesses or sexual beings. In Freud's studies, the libido is usually presented as masculine, which is in contrast to Salome's character, who is a woman with a clear sense of lust and desire in Strauss' opera. Freud also believed that 'culture burdened women with a heavy share in sexual and reproductive life and for this reason, they had less chance of sublimating their sexual desires in the pursuit of learning'.[30]

However there were women intellectuals who were making progress in the field of psychoanalysis. Lou Andreas-Salomé (1861–1937), a friend of Freud and fellow psychoanalyst, tried to define a new culture for women. Her essay on female sexuality in 1904, *Die Erotik*, proposed the psychological differences between the sexes, and constructed an independent feminine psychology. Likewise Helene Stöcker (1869–1943), another German intellectual and friend of Andreas-Salomé, fought for female political and social equality. After a strict girls' school education she became one of the first German women to receive a doctorate. In 1905 she helped found the League for the Protection of Mothers and Sexual Reform, whose campaigns included support for unmarried mothers. Stöcker was actively involved in lobbying the German parliament against criminalizing homosexuality. Her influential new philosophy, called the New Ethic, advocated the equality of illegitimate children, the legalization of abortion, and the importance of sexual education.[31]

189

On another side of the feminist spectrum, the socialist women's movement in Germany used the struggle of the working classes to stress issues of gender equality and advocate women's rights. It was led by Clara Zetkin (1857–1933) (pl.189), a Marxist from a town close to Dresden and member of the Women's German Social Democratic Party. She published *Die Gleichheit*, a journal that debated issues such as divorce and gender inequality.[32] Zetkin was instrumental in establishing the first International Women's Day in 1911 (pl.190).

The intellectual discourse that surrounded the question of women's sexuality and equality naturally affected contemporary attitudes to women in Germany prior to emancipation. They explain how and why Strauss' choice of subject captured such a strong hold on the public imagination, and on the minds of the artistic, literary and intellectual circles in Europe.

190

A CITY OF EXPRESSIONISM – A MODERN OPERA?

At the beginning of the twentieth century, many artists in Dresden were turning their backs on romanticism; instead embracing modernism and expressionism across all art forms. Architectural students at Dresden's Königlich-Sächsischen Technischen Hochschule included Fritz Bleyl, Erich Heckel, Ernest Ludwig Kirchner and Karl Schmidt-Rottluff, who all formed part of Die Brücke (The Bridge) artists' group in 1905. Studying in the city, the Die Brücke artists rejected bourgeois social conventions and academic traditions, and sought a new, more empathetic way of representing the world. They saw themselves as a bridge to the future and believed that art could express radical and social views through its depictions of the modern city, landscapes and people. Working as a group, the artists shared a studio and holidays together – and their work often depicted the same subject matter and collective style, frequently incorporating garish and bold palettes, direct compositions and thick outlines.[33]

The Die Brücke manifesto of 1906 (pl.191) stated: 'as young people who bear within themselves the future of humanity, we wish the freedom to live and work as we choose, in opposition to the well-established older forces'.[34]

These artists wanted to capture modern life, but also to represent traditional subjects in new formats. Their visual representations of the female body reflected a new modern woman, and therefore an expression of modern femininity. Kirchner's painting *Street, Dresden* (1908, reworked 1919; date on painting 1907), for example, shows fashionable urban women (see pl.179). Die Brücke artists were not interested in presenting an idealized female form, as painted in the academic tradition. Their work was much freer and more immediate; their forms were liberated from the constraints of the nineteenth century.

In Kirchner's woodcut *Melancholisches Mädchen* (1928) (pl.192) the artist paints himself looking over the shoulder of his partner who confronts us with her ankles crossed. While the image was created after the Die Brücke movement finished and the style probably reveals much of their personal relationship, it is the raw, crude expression of the woman's sexuality, her nipples highlighted in red, combined with her melancholic expression, that is evocative of *Salome*'s core themes. This idea of the expressionist woman, especially images depicting the female nude, resonates with Strauss' empathy with Salome in his modernist opera. It also reflects the artists' sensitivity to the new roles for women that were gradually emerging at that time. Many early subscribers of the Die Brücke movement were indeed strong women, including Rosa Shapire. One of the first women to receive a PHD in 1904, she later bequeathed part of her collection of woodcuts by Karl Schmidt-Rotluff to the V&A.

Strauss' own views on making modern music echo the manifesto of the Die Brücke expressionist movement. He aimed to break away from the tradition now embodied by Wagner, and sought to create new forms of musical expression. While he was a little older than the coming generation of artists – 41 at the time of the *Salome* premiere in 1905 – he shared much of their youthful, experimental approach and their awareness of modern twentieth-century life.

191
Die Brücke Manifesto
Ernst Ludwig Kirchner (1880–1938)
Woodcut, 1906
The Museum of Modern Art, New York

192
Melancholic Girl (Melancholisches Mädchen)
Ernst Ludwig Kirchner (1880–1938)
Colour woodcut on Japanese paper, 1928
V&A: E.5332-1960

But the idea behind this noble intention of the great master, namely that even a perfect work of art should only be considered as one stage in a great organic development, that it should be planted as seed in the souls of our descendants, to inspire and assist in the birth of even higher and more perfect creations, this wonderful idea we will honour ... and never forgetting, over and above the love and admiration we owe to the masters of the past who have found perfection, that art is subject to the self-same laws as ever-changing life.[35]

192

DRESDEN

Strauss was in tune with the artists of his age, but it is also clear that he was aware of the demands being made of the citizens of the new century. He described and defined the challenges faced by opera in the age of cinema, and had an astute, entrepreneurial sense of the need to create a blockbuster to meet the demands of a mass market. Yet he still stated: 'We are all children of our own age and can never jump over its shadow'.[36]

The visual nature of the Dresden *Salome* premiere was in fact representative of nineteenth-century theatrical design, with a strong sense of naturalism. Indeed, the photographs of the original production show a staging disconnected from both the music and the work of other artists working in the city (pl.193). This perhaps reflects the position of Die Brücke and Strauss at the edge of the avant-garde, with their artistic vision yet to be fully grasped by the traditional design department of the 1905 Semperoper.

For Strauss, the creation of a truly modern stage aesthetic was to come a little later. Mahler, who desperately tried to host *Salome* at the Vienna State Opera, introduced Strauss to the Austrian artist Alfred Roller (1864–1935). Roller was a key player in the Viennese Secession movement, alongside the artist Gustav Klimt (1862–1918). In 1905, he produced a modernist design concept for *Salome* in Vienna (pl.194). Subject to the power of the Viennese censor, however, a Viennese staging of *Salome* was not realised until 1918. Roller's monochrome, simplified design would have provided a strongly architectural, yet minimal environment through which to reveal the emotional extremes of the opera. It was not until *Elektra*, in 1909, that Strauss was able to fully cooperate with Roller to create a modernist staging for his work.

The 1906 Austrian premiere of *Salome* in Graz was attended by Mahler, along with many young composers including Arnold Schönberg (1874–1951) and Alban Berg (1885–1935).[37] Giacomo Puccini (1858–1924) himself saw *Salome* one year later. Strauss' music was an inspiration for a new generation at the beginning of the twentieth century, and remained an inspiration throughout it. Although Strauss never wrote for cinema, his expressive depiction of set-pieces was particularly suited to accompanying moving pictures. In 1926, Strauss conducted a live orchestra performance for his opera, *Der Rosenkavalier*, which was written in 1911, to the premiere of a silent movie on the same subject.

Other film composers who have been influenced by Strauss' music include John Williams, whose epic soundtracks for *Star Wars* and *Superman* echo Strauss' orchestral works. Stanley Kubrick selected 22 bars from Strauss' tone-poem *Also sprach Zarathustra* for the opening of his iconic movie, *2001: A Space Odyssey*.

Strauss' compositions also continue to influence contemporary musicians, who have been fascinated by the story of his music; David Bowie (1947–2016), for example, expressed a deep connection to Strauss' *Vier letzte Lieder* (*Four Last Songs*), which were created shortly before his death and used mortality as their subject.

SALOMANIA

The term 'Salomania' was used in the *Theatre Magazine* in April 1909 in an article entitled 'All sorts of Kinds of Salomes'. The article was accompanied by images of this 'evil and fascinating' woman and responded to the wave of interest in the 'Dance of the Seven Veils', which was busily being performed by dancers such as Maud Allan, Loie Fuller (pl.195) and Isadora Duncan. Salome's dance, often performed to music by different composers, provided a way for dancers to express themselves, inspiring new movements liberated from tradition. Its popularity spread across the Atlantic, and in 1908 there were 24 different performances of Salome's dance in New York alone.[38] Many have been captured on film – including Charlie Barber's 1923 production starring Alla Nazimova. Often described as the first American art film, it took inspiration from Aubrey Beardsley's illustrations.

193
Postcard for the premiere of *Salome* at the Semperoper, Dresden
9 December 1905
Dresden Semperoper Historical Archive

194
Stage sketch for *Salome*
Alfred Roller (1864–1935)
Indian ink on paper, 12 December 1905
Theater Museum, Vienna

193

194

DRESDEN

The *Salome* created by Strauss is a shocking love story, and one of the most extreme operatic experiences ever made – allowing each generation in turn to live out its own interpretation of his masterpiece. The focal points of the opera – the 'Dance of the Seven Veils' and Salome's kiss of the separated head of John the Baptist – present iconic moments of interpretation for dancers, singers, directors and designers, including, for example, the pioneering fashion and theatre designer Mariano Fortuny (1870–1941). Here, Fortuny depicts Salome from behind, her body draped in transparent and thin fabric, which evokes a sense of movement (pl.196). Salome and her veils later became a source of inspiration for Fortuny's innovative style. Audiences and critics are seduced and provoked by Salome over and over again.

In 1949, Strauss' opera was directed by a young Peter Brook, with the set and costume designs by Spanish artist Salvador Dalí (1904–89) (pl.197), at London's Royal Opera House. The radical, ground-breaking duo challenged the conventions of the Royal Opera House with their production, bringing theatre practice to opera and resulting in the production being closed after just six performances. Brook described Strauss' music as the: 'hallucination-producing drug, which induces the same emotional reaction as the highly stylized, artificial, rhetorical and elaborate visual imagery of Wilde's original…. The task of the producer and designer is to find the same approach in "theatre style" which Wilde supplies in his dialogue'.[39]

Brook and Dalí certainly upset their London audience: 'The critics all decided that Dalí and I were only out to annoy them. There, at least, I might claim that they underestimated us; if that have been our intention I think that between us we might have done much worse'.[40]

Robert Carsen's production of *Salome*, created in 2008 for the Teatro Regio in Turin, offered an ironic and contemporary view of Wilde's drama. Herod's palace was designed as a gambling house in Las Vegas – an extreme setting for an extreme story. Salome was portrayed as a rebellious adolescent, who moves through a society obsessed with money, gambling and sex. Carsen's production was rich in deadly and addictive eroticism, where the beautiful, sensual and barefoot princess bewitches all the men she encounters. Finally, Herod is disgusted by Salome kissing the lifeless mouth of the severed head of John the Baptist.

In 2008, David McVicar staged his *Salome* in early twentieth century Germany, inspired by Pier Paolo Pasolini's 1975 film *Salò, or the 120 Days of Sodom*. The set was divided into two parallel worlds, designed by Es Devlin: on the top level, Herod revels with the banqueters while below a dingy basement is full of kitchen workers, off-duty soldiers and prostitutes. The climactic kiss scene is macabre and visceral, conveying the grim reality of Salome's grotesque act. For McVicar, the kiss was more important than the dance.

The different interpretations highlight how *Salome* and its music has successfully crossed generations as well as cultures, inspiring creativity and expanding cultural and social boundaries. Throughout the twentieth century, opera premieres have increasingly had to connect to the cultural background in which they are first performed. Where will directors and designers take *Salome* next?

Salomé, Salomé, dance for me. I pray thee dance for me. I am sad to-night.
When I came hither I slipped in blood, which is an evil omen; and I heard,
I am sure I heard in the air a beating of wings, a beating of giant wings.
I cannot tell what they mean…. I am sad to-night. Therefore dance for me.
Dance for me, Salomé, I beseech you. If you dance for me you may ask of
me what you will, and I will give it you, even unto the half of my kingdom.[41]

196

195
La Loie Fuller dans sa création nouvelle Salomé
(Loie Fuller in her new creation Salome)
Georges de Feure (1868–1943)
Colour lithograph, c.1895
V&A: E.161-1921

196
Salome holding the Head of Saint John the Baptist
Mariano Fortuny (1871–1949)
Pastel, black stone and white gouache
Musée d'Orsay, Paris; deposited at Musée Rodin

197 (pp.220–1)
Costume design for The Executioner
Salvador Dalí (1904–89)
Ink on paper, 1949
Royal Opera House Collections, London

DRESDEN

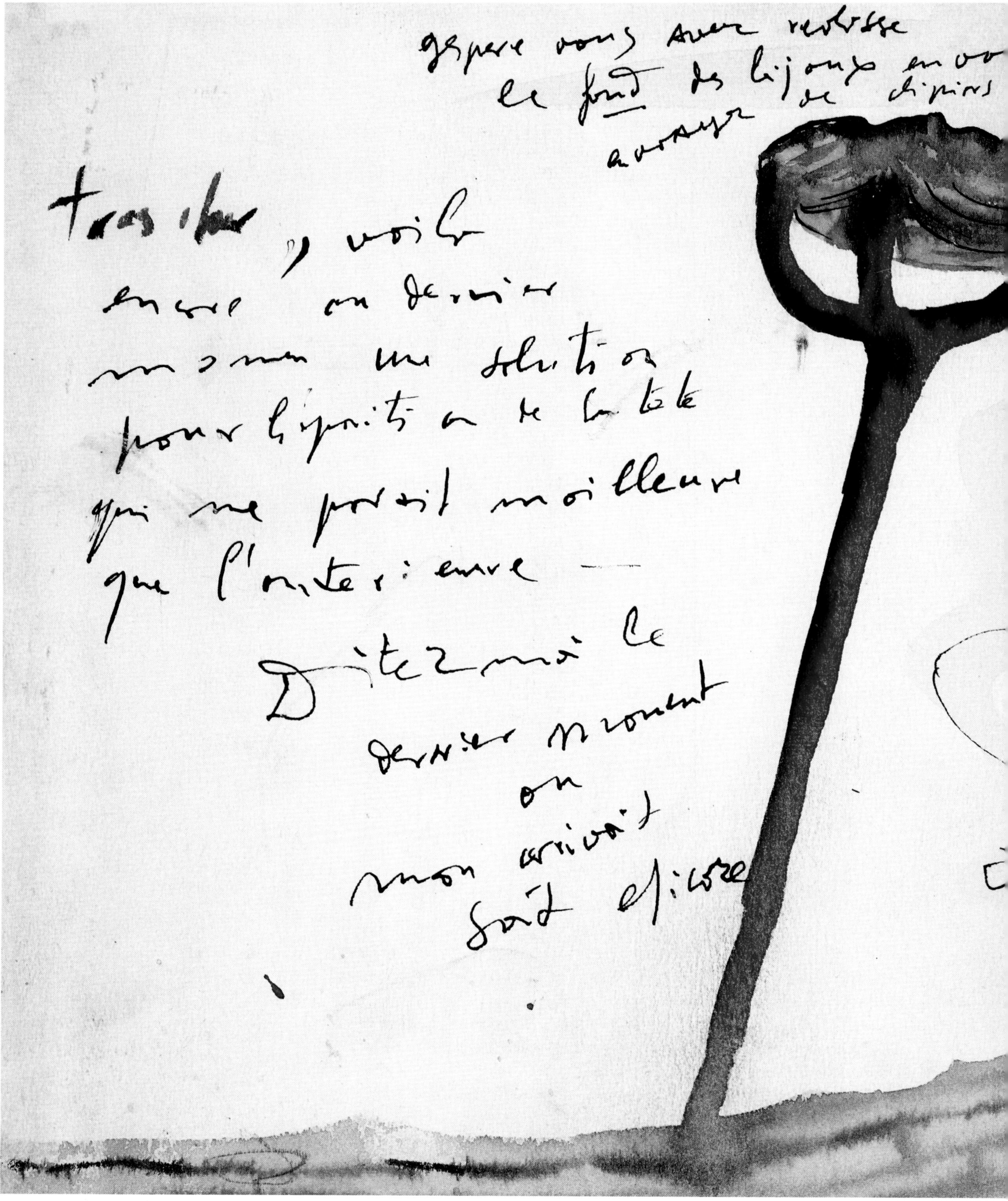

j'espère vous avez retrouvé
le fond des bijoux en or
avec de chiens

Très cher, voici
encore un dernier
moment une solution
pour liquidité ou de la tête
qui ne paraît meilleure
que l'intérieure —

Dites-moi le
dernier moment
ou
mon arrivant
soit efficace

197

198

199

DRESDEN

200

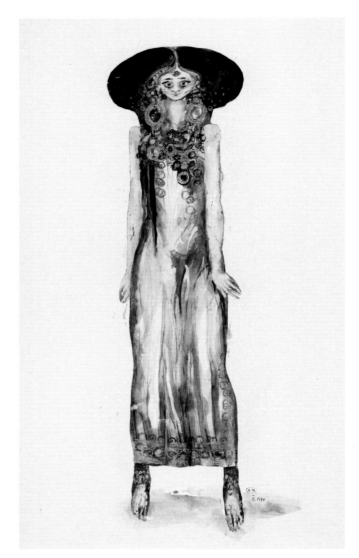

201

198 (p.222)
The Dancer's Reward, Plate XIV
Aubrey Beardsley (1872–98)
Line block print on Japanese vellum
V&A: E.435-1972

199 (p.223)
The Climax, Plate XV
Aubrey Beardsley (1872–98)
Line block print on Japanese vellum
V&A: E.436-1972

These plates are from the 1907 edition of *Salome*
published by John Lane, using the original 1894
drawings by Aubrey Beardsley. The first shows the
crazed Salome just after the 'Dance of the Seven
Veils', when she is given John the Baptist's head on
a platter, while the other shows the culmination of
the play as she kisses his severed head.

200
The Toilette of Salome II, Plate XII
Aubrey Beardsley (1872–98)
Line block print on Japanese vellum
V&A: E.433-1972

This print, from the 1907 edition of Wilde's play,
shows the young princess at the beginning of the
story, before she encounters John the Baptist.
On the bookshelf in the foreground are books
by authors such as the Marquis de Sade and Émile
Zola (*Nana*), a reference to Salome's dawning
sexuality.

201
Costume design for *Salome*
Andrezj Majewski (1936–2011)
Various techniques on paper, 1970
Royal Opera House Collections, London

Polish designer Andrezj Majewski created
this costume in 1970 for Grace Bumbry, who
performed the role of Salome in the Royal Opera
House production in London. This light-coloured
dress was designed for her first appearance,
suggesting Salome's purity before Herod's
perversity leads her to madness and the
unleashing of her own desire.

202
Costume for Herodias
Gianni Versace (1946–97)
1986–7
Versace Archive, Milan

Director Robert Wilson asked Versace to design
the costumes for the Teatro alla Scala production
of *Salome* in the 1986/87 season. This dress was
worn by Helga Dernesch, who played Salome's
mother Herodias. The dark colour and sharp
outlines of Versace's design echo the aesthetic
of Beardsley's illustrations, as seen in plate 200.

202

DRESDEN

203

204

203
Dresden Suburb
Erich Heckel (1883–1970)
Oil on canvas, 1910
Chemnitz Gemäldegalerie

The Die Brücke artistic group was founded in
1905 by Erich Heckel, Ernst Ludwig Kirchner,
Karl Schmidt-Rottluff and Fritz Bleyl. These
young artists looked for a more expressive way to
represent the world, turning to influences such
as Van Gogh or Gauguin and techniques such
as woodcut. This view of Dresden, created just
before the artists moved to Berlin in 1910, shows
the opulent, Baroque city in a new light.

204
The Lovers
Ernst Ludwig Kirchner (1880–1938)
Pastel, c.1906–9
V&A: P.6-1964

Pastel was one of the many drawing methods used
by the Die Brücke artists in order to capture their
models quickly, and to express the spontaneity of
the human body. Kirchner wanted to free not only
his art but also his own life from convention.
He never married his girlfriend Doris Grosse
('Dodo'), who was his favourite model between
1906 and 1911.

LENINGRAD

7

DMITRI SHOSTAKOVICH
1906–75

Lady Macbeth of the Mtsensk District

Katerina is unhappily married to
the merchant Zinovy. While he is away,
she falls in love with his worker Sergey,
and murders her controlling father-in-law
Boris after he becomes suspicious.
When Zinovy returns the couple kill him
and plan to marry. But the wedding
is interrupted when Zinovy's corpse is
discovered. Both Katerina and Sergey are
sent to a Siberian labour camp, where
Sergey finds another lover. A despairing
Katerina drags her rival into
a lake, where both women drown.

206

INTRODUCTION

GRAHAM VICK

THE WOMAN OF HIS DREAMS

If I could choose one period to visit via time travel it would be post-revolutionary Moscow, where every rule, every assumption was questioned and redefined — the family, the state, education, art, society, morality: let's banish the tyranny of religion and the sanctity of childbirth and look at alternatives; let's assume our fate is not written in the stars, in our birth, our nationhood. Let every man be Prometheus.

In this heady intoxicating atmosphere, revisionist theatre director Meyerhold challenged the naturalistic approach of Stanislavsky; tradition was thrown out as lazy entrapment — and women found a voice.

Katerina Ismailova is one of the most remarkable women in all opera — only Janáček's Elina Makropoulos is up there with her. Shostakovich took a dark sombre tale and created a raucous statement on gender oppression — *Lady Macbeth of the Mtsensk District* is an opera not so much about Russian authoritarianism as universal male power. The magnificent horror, the sexual longing transformed into physical power, the scream of a vivid creature longing to love and be loved howling like an animal and destroying like a lioness — all this adds up to a veritable Kali, the ravishing Hindu goddess of destruction.

Inspired by the theatrical experiment of constructivism, Shostakovich's experience in cabaret and playing the piano for silent movies drew from him a magnificent pastiche in which barely a phrase carries conventional opera sentiment. Only the writing for the Old Convict and the final convicts' chorus presents the traditional sentimental Mussorgsky view of an eternally suffering Russia — but Katerina will have none of it. She chooses to drown herself while taking her rival down with her: a triumph of freedom and revenge beyond any morality or decency. This is nature in all its tooth and claw.

Lady Macbeth of the Mtsensk District belongs in that new world of popular music, and popular culture that was subsequently hijacked by the classical elite and softened under the dust of its Stalinist fate, screaming its transgressive desires which mirror the darkest corners of our own longings and desires … to fuck to the death. Let's not sentimentalize this magnificent subversion. Let's not delude ourselves — it is the self-congratulation of our liberal values' triumph over Stalinism that has, paradoxically, given *Lady Macbeth of the Mtsensk District* its success, sanitizing its glorious filth under the dignity of repression.

I've directed *Lady Macbeth of the Mtsensk District* twice. The first time at the Metropolitan Opera in New York in the early nineties, in the wake of the fall of Communism. The optimistic hedonism of that era of joint ventures provided a convenient parallel with the cliché of the American housewife stifled by traditional family values and a lack of sexual fulfilment. As the phenomenal Maria Ewing rolled on the perfect lawn under a sprinkler trying to drown her desires, naked workmen taking showers after work called her into their yard for her habanera-like riff on men. This number — a cabaret song — is just one of many 'numbers' knitted into this crazy kaleidoscope of musical irony. For the interlude that follows, I asked the conductor Valery Gergiev if the tempo really needed to be that extreme. 'This interlude needs to go slightly faster than the orchestra can manage to play it — and this is a very good orchestra', was his reply. Transgression, risk, daring on every front.

Not having a river onstage, the final act was punctuated by prisoners emptying their slop buckets (in reality, floating Mars Bars) into a cesspit in the centre of the stage. So it was that Katerina slid silently into the shit, dragging the screaming sex worker Sonyetka down with her.

In Gothenburg, Sweden, we began in a perfect fitted kitchen … all shiny white and stainless steel — no food in sight — Katerina in a fake fur coat, stultified, with an ostensibly perfect life. The oppression of Scandinavian values, of 'Hygge', of work-life balance and legalized pornography … a Katerina longing to be the wild creature she felt inside … not the perfect cosy homemaker lighting candles and perfecting her soft furnishings.

Here the prison was the rooms of Katerina's world, filled with characters from her life: the prisoners condemned to the endlessness of being trapped in conventional formality, inhabiting the kitchen, the garage, the bedroom, the roof, the basement. Katerina finally escapes from the prison of her society, this time by filling her mouth with rat poison and seducing her rival to death with a long lingering deep-tongued passionate kiss.

207

205 (pp.228–9; detail)
Map of Leningrad from *A Pocket Guide to the Soviet Union*
Issued by Intourist, etc.
(ed. L. A. Block), 1932
British Library, London,
010290.df.21.

206 (p.232)
Scene from *Lady Macbeth of the Mtsensk District*
Directed by Graham Vick
Metropolitan Opera House,
Lincoln Center, New York, 2014

207
Gitta-Maria Sjöberg as Katerina
in *Lady Macbeth of the Mtsensk District*
Directed by Graham Vick with
set designs by Paul Brown
Gothenburg Opera, 2012

208
Anatoli Kotscherga as Boris (left)
and Eva-Maria Westbroek as
Katerina in *Lady Macbeth of the Mtsensk District*
Directed by Graham Vick with
set designs by Paul Brown
Metropolitan Opera New York,
Lincoln Center, New York, 2014

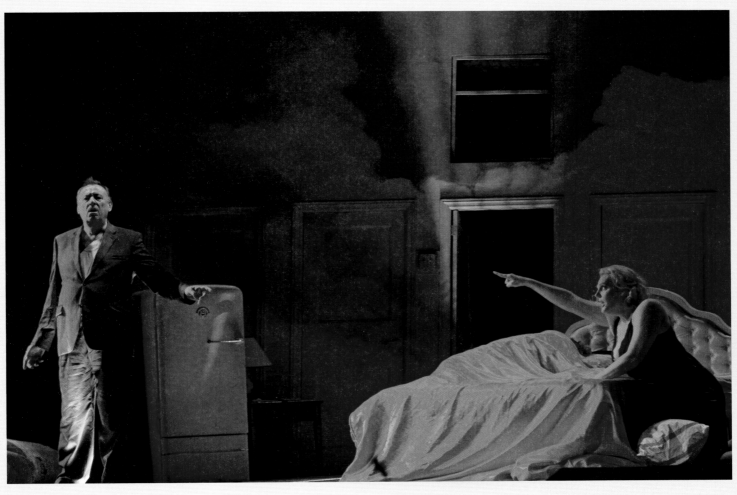

208

HEROINE, VICTIM OR CRIMINAL? SHOSTAKOVICH'S *LADY MACBETH OF THE MTSENSK DISTRICT*

ELIZABETH WILSON

210

Dmitri Shostakovich was born in St Petersburg, then the capital of the Russian Empire. The city was to undergo momentous change during his youth, as was reflected in the alteration of its name twice within a decade. The young Shostakovich (pl.211) went to school in St Petersburg, was a Conservatoire student in Petrograd and lived in Leningrad until the start of the Second World War. St Petersburg/Petrograd was Russia's cultural centre – its musical life was second to none and opera thrived in the Imperial Theatres (the Mariinsky and Mikhailovsky). Indeed, it was at the Mariinsky that Diaghilev worked (and was sacked from) before setting up the Ballets Russes; where operatic productions by Wagner and Strauss were magnificently staged; and where Vsevolod Meyerhold first worked as an opera director. In fact, his production of Sergei Prokofiev's first mature opera, *The Gambler* never reached the stage because of the breakdown of order after the first February revolution in 1917. Petrograd itself thus became the principle stage for the cataclysmic events of that year.

Many of the city's cultural institutions remained open even after the Bolsheviks seized power during the October Revolution (pl.210), including the Petrograd Conservatoire where Shostakovich studied from 1919. The young student was fully immersed in the city's musical traditions, and was an avid frequenter of the Mariinsky Theatre, particularly enjoying the ballet productions while also falling in love with the ballerinas. After 1924, when the city was renamed Leningrad (or 'St Leninsburg' as Shostakovich sarcastically called it),[1] its musical life diversified, allowing for visits and performances of modernist Western composers such as Alban Berg (1885–1935), Paul Hindemith (1895–1963) and Ernst Krenek (1900–91), which had a notable influence on Shostakovich's subsequent musical formation. Many of Europe's best performers also came there to work with the renowned Leningrad Philharmonic Orchestra in its beautiful hall (formerly the Noblemen's Hall). The same orchestra in the same hall gave the premiere of Shostakovich's own First Symphony (constituting his Conservatoire diploma work) on 12 May 1926.

The Shostakovich family flat on Nikolaev St (renamed Marat street after the Revolution) was centrally placed, just round the corner from Nevsky Prospekt and only minutes away from the Moskovsky railway station. After the death of Dmitri's father in 1924, the family had to give up three of their rooms, and share their kitchen and bathroom. From his home Shostakovich could walk (or run!) to the city's concert halls and also to the cinemas, where he earned money as an illustrator of silent films. To reach the Conservatoire and Mariinsky Theatre (now renamed GATOB) required taking a tram, but more often than not, with no money for the fare, Dmitri would walk the good half hour to attend lessons and performances.

This then was the city in which Shostakovich was formed as an artist. It was where he would go on to create his first masterpieces, get married and start a family. Not least, it was where he enjoyed unsurpassed success as an opera composer, a success that was rudely interrupted when on 26 January 1936, Stalin demonstratively walked out of the Bolshoi Theatre production of his second opera, *Lady Macbeth of the Mtsensk District*.

ART AND RHETORIC, IDEOLOGY AND MUSIC

In an article entitled 'Declaration of a Composer's Duties' published on 20 November 1931, Shostakovich testified to what he perceived to be a 'catastrophic' situation on the musical front: 'I am convinced that it is the wholesale flight of composers into the theatre which has created this situation'.[2] He lamented the low quality demanded of theatre music, the banal clichés and illustrative techniques that composers resorted to.

211

209 (pp.236–7)
Mikhailovsky Theatre auditorium, St Petersburg
Built in 1833, the auditorium was refurbished in 1859 and restored in 2001

210
Part of the design for a square,
14th anniversary of the October Revolution
Unknown artist
Postcard, 1930
State Museum of the History of St Petersburg

211
Dmitri Shostakovich
A.A. Temerin
Photograph paper on cardboard, 1929
Russian Theatre Museum, St Petersburg

Shostakovich admitted that over the last three years he himself had written music for ten theatrical projects in Leningrad alone – for music-hall, theatre and ballet productions, as well as for cinema. This did not include commissions that he failed to complete and his on-going work on his second opera *Lady Macbeth of the Mtsensk District*. Shostakovich now swore to forego further commissions for the next five years – a promise which he did not maintain. In his view, composers were renouncing their responsibilities, leaving the choice of theme to theatre and cinema directors, and choreographers. Without stating it in so many words, he pointed to the sad dearth of any representative Soviet opera.

Shostakovich's declaration has to be understood within the context of its timing, which coincided with the peak of the Proletarian Cultural Revolution, when Associations such as RAPP (Russian Association of Proletarian Writers) or RAPM (Russian Association of Proletarian Musicians) hounded the more liberal cultural associations into closure in the name of the proletariat. Shostakovich belonged to LASM (the Leningrad Association of Contemporary Music); he shared this organization's views on maintaining high professional standards, and approved of its propagation of Western 'modernism' as well as Russian contemporary music; he was less happy that the 'Rimsky-Korsakov clan' was in charge. After the closure of LASM early in 1931, RAPM demagogues subordinated all debate on musical matters to its lowest common denominator – the mass song.

INDUSTRIALIZATION: TOWARDS A HEROIC AGE

In an age of momentous projects of industrialization and collectivization upon which the country had embarked already in 1927, the general rhetoric of the moment tended towards the heroic (pl.212). The introduction of the Five-Year Plan produced new linguistic imagery: the ability to surmount the impossible, over-fulfilment of plans, the creation of counter-plans – all of which involved shock work tactics. The new language also implied class warfare, the need to fight sabotage, to stamp out religion and petty-bourgeois deviations. Yet the situation was not straightforward – collectivization of the land had been imposed by brute force and resulted in famine, the rich (or slightly better-off) peasants, dubbed 'kulaks', were victimized, while on the industrial front, campaigns against the 'bourgeois' specialists and their suspected attempts at 'wrecking' led to the first show trails in 1928. Heroic concepts, which also admitted the idea that every small man was an important cog in the machine, vied with grotesque caricature of archetypal class enemies in the agit-prop art and posters of the day. And these concepts not only influenced writers, cinema-directors and composers in their choice of theme, but had a real effect on everyday life. When 'class rationing' was introduced in Leningrad by the Party boss Sergei Kirov, it favoured the working class, while 'specialists' and 'intellectual' labourers were befittingly allotted a more modest share; other sections of society were deprived of rations, and effectively reduced to near-starvation.

Nevertheless within a few months of Shostakovich writing his article, the situation on the cultural front had changed radically. In April 1932, through direct Party intervention, the proletarian associations were dissolved, together with any remaining independent groups. In their place the 'Creative Unions' were founded, designed to defend the rights of each artistic group, defined as: Writers, Visual Artists, Cinema Workers and Composers. The Party now drew up the guidelines for creativity, enforcing the doctrine of socialist realism, and imposing complete control. It took some time before the consequences of these steps were fully felt.

In essence this was the backdrop against which *Lady Macbeth of the Mtsensk District* was conceived in 1930, created over the next two years, and first staged in January 1934. It was then performed for two seasons with unheard-of popular success,

212

before being unceremoniously gunned down and laid to rest after the appearance of the editorial article in *Pravda*, 'Muddle Instead of Music', which ferociously attacked not only the opera but also its composer.

CREATING AN IDEOLOGICALLY ACCEPTABLE SOVIET OPERA

In 1930 when his opera *The Nose* was premiered, Shostakovich claimed it was intended to satirize the Russia of Alexander I. Interpretation through the lens of Marxism was a necessary form of self-defence. Yet in choosing another nineteenth-century story, Nikolai Leskov's *Lady Macbeth of the Mtsensk District*, the composer seemed to be once again ignoring the challenge of using an appropriate Soviet theme, just at a time when the need for a rousing Soviet opera had become ever more pressing. Initially in the mid-1920s, the idea of making opera accessible to the masses involved the simplistic solution of re-hashing librettos and titles of existing 'classic' opera, as when *Tosca* became *Life for the Commune*. But by the mid-1920s, operas on suitable historical subjects were being written, such as Andrei Pashchenko's *Orliny Bunt* (*the Mutiny of Eagles*), dealing with Pugachev's rising, and premiered at Leningrad's GATOB.[3] The first proletarian opera was considered Vladimir Deshevov's *Lyod I Stal'* (*Ice and Steel*) based on the events of the Kronstadt rising which was produced during GATOB's 1929 season. Deshevov liquidated the 'class divisions' between soloists and choir, giving each chorus member a specific role, while the soloists were banished from the grand world of arias to basic recitative roles. As far as GATOB was concerned these first Soviet operatic experiments were not a great success, and could not match in quality or appeal the operas that, for instance were staged in its 1927 season: *Der Rosenkavalier* and *Salome* by Richard Strauss (1864–1949), Prokofiev's *Love of Three Oranges*, *Der ferne Klang* by Franz Schreker (1878–1934), and Berg's *Wozzeck*.

More successful was the creation of a Soviet ballet: *Krasnyj Mak* (*The Red Poppy*) by Reinhold Glière (1875–1956) was produced in 1927 at Moscow's Bolshoi Theatre and greeted as the first Soviet ballet on a revolutionary theme. GATOB quickly staged its own production, and then in 1932, to celebrate the fifteenth anniversary of the Revolution, presented *Plamya Parizha (The Flame of Paris)* by Boris Asaf'ev (1884–1949) – hailed as an exciting new genre, the 'drama-ballet'.

With the emigration of such celebrated Russian composers as Igor Stravinsky (1882–1971), Prokofiev and Nikolai Medtner (1880–1951), the rising star of Soviet music was without question Shostakovich. After the rousing success of his diploma work, the First Symphony premiered at Leningrad's Philharmonic Hall in May 1926, he was caricatured as a victorious Triton forcing open the jaws of a sea monster, a motif borrowed from the gilded statue, part of the grandiose fountain complex of Peterhof Palace, built on order of Peter the Great. His first opera *The Nose* was produced in 1930 at Leningrad's second opera house the Malyj Leningradsky Opernyj Teatre known by its acronym MALEGOT (Leningrad Small Opera Theatre, formerly the Mikhailovsky Theatre see pl.213). As the Russian music expert Gerard McBurney has stated, the opera, based on Gogol's story, was 'an electrifying tour de force, vocal acrobatics, wild instrumental colours and theatrical absurdity'.[4] Its kaleidoscopic range of influence borrowed techniques from theatre and cinema as well as modernist composers. It would not have escaped the attention of Leningrad audiences that both Berg's *Wozzeck* (staged at the GATOB in 1927) and *The Nose* open with a man being shaved – something difficult to imagine in classic opera. The whole work is intimately tied up with St Petersburg/Leningrad, where fantastical and unsettling events occur against the familiar setting of the streets and canals, within the very city centre where novelist Nikolai Gogol (1809–52) lived, and with which Shostakovich was intimately connected.

213
Model of Mikhailovsky Theatre painted red by the Bolsheviks as in 1927
Unknown artist
The Mikhailovsky Theatre Museum, St Petersburg

214
Leaflet advertising a production of Vladimir Mayakovksy's comedy *Klop* (*The Bedbug*), by Vsevolod Meyerhold
Aleksandr Mikailovich Rodchenko (1891–1956)
Printed by Moscow Polygraphy
Lithograph, 1929
V&A: E.1282-1989

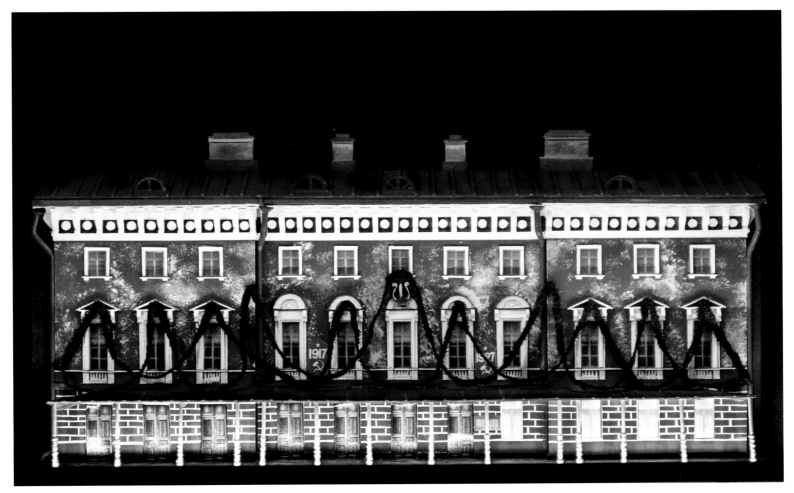

213

214

LENINGRAD

215

Other gifted Soviet composers were also writing opera. Already in the mid-1920s Yuri Shaporin (1887–1966) announced his opera *The Decembrists* based on a libretto by novelist Alexei Tolstoy. It took him nearly 30 years to complete the work, although in the meantime he was receiving handsome advances. Between 1926 and 1930, Alexander Mosolov (1900–73) wrote two operas: *Geroj* (*The Hero*) was planned for staging in Germany, and *Plotina* (*The Dam*), went into rehearsal at the Bolshoi Theatre, but was taken off just before the premiere in December 1930. Mosolov jeopardized his chances by using a risky subject based on the conflicts arising in a rural community over-taken by industrialization, and to add to his sins employed daring orchestration and heightened expressionism. A planned production of *The Nose* at the Bolshoi under Meyerhold's direction was likewise cancelled in 1931. As for Mosolov, neither of his operas was performed during his lifetime.

TOPICAL THEMES AS A MEANS OF SURVIVAL

Guided by a strong survival instinct and an acute awareness of the political situation, Shostakovich learnt to juggle his options, even when working in genres not necessarily close to his heart. Such works as his Second Symphony (1927), dedicated to the October Revolution with verses by the proletarian poet Alexander Bezymensky and Third 'Mayday' Symphony (1930) appeared to serve the Party line. Yet their inaccessible and avant-garde language perplexed members of RAPM. The best opportunity to ally himself with topical themes lay in writing scores for theatre and cinema, which included music for Meyerhold's production of Mayakovsky's play *The Bedbug* (pl.214) – and Kozintsev and Trauberg's film *New Babylon*. He joined Leningrad's TRAM theatre collective, created on Brechtian agit-prop principles, and was quick to learn how to pepper his declarations with political clichés. For instance, he instructed that a proletarian composer should not just write illustrative music representing the churning and clatter of machinery, but that his duty was to depict 'the pathos of socialist labour, the dynamic energy and creative force of the working class'.[5] This attitude was carried over in his film music, when he worked at LenFilm (Leningrad's film studios) with directors like Sergei Yutkevich, Fridrikh Ermler and the Kozintsev-Trauberg team.

Still avoiding opera, Shostakovich wrote two ballets for GATOB, *The Golden Age* (1930) and *Bolt* (1931) (pl.215 and 216). In the first, the conflict between Soviet and capitalist football teams served to demonstrate Soviet superiority, not least in the idea of physical culture as an art form, as manifested in the street spectacles and parades that were such a prominent feature of Stalinist Russia. *Bolt* dealt with sabotage in industry, but the exaggerated typecasting of the roles, wittily and sarcastically illustrated in the music was deemed 'un-proletarian'. *Bolt* was given one single performance on 8 April 1931. Tragically Fyodor Lopukhov's choreographic plan and Tatyana Bruni's constructivist sets were lost, although Bruni was able to reconstruct the costume designs for a later Leningrad production of the ballet in 1979.[6] Despite the brilliance of the music, Shostakovich was not forgiven for his 'anti-utopian' attitude. The proletarian journal *Rabochii i Teatr* (*The Worker and the Theatre*), wrote a menacing review: '*Bolt* was a flop and should serve as a last warning to its composer'.[7]

Shostakovich reused *Bolt's* music in other scores and produced two popular orchestral suites, which must have reminded his contemporaries of the fun-loving aspect of the young composer, happy to amuse his friends improvising foxtrots at night-long parties, and with a predilection for 'The American mountains' roller-coaster at Leningrad's GosNarDom (State People's House).

216

LENINGRAD

217

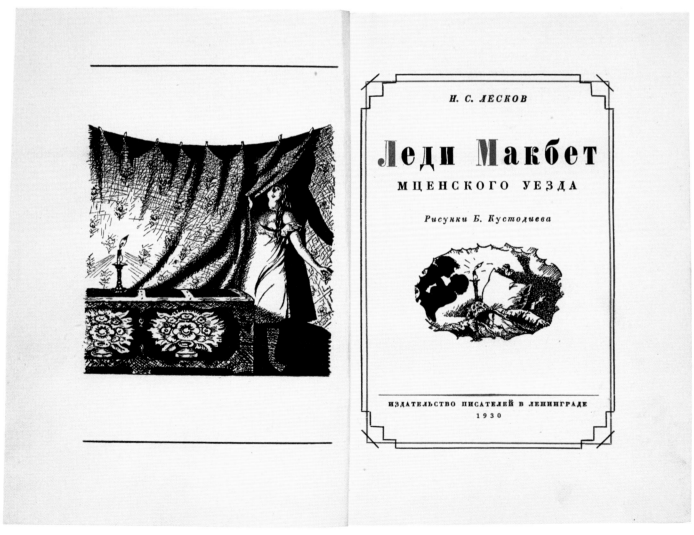

218

As he started work on *Lady Macbeth of the Mtsensk District*, Shostakovich was following RAPM's attacks in the national press very closely. This is evident from his correspondence with his friend, Ivan Sollertinsky, his confidant in regard to his compositional progress and amorous adventures (pl.217). Ivan Ivan'ich, in exchange, kept 'Dmitri Dmitr'ich' up to date on ideologically delicate matters at home. (The two men were inseparable and addressed each other formally by name and patronymic while using the informal 'thou'.)

Thus, we learn that the Ukrainian Association of Proletarian Musicians (UAPM) had reacted negatively to a new production of *The Golden Age* in Kiev in 1931.[8] In the same letter from Odessa, Shostakovich describes his dealings with a female representative of UAPM who wished to convert him to Mass Song:

> Just think she says, 'we of the UAPM heard your ballet – such decadence – Tahiti Trot – the light genre – capitulating to contemporary-ism, Western-ism....' And so as the words kept flowing form her – mmm – delightful little mouth, I listened in delight.... 'Why talk of this? Life is wonderful,' I intervened, and putting my arms round her attempted to kiss her. At that moment I felt a hard slap on my cheek. With a shriek she cried out 'I will write about this in the journal *Proletarian Music*' and stormed out.

Shostakovich hastened to inform Ivan Ivanich that her other catchwords included not just 'Modernism' and 'formalism' but also 'Sollertinsk-ism' (*Sollertinshchina*).[9]

A SUBJECT FOR AN OPERA; LESKOV'S *LADY MACBETH OF THE MTSENSK DISTRICT*

On a more serious note Shostakovich reported his progress on *Lady Macbeth of the Mtsensk District*, on which he could only work sporadically, mostly when away from Leningrad. He had great ambitions for his second opera, intending it to stand as his compositional credo. After the avant-garde experiment of *The Nose,* he now wished to return to more conventional operatic techniques. This was implicit in his declaration that the musical language of *Lady Macbeth of the Mtsensk District* had to be based on the maximum expression of the voice and use of cantilena line, where 'singers must sing, and not speak or declaim'.[10] Leaving behind the grotesque absurdities of Gogol's world and ignoring topicality, Shostakovich searched for a theme of 'eternal' significance. In 1930 he came across a new edition of the nineteenth-century writer, Nikolai Leskov's story *Lady Macbeth of Mtsensk District* in a new edition with pen and ink illustrations by the artist Boris Kustodiev (pl.218).

Leskov's understanding of provincial Russia was influenced by his work as chairman of the Orlov criminal courts commission. (Originally titled *Lady Macbeth of Our District*, the story bears the subtitle 'Sketch for notes on a Criminal Court case'.) In the court hearings Leskov encountered weird and extraordinary incidents, and himself was witness to a young bride pouring boiling sealing wax into her sleeping father-in-law's ear, an unusual form of murder, but one which may have provided a prototype for the story's chief protagonist, Katerina Izmailova. When it came to writing about the unfamiliar – namely the final chapters set in Siberia – he reported with pride that the novelist Fyodor Dostoevsky (1821–81) had praised him for having accurately reproduced this reality.

Leskov's narration is characterized by its cool detachment, while his use of colourful speech patterns and country dialect impart validity to the story's provincial character. Lacking is the biting irony of a Gogol or Dostoevsky, two authors whom

217
Dmitri Shostakovich, Nina Varzar and Ivan Sollertinsky
Unknown artist
Photograph, c.1930s
The Archive of Dmitri Shostakovich, Moscow

218
Lady Macbeth of the Mtsensk District
Nikolai Semenovich Leskov (1831–95)
Illustrations by Boris Mikhailovich Kustodiev (1878–1927)
Leningrad, 1930
British Library, London, X.989/15290

219

Shostakovich revered above all others. Rather, Shostakovich borrowed the techniques of Russian's greatest satirist, Saltykov-Shchedrin (1826–89). In claiming that 'there is no story in Russian literature that more vividly or expressively characterizes the position of women in pre-revolutionary times' Shostakovich constructed his ideological platform for the opera.[11] Yet, in his portrayal of Katerina's awakening sexuality, the violence of her passion and her doomed love, his models derived not so much from Leskov as from contemporary operas such as Berg's *Wozzeck,* and *Katya Kabanova* by Czech composer Leoš Janáček (1854–1928), based on *The Storm* – a play by Alexander Ostrovsky (1823–86).

While writing *Lady Macbeth of the Mtsensk District* in 1864, Leskov deliberately referred to *The Storm,* written some five years earlier. His use of impartial narration acts as a conscious antidote to Ostrovsky's sentimental treatment of his unfortunate heroine. Indeed, the two Katerinas have much in common: both are childless merchants' wives living in the stultifying environment of provincial Russia, both suffer from despotic in-laws, both commit adultery, and both perish, but for different reasons. Katya Kabanova repents, confesses her sin and then commits suicide, while Katerina Izmailova for the sake of love commits cold-blooded murder, finally killing herself and her rival. As the music historian Richard Taruskin observed, in order to justify his Katerina Shostakovich discarded Leskov's neutrality and restored Ostrovsky's 'sentimental' mode, seemingly 'switching heroines'.[12]

220

LESKOV, ZAMYATIN AND KUSTODIEV: THEIR 'RUSSIAN TYPES'

Russian painter Boris Kustodiev (1878–1927) shared Leskov's intimate knowledge of provincial Russia, and was best known for his 'portrait types', where he summons up not just a person's exterior image, but their whole inner world (pl.219 and 220). His drawings for *Lady Macbeth of the Mtsensk District* are sombre as befits the story, standing worlds apart from his better-known portraits of luxuriant Russian Venuses and merchants' wives. Created some four years before Kustodiev's death in 1927, the *Lady Macbeth* illustrations were intended for publication by the short-lived Petrograd publishing house Akvilon. Whereas *Lady Macbeth of the Mtsensk District* did not appear in print then, two other stories with Kustodiev's illustrations were published in 1922 and 1923: Leskov's *The Darner,* and *Rus'-Ruskiye Tipy* (*Russia – Russian Types*) by Evgeny Zamyatin (1884–1937). The latter borrowed its title and drew inspiration from Kustodiev's recent series of portrait-types. And there is a further borrowing: Zamyatin's *Rus'* is strikingly similar to Leskov's *Lady Macbeth,* but is characterized by its soft-edged Kustodiev-like lyricism, while avoiding the sentimentality of Ostrovsky's *The Storm,* and negating the violence of Leskov's story. Zamyatin's heroine, Marfusha, a girl of few words and docile temperament, from a town named Kustodievo on the Volga, is married to an elderly well-off merchant, who dies from a surfeit of toadstools. Although poison is hinted at, no accusations are passed, allowing Marfusha to legitimately marry the young gypsy with flashing eyes, with whom she had dallied before her husband's death.

Through his school friend, Irina Kustodieva, the artist's daughter, Shostakovich got to know Kustodiev in 1919. A touching friendship developed between the young boy and older artist. As Shostakovich sat at the piano and played, Kustodiev would observe and sketch; his best-known portrait shows the 13-year-old Shostakovich in sailor suit, clutching a volume of Chopin. The Kustodievs' hospitable household was a meeting place for Leningrad's intelligentsia, and it was there that Shostakovich first met Zamyatin, whom he was soon to invite to collaborate on the libretto of *The Nose.* The two men remained on friendly terms – and enjoyed playing poker together – until Zamyatin's emigration from the Soviet Union in 1931.[13]

219
Merchant's wife
Boris Kustodiev (1878–1927)
Oil on canvas, 1915
State Russian Museum, St Petersburg, Inv. 1870

220
By the Samovar
Kuzma Petrov-Vodkin (1878–1939)
Oil on canvas, 1926
The State Tretyakov Gallery, Moscow, Inv. 9367

THE PLIGHT OF WOMEN IN TSARIST RUSSIA

Leskov's tale grew from his concern for the plight of women in nineteenth-century Russia. On completing the story, he sent it to the renowned literary critic, Nikolai Strakhov: 'I beg your attention for this small work *Lady Macbeth of our District* which is the first in a series of sketches of the singular type of female character to be found in these areas (around the Oka and in part the Volga rivers)'.[14] Leskov planned 12 such sketches, eight of which were based on merchant and folk life. And likewise, Shostakovich decided to devote a trilogy of operas on the fate of extraordinary women (pl.221). But the crass denunciation of *Lady Macbeth of the Mtsensk District* in 1936 killed the opera writer in Shostakovich, despite his obvious predilection for the genre. In 1940 he considered a commission from Leningrad's Kirov Theatre for an opera entitled *Katyusha Maslova,* Tolstoy's heroine from his novel *Resurrection.* The project backfired when in the following year Anatoly Mariengof's libretto (approved by Shostakovich), was banned by the State repertoire committee. More than 20 years later the renowned soprano, Galina Vishnevskaya, arguably the best interpreter of *Lady Macbeth of the Mtsensk District's* title role, also suggested that Shostakovich write an opera for her inspired by Katyusha Maslova. Despite his devotion to Vishnevskaya's artistry, Shostakovich adamantly refused: 'No, no, not another Katerina, that's an ill-starred name'.[15]

But back in 1930, Shostakovich was drawn to Leskov's story by its extreme drama. In order to justify the murders committed by the heroine, Shostakovich fashioned Katerina's image according to his need to identify with her. His success in this may have been conditioned by being in love himself. In May 1932 he married after a long and complex romance the fascinating and intelligent Nina Varzar, a physicist by training, to whom he dedicated his opera. Galina Vishnevskaya was convinced that 'Katerina Izmailova ... is not the heroine of Leskov's story, she is Shostakovich's Nina'.[16] Another Galina, the Marxist writer, Galina Serbraykova (1905–80) left an account of her visit in 1932 to the Shostakovich family home in Marat Street:

> In a murky room he was composing his new opera, *Lady Macbeth of Mtsensk* at a large desk. He would play bits of it through on the piano.... The young composer admitted to me that he was about to get married. He was unable to hide his agitation, and gulping down his words, he told me about his fiancée, trying to remain cool and objective, an impossible feat for those in love.[17] (pl.222)

A LIBRETTO ON A SHAKESPEAREAN SCALE

As Shostakovich noted, the very title of Leskov's story implied 'an insignificant territory, heroes who are little people with passions and interests that are much smaller than in Shakespeare'.[18] Shostakovich needed a libretto where dramatic tension was paramount and Shakespearean passions could hold sway. It is unknown whether the significant changes made to Leskov's story all originated with Shostakovich or with his librettist Aleksandr Preys; but they served time-honoured theatrical principles: the creation of contrast and expanded characterization, which showed the influence of current Soviet ideology and class warfare. Thus Katerina's father-in-law, Boris Timofeevich, is transformed from the 80-year-old patriarch of Leskov's story into a lusty and sadistic despot, who forces Katerina to her knees to swear fidelity to her departing husband, and later decides to satisfy his lust with her but is pipped to the post by the worker,

221

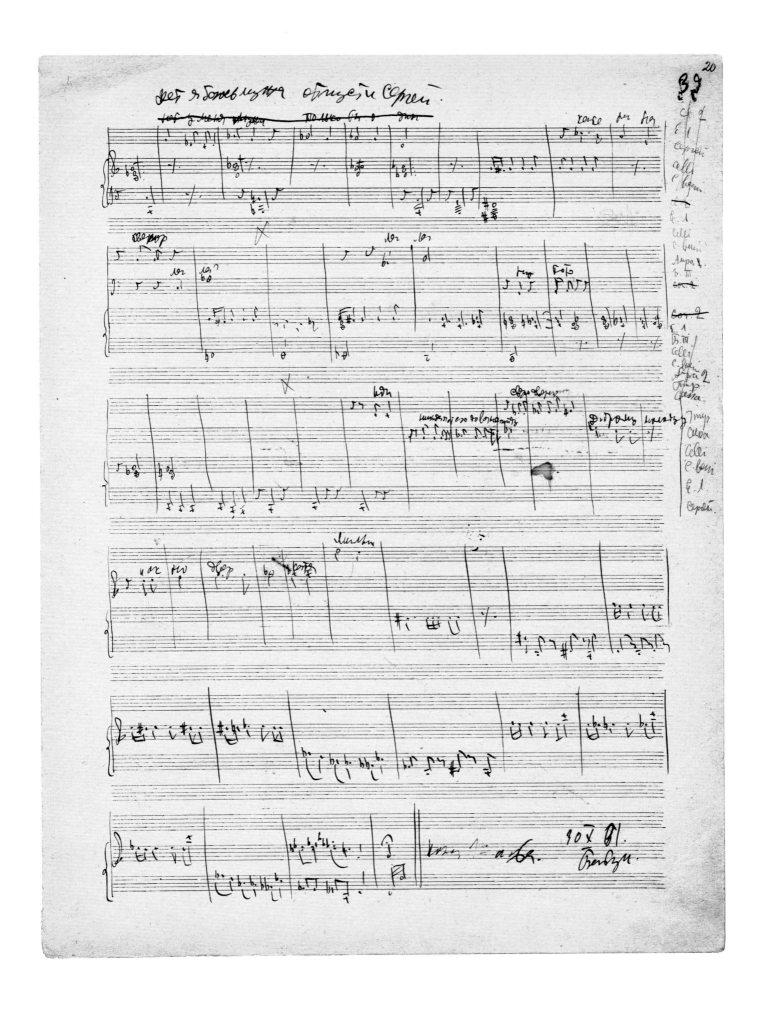

223

224

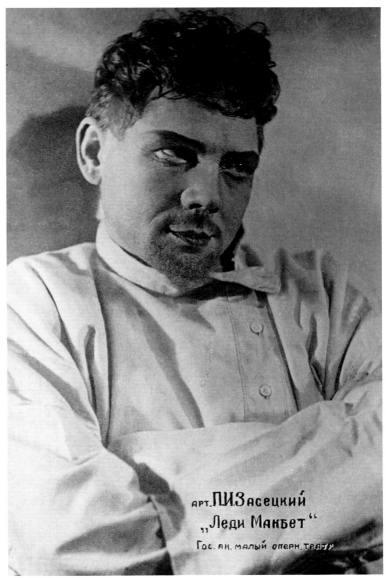

225

Sergey (pl.225). Likewise, he is determined that Katerina should witness his sadistic whipping of her new lover after catching Sergey leaving her room. Throughout the opera, Shostakovich pits Katerina's 'genuine' emotions against a world of crass male brutality, illustrating such scenes as the molesting and near-rape of Aksinya or the flogging of Sergey with music of unrelenting energy and violence (pl.223 and 224).

The whole of Act III deviates completely from the original story. Shostakovich and Preys' new version of events (the Shabby Peasant's discovery of Zinovy Borisovich's corpse, the scene at the police station, the rudely interrupted marriage ceremony, and arrest of Katerina and Sergey) provide enormous dramatic impetus, pushing satire to the point of grotesque. The Shabby Peasant, (variously translated as 'Tattered Peasant', 'Seedy Lout' and 'Village Drunk') fulfils a role absent from Leskov's story – that of the comic figure. Other changes to the libretto involved excising the murder of Zinovy's young, religiously inclined nephew, seen as an impediment to Katerina's inheritance. Additionally Katerina's pregnancy is suppressed, as well as her total indifference to the fate of her baby, born after her arrest. For Shostakovich's heroine needed to preserve her status of victim or 'innocent' murderess. 'Katerina is the only positive character in my opera. Her love for Sergey is the only thing that exists for her, and in her love she finds the sole aim of her existence.'[19]

The composer's case succeeds because of the ravishing music of her part, soaked in Russian intonations, always captivating whether sad, lushly beautiful, tender or

223
A.I. Sokolova as Katerina
Photograph, 1934
St Petersburg Museum of Theatre and Music

224
S.V. Balashov as Zinovy
Photograph, 1934
St Petersburg Museum of Theatre and Music

225
P.I. Zasetsky as Sergey
Photograph, 1934
St Petersburg Museum of Theatre and Music

despairing. In contrast, Shostakovich depicts his heroine's victims and persecutors as shallow or depraved with music that is either trivial or grotesque.

In calling the opera a 'satire-tragedy' Shostakovich invented a new artistic genre, which was open to political interpretation. The only character to whom the word tragedy can actually be applied is Katerina, while all the others are subjected to satire, if not primitive caricature. But as the 1930s advanced, the Soviet Union became increasingly plunged into a tragedy of repression, living a sort of parallel world to that of the opera, where it was no longer clear whether one was talking about iniquities in Tsarist or Stalinist Russia. Indeed, the borderline between satire and parody in Shostakovich can be so blurred, that at times it degenerates into topical propaganda. Daniil Zhitomorsky, a musicologist and one time adherent of RAPM, pointed out how the scenes involving the priest and the police reminded him of the agit-prop techniques of the 'Blue Blouses' – brigades of actors and musicians who performed theatrical scenarios in factories and workers' clubs in order to hammer home political messages.[20]

MARXIST INTERPRETATION OF CHARACTER

In order to ensure his cherished opera's path on to stage, Shostakovich paid lip service to the ideology imposed by the Cultural Revolution. The merchant class in the second half of the nineteenth century represented a rising capitalist class. Shostakovich presents the Izmailovs as exploiters, the priest as a drunken nonentity who believes equally in vodka and religion as the 'opium of the people', the teacher (a Bazarov-like nihilist) at the police station as an atheist who thinks that frogs have small, but mortal souls, and the Tsarist police forces as corrupt and all too eager for bribes.

Even the shabby (and drunken) peasant's role is extended from the comic to the treacherous once he discovers Zinovy's stinking corpse. Galina Vishnevskaya recalls Shostakovich saying with venom: 'that bastard ran to the police, overjoyed that he could inform on "Katerina". That now is a hymn to informers'.[21] In print, he dubbed the Shabby Peasant 'heir to Grishka Kuterma' – the duplicitous drunk from Rimsky-Korsakov's (1844–1908) opera, *The Legend of the Invisible City of Kitezh and the Maiden Fevroniya*.[22]

Shostakovich's caricature-role for the priest is legitimized in the wake of the ferocious anti-religious campaign of 1929 (pl.226). Not only were an enormous number of priests and congregation members arrested but the Josephine branch of the Orthodox Church, which was particularly active in Leningrad and which refused to compromise with the Soviet authorities, was completely decimated. As 'scientific' atheism was propagated to replace religion, a Museum of Atheism was created in 1932 in Leningrad's Kazan Cathedral.

As for Katerina's lover, he too was characterized in accordance with ideological placard art of the day: 'Sergey is a potential KULAK, and only the accident of discovery turns him into a prisoner instead of a merchant-exploiter. But in prison he remains the same. The music exposes and unmasks him. He uses his good looks to seduce women, he has pretentions to culture'.[23] Indeed it is on the unlikely pretext of borrowing a book that he first knocks at Katerina's bedroom door.

Although Shostakovich took responsibility for the dramatic structure of the libretto, credit for its literary quality was due to Preys. He imitated the folksy quality of Leskov's prose with the same ease as witty, rhyming verses for the Shabby Peasant's hymn to vodka, or the Chief of Police's pompous musings. However it was Shostakovich's understanding of the pre-eminent role of the orchestral score and its symphonic development, which raised the opera to the level of a masterpiece. The extraordinary orchestral entr'actes, Shostakovich explained, 'serve not only for mechanical scene changes but as a way of continuing musical ideas from the previous scene, and they play

Помещичий двор господа бога отца, вседержителя, творца небу и земли, видимым всем и невидимым.

226

an important role in the characterization of the events taking place on stage'.[24] Most famously the entr'acte after scene III is a graphic illustration of lustful love-making, with the trombone's descending glissando signifying post-climax (dubbed in 1935 by a New York critic as the first example of 'Pornophony'). In contrast the weighty passacaglia entr'acte (originally written for organ) between scenes IV and V (the two Ismailov killings) plunges us into a world of dark premonition.

THE RIGHTS TO PREMIERE

From early 1932, with *Lady Macbeth of the Mtsensk District's* completion in sight, Shostakovich set about negotiating the rights of first performance, and soon found himself entangled with three opera houses: two in Moscow and one in Leningrad. The fifteenth anniversary of the Revolution was being celebrated in November 1932, and with this in mind Shostakovich had signed two agreements with the Bolshoi Theatre for a heroic fairy tale opera *Razgadka* (*The Riddle*) with a libretto by Demyan Bedny, and the tragedy-farce *Orango*, set to a libretto by Aleksandr Starchakov and Alexei Tolstoy. He had also announced a grandiose Choral Symphony '*From Karl Marx to our own days*', of which he claimed the first movement was completed. He had also undertaken promises to write another opera (*The Great Lightning*), and an operetta, as well as stage and film music. Ultimately the only project that reached completion was his music for Ermler and Yukevich's film *Counterplan*, which received its triumphant first showing on 7 November, the very day of the anniversary celebrations. (The film's title-song, *The Song of the Counterplan*, became Shostakovich's single most popular piece.)

226
Bezbozhnk u Stanka (*Godless at the Workbench*)
'This is what happens in the backyard of our landlord, God the father, creator of heaven and earth, of all that is visible and invisible.'
Dmitri Moor (1883–1946)
Moscow, 1923
David King Collection, Tate, London

227

228

In early October, the Bolshoi Theatre realized that none of their commissioned projects were going to be ready for the following month's celebrations. Shostakovich, having received – and spent – the advances for his two unwritten operas, probably thought that in compensation he could offer the Bolshoi first performance rights of *Lady Macbeth of the Mtsensk District,* and signed a contract on 10 October. In doing so he ignored that he had already promised these rights to the Nemirovich-Danchenko Musical Theatre. Two days later, trying to extricate himself from this quandary, Shostakovich wrote to Boris Arkanov, artistic director of the Bolshoi, questioning their decision to subject *Lady Macbeth of the Mtsensk District* to official audition (such vetting was in fact normal procedure). 'Imagine if Avel Sofronovich Enukidze[25] came and said "I don't like this work, I would rather you put on *Pagliacci*." I need to know how you would react in such circumstances.'[26]

Simultaneously he wrote to Pavel Markov, artistic director at the Nemirovich-Danchenko Musical Theatre:

> I know you are furious with me for signing with the Bolshoi Theatre.
> But listen to me – the destiny of *Lady Macbeth* is very dear to me. But our friendship and relations are even dearer.... If you want I will tear up that contract immediately, although it will put me in a difficult financial situation – I owe them 5,400 roubles.[27]

In the end, two simultaneous productions were authorized, one in Shostakovich's native city, the other in Moscow. Leningrad's MALEGOT won the rights to world premiere on 22 January 1934 (pl.229), with the same team that produced *The Nose* (conductor Samuil Samosud, producer Nikolai Smolich and set designer Vladimir Dmitriev, see plates 227 and 228). Two days later the Moscow premiere followed at the Nemirovich-Danchenko Musical Theatre where the opera was presented under the title *Katerina Izmailova.* In the spirit of the day, the Moscow performances were announced as part of the Theatre's production campaign for the seventeenth Party Congress, to keep on par with the Donbass coal miners' production quota.

LADY MACBETH/KATERINA IZMAILOVA: AN UNPRECEDENTED OPERATIC SUCCESS OR A CATASTROPHE?

Both productions enjoyed unprecedented success and a large number of performances.[28] There was heated discussion as to which production was the best. Shostakovich himself was loath to express a preference, but praised Smolich for his understanding of how opera works. 'Overall I have to say that your production of *Lady Macbeth* reaches the audience, sustains the tension and interest throughout and evokes sympathy for Katerina.'[29] At the same time he admitted that, 'Nemirovich-Danchenko, with his great talent, has infused his production with the whole dramatic concept and culture of the Moscow Arts Theatre system. There are moments where he achieves quite shattering results'.[30]

As for the musical aspect, Nemirovich-Danchenko himself admitted the superiority of MALEGOT'S version:

> Our conductor Stolyarov does not possess the masterful poise of Samosud.
> This is the main difference between our and the Leningrad productions.
> We show a tragedy; in Leningrad they play a lyrical opera. Our production is filled with strong emotion and suffering, theirs shows caution, a fear of exaggeration, of upsetting the nerves.... Somebody cracked a witticism: in Moscow the opera is called *Katerina Izmailova* but they play *Lady Macbeth,* and in Leningrad it is called *Lady Macbeth* but they play *Katerina Izmailova*.[31]

A third home production opened at Moscow's Bolshoi Theatre some two years later on 28 December 1935, conducted by Aleksandr Melik-Pashayev. An unprecedented situation now occurred when, in January 1936, three productions of the same opera were being performed in Moscow to full houses – the two Moscow productions were joined by Leningrad's touring MALEGOT production.

It was the Bolshoi's new production of *Lady Macbeth of the Mtsensk District* which Stalin went to see on 26 January 1936 and which he and his suite walked out of before the last act, without having spoken to the composer. (Shostakovich used to say that Stalin must have had forebodings that the final 'Siberian Act' was too close to the bone.)

Two days later the editorial article 'Muddle Instead of Music' appeared in *Pravda* (pl.230) with devastating effect, not just for Shostakovich and his opera, but for the whole of Soviet musical society. Although the damning article carried no signature, it can be safely assumed that it was written at Stalin's behest and with his approbation – if not actually penned by him (pl.231). The real authorship is usually attributed to *Pravda's* leading journalist, David Zaslavsky. 'Muddle Instead of Music' was a direct attack not only on Shostakovich's opera but on his person, and accused the composer of not meeting the country's need for 'good operas', but instead shocking the listener through 'deliberate dissonance, confused streams of sound'. The 'grinding and squealing' of music with no melody is equated to a 'wilderness of musical chaos' and dubbed as 'leftist confusion instead of natural human music'. The composer is effectively charged with sacrificing good music to 'a petty-bourgeois, formalist attempt at originality'. It ends with the threat that this 'game may end very badly', which made clear that Shostakovich would either be punished or expected to recant.

Only in the late 1950s did Shostakovich decide to save the work from oblivion by making a new version, with offending texts expurgated, the more grotesque musical ideas softened and two new entr'actes written. His opera saw the light again in 1963 in this version, under the name of *Katerina Izmailova,* with a new Opus number 114. The original version of *Lady Macbeth of the Mtsensk District* Op. 29 had to wait another 33 years to be performed again in Russia, when, in 1996, Mstislav Rostropovich conducted staged concert performances in Moscow and in Shostakovich's native city, which had recently reverted to the its original name: St Petersburg.

230
'Muddle Instead of Music'
Pravda
28 January 1936
Library of Congress, Washington

231
Politbureau ZKVKP (B) (Central Committee of the All Russian Communist Party (Bolshevik))
Gustav Klutsis (1895–1938)
1935
V&A: E.1267-1989

230

231

232
Panorama of the sets for the
7 November 1931 celebration
Photograph, 1931
The State Museum of the History of
St Petersburg

The city of Leningrad hosted annual festivities to
celebrate the Bolshevik insurrection in 1917, which
led to the October Revolution. On occasions such
as these, the whole city would be transformed into
a stage, with public parades and performances
celebrating the Soviet workers. This photograph
shows the spectacular staging in front of the Winter
Palace, as depicted in the set design in plate 210.
Shostakovich's second symphony *To October*
was composed for the 10th anniversary
celebrations in 1927.

LENINGRAD

233

233

Worker and Kolkhozian Woman
Vera Mukhina (1889—1953)
Bronze cast in 1961 from the original 1937 model
The State Tretyakov Gallery, Moscow, CKC-272

Vera Mukhina developed her dynamic style during
the years of the Russian avant-garde movement
(1917—33), and later adapted to socialist realism
following a change in state policy after the Soviet
Writer's Congress in 1934. *Worker and
Kolkhozian Woman* is her most famous work, and
was presented in the USSR pavilion at the World
Exhibition in 1937. The man and woman are holding
the hammer and sickle, symbols of the Soviet Union.

234

*Towards the Reconstruction of Transport! —
We Shall Give*
I. Gromitsky (1904—91)
Printed by Typo-Lithography Vorovsky,
Moscow and published by Oqiz-Izoqiz
(State Publishing House)
Colour lithograph, 1931
V&A: E.405-1988

Under the new regime, Soviet workers were
glorified as instrumental to the implementation
of a new five year plan launched in 1928. This
poster emphasizes the need to invest in the radical
industrialization of the Soviet Union, in this
case transport.

234

235
Three photographs of the premiere of *Lady Macbeth of the Mtsensk District*
Scrapbook, 1934
The Mikhailovsky Theatre Museum,
St Petersburg

These images come from a scrapbook containing production pictures of various operas that were performed at MALEGOT (Teatr Maly Operny, today the Mikhailovsky Theatre). These photographs show the premiere of *Lady Macbeth of the Mtsensk District* on 22 January 1934. The stage setting of Act I was created following the set model in plate 228 (p.258).

236
Set design with stage directions showing the movement of actors for Act IV
N.G. Shul'gin
Pencil and ink on paper, 1934
St Petersburg Museum of Theatre and Music

237
Set design with stage directions showing parts of the set for Act IV
N.G. Shul'gin
Pencil and ink on paper, 1934
St Petersburg Museum of Theatre and Music

These two diagrams depict the stage set or *mise-en-scène* in Act IV of *Lady Macbeth of the Mtsensk District*, which takes place near a lake in a Gulag (prison camp) in Siberia. Plate 237 shows the empty stage, with labels indicating different areas such as 'Male camp' and 'Female camp'. Plate 236 shows the movements of the cast on stage during the final scenes of Act IV. The dots represent singers, most of them chorus members (the prisoners). The arrows indicate the movements of the principal singers — Sergey, his new lover Sonyetka and Katerina — throughout the scene.

235

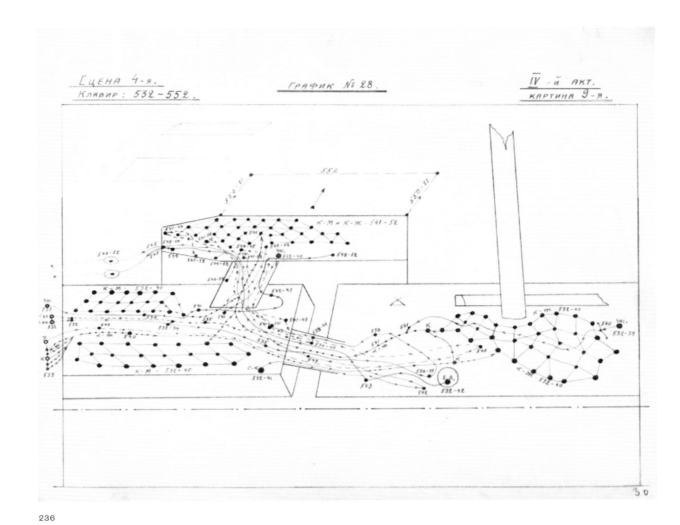

236

237

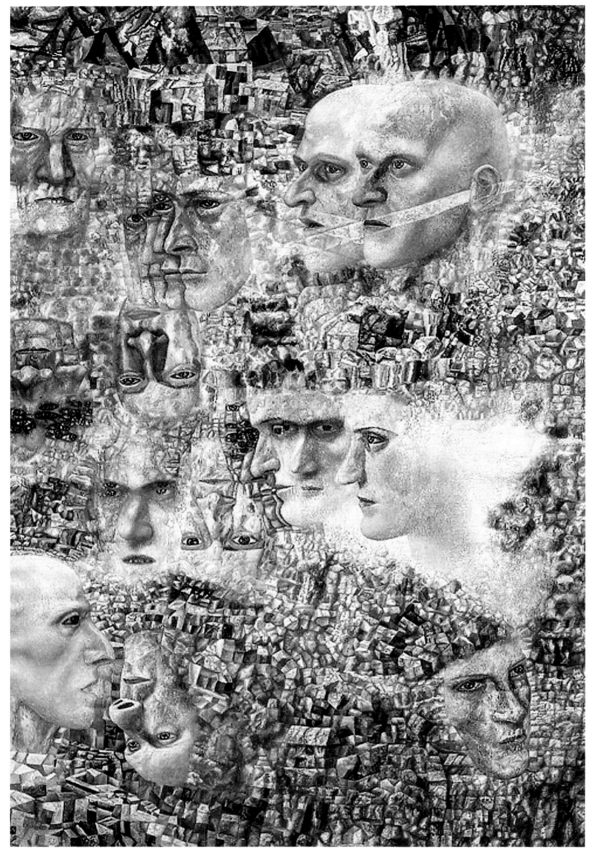

238

239

238
Shostakovich's First Symphony
Pavel Filonov (1883–1941)
Oil on paper, 1935
The State Tretyakov Gallery, Moscow

Following the 1917 revolution, artist Pavel Filonov
developed a unique view on the role of art in
society. He believed in the concept of 'Universal
Flowering', a metaphysical ascent of human kind
where the people take power. His compositions in
the 1920s and 1930s reflect the idea of individual
parts forming a whole, creating a new style of
multifaceted paintings.

239
Katerina Ismailova, The Royal Opera
Houston Rodgers (1902–70)
London, 1964
V&A: THM/245

Following the failure of *Lady Macbeth of the
Mtsensk District* in 1936, Shostakovich tried
several times to revise and revive his opera.
Working together with his third wife Irina
Antonovna, he finally succeeded in 1963 and the
opera came back to the stage under the name
Katerina Ismailova. It was performed in London
one year later at the Royal Opera House.

8

OPERA:
Today and Tomorrow

JOHN FULLJAMES Opera has a long, wonderful and sometimes daunting past, that has been much celebrated and studied. It is just as important that we study its present and envision its future. So we decided to ask a group of people who are working in opera around the world to share their perspectives on the future: what next, where next, who next? This book has explored how opera can be seen as a meeting place; in this section composers, writers, singers, directors and architects contribute their views on where opera is heading and how its relationship with its cities and citizens will continue to evolve.

Why is opera important to world cities in the twenty-first century?

ALEX BEARD Opera is a universal medium of unparalleled force. It shines a light on the fundamentals of what it means to be human, of what it is to love, to betray, to mourn, to delight. Opera explores conflicts between personal urges, the conventions of society and the demands of politics.

The presentation of opera demands creative flair, technical expertise, brilliant craftsmanship and considerable financial resources. World cities attract many of the most talented people from around the globe, and it is perhaps in world cities that their skills and resources can come together via opera.

As a centre for creativity and a powerful symbol of cultural vision and creative ambition, the opera house is the perfect space for the genuinely international art form that is opera in the twenty-first century. There is an increasingly diverse talent performing across the world, and great opera houses can now be found in Shanghai, Beijing, Seoul and Muscat as well as Milan, Paris, Vienna and New York.

Opera is a powerful antidote to an increasingly frenetic, always switched on, multi-tasking city lifestyle. It allows 300 people to pause for a moment, to suspend time, to force reflection.

UNSUK CHIN Good opera is a 'power plant of emotions' (Alexander Kluge) and an indispensable remedy against technocracy and information overload: it offers us something we cannot completely grasp with reason, and yet it stimulates reflection. Opera has the capacity to uplift the spirit, but it is also a mirror. By invoking extreme emotions in a highly nuanced manner, it is cathartic in nature, confronting viewers with those parts of themselves they have suppressed: hence, it is an antidote to particularisms and echo chambers of all kinds.

By bringing different arts together, opera might often seem surreal and over the top, but still, in an almost magical way, it succeeds in reconciling the irreconcilable. It is not an escapist and elitist entertainment of a few – on the contrary, opera can and should be a highly popular (but not populist!) art, attracting different social strata from different cultures and transcending time and place. In fact, opera has always been a cosmopolitan enterprise; great operatic works – from Monteverdi all the way to our time – could be likened to agoras of ideas and emotions, where essential issues related to the human condition are being dealt with in deeply affecting ways. With all its glorious ambiguities, opera feels perfectly suited to our ever-globalizing world of syncretisms and coexistences.

DAVID HENRY HWANG Of all our dramatic forms, opera remains the most highly theatrical, the one that utilizes all elements available to the stage: music, story, acting, design, dance. It is the form that most fully invites audiences to suspend their disbelief. In real life, we do not go around singing. So to go to an opera is to accept a more fantastical vision of the world, establishing a framework that allows artists to create stories that expand the mind and the heart.

In the twenty-first century, opera must reflect the more international, cosmopolitan world in which we live. It should embrace stories from around the world, created by artists who know those cultures and characters, and can imbue them with complexity and humanity. Opera is epic and elastic enough to incorporate new forms and traditions from outside its historical home in Europe and America. Opera in the twenty-first century will be important to the world as it expands to include the world.

FIONA MADDOCKS

In part it's the opera houses themselves, so often – new or old – the most beautiful landmark buildings in a city. Many of the world's top theatres are now open for tours, to show off their interiors, whether elaborate icing-cake affairs, rich with red plush and gilding, or examples of modernist architectural vision. They carry with them an aura of hope and grandeur, pride and glamour, a link with traditions past, both local and international.

They also hold the promise of extraordinary music, high drama, visual entertainment, escapism, a shared experience with several hundred other people, all of which is part of going to the opera. In a time of increasing social polarization and lone curating – sitting at home alone with a tablet or smartphone choosing what to see or listen to – the chance to concentrate, uninterrupted, for three hours or more, has acquired greater value.

Today, when every aspect of old cultural habits is being challenged, opera is no longer confined to theatres built for that purpose. Now there are alternatives, seeping into unexpected corners of urban life. A pop-up performance up close in a pub (as in *La bohème* at the King's Head, Islington), or a warehouse, a train tunnel or a studio space – any city building you like – has the power to attract entirely different audiences, who want more edgy attitudes and less fuss. This kind of opera is seeping into the nooks and crannies of city life, far from civic centres, and it is burgeoning.

One of the great pioneering examples, in a radical and adventurous way – is Birmingham Opera Company (BOC), founded in 1987 by the director Graham Vick and the choral conductor-trainer Simon Halsey. They took opera to places that had none, and found audiences who had never been to opera, persuading hundreds to join in. Audiences were made (some were reluctant but most soon got the point) to promenade around, say, a cavernous carpet warehouse, and follow the action. BOC led the way. This was social change in action for the citizens of Birmingham.

Still, the excitement of entering a traditional opera house never fades. It's always a pleasure to visit the Theatre Royal in Glasgow, home of Scottish Opera, the oldest theatre in the city and one of the longest-running in Scotland. Or the Wales Millennium Centre, close to the heart of one of the world's greatest singers, the Welsh bass-baritone Bryn Terfel. Or the Grand Theatre Belfast, build by the great and prolific theatre architect Frank Matcham, starting as a music hall, turning for a time into a cinema, badly damaged by bombs during the 'Troubles' and reverting to an opera house. In 1963 Pavarotti gave his UK debut there, performing in his first *Madama Butterfly*. So the building has associations with one of the greatest singers of the twentieth century.

From the old to the new – from Taichung to Linz, Kushan, Oslo, Dubai – new opera houses are being built, often by some of the most adventurous and stylish architects of our day. The grand theatres of the (mostly) nineteenth century were shaped by underlying social divisions which have – or should have – no place in twenty-first century life. This means new ideas for public spaces, seating, purpose. Among the recent is the Royal Opera House in Muscat, Oman, so far a receiving house for productions from all over the world, seeking out global partnerships for Western classical music (in 2019, it launches a production which will tour twelve opera houses) but with plans to nurture own home-grown Arabic musical traditions too. A new facility for a library, exhibitions and digital exploration will extend its purpose and reach. Out of this, eventually, some greater spirit of cultural unity may arise: a new dream of what opera can and must do to have a purpose in our own times but with much work yet to be done.

YUVAL
SHARON

My answer to this question, as an American director, will surely be quite different than that of my European colleagues. Opera houses are anchor points in European cities, similar to cathedrals or government buildings. There is not a single city in America where the opera house is situated like the commons, as in Vienna, Paris or London. As a result, opera houses offer the psychogeographic suggestion of opera itself remaining central to a sense of civic identity. This is simply not the case in America, where opera companies spend no small amount of time or resource advocating for acceptance, asserting that they are important to their city. Opera for us is not a given, and the form must constantly justify its presence and price tag.

We can only assert opera's continued importance to world cities if the life of the opera company and its interpretational originality can be seen to shape the audience of its specific time and place. Opera in my city, Los Angeles, should not be an internationally homogenized product, interchangeable with what you can experience in New York, Detroit or Florida. That's precisely why The Industry, my own company in LA, eschews the traditional architecture of the opera house, preferring to hold new operas at an operating train station, inside moving cars, or at 'non-spaces' such as escalator hallways, warehouses or parking lots. This isn't done for novelty's sake, but instead as an inquiry into how the hybrid art form of opera can be resonant and responsive to the life of this particular city – and thus central to civic discourse and civic identity. In America, where opera houses do not occupy a central place in urban organization, the most vital experiments seem to be happening outside the confines of the traditional opera house. The art form and the artists bringing it to life are then forced to engage with their surroundings, rather than stay safely perched away on their inaccessible magic mountain. I think this will be crucial for opera's twenty-first century relevance in American cities.

FRED
PLOTKIN

Like a museum, an opera house is now a place where persons of disparate interests, backgrounds and expectations can gather in the presence of arts drawn from many disciplines to have a new experience. And, in so doing, these people discover more about their own humanity and about things they never imagined. In these great venues, the human mind and soul know no boundaries.

The opera house and the museum are much more than custodians of the past. They are the essence of multiculturalism. Precious treasures are found in their grand spaces that remind us that we are part of a larger whole. And they ask us to think, to feel, to create in new ways. Their doors are open to all and they beckon the most talented, restless, audacious and passionate among us. Their presence in cities permits an ongoing dialogue between the temporal and the eternal.

As cities become more densely packed and move at dizzying speeds, their citizens per force use their senses less fully. To see less, to hear less, to feel less becomes a defence mechanism against sensory overload. This denial of information and experience makes life less rich. As such, the opera house becomes the place where the city dweller can activate the senses in ways only this art form can provoke. The insights that we can derive at the opera house – some readily evident and others more subtle – are among its most precious rewards. Opera makes us more richly human, and more compassionate neighbours.

DAVID
STAPLES

Let's first step back and think about a historical context. The first public opera house, Teatro San Cassiano, opened in Venice in 1637. Previous opera houses had been private but this was the first public venture. It moved opera from a private aristocratic audience to a more public one.

241

242

243

240 (pp.270–1)
Rise and Fall of the City of Mahagonny
by Kurt Weill and Bertolt Brecht
Directed by John Fulljames
Royal Opera House, London, 2015

241
Oslo Opera House, Norway
Designed by Snøhetta architects, 2007

242
Sydney Opera House
'Vivid Sydney' (a colourful Aboriginal design) is
projected on the western façade, 2016

243
National Centre for the Performing Arts, Beijing
Designed by Paul Andreu, 2007

In many respects the subsequent history of opera and opera houses has been a balancing act between something for the elite and something for the public. Many of the great European opera houses have been unashamedly grand buildings located on major public square or piazzas. The Paris Opéra Garnier is a magnificent building located at the head of one of Baron Haussmann's grand boulevards. (By contrast the Royal Opera House in Covent Garden, London is located on a side street and for many years faced Bow Street police station.) Buildings constructed for opera have been imposing, formal and well-suited to an educated and self-confident elite. They were not open, welcoming or accessible buildings.

In the latter part of the twentieth century, communities and governments kept building opera houses. Why? Perhaps for two or three quite different reasons: first of all there was a demand from the public for a new or renovated space for opera (and ballet); secondly, there was a growing realization that cities are not simply places for work, but must also offer a quality of life and educational opportunities for residents that include the performing arts and opera; finally, many developing cities desired the trimmings of a major city, which could include a significant airport, a major league sports franchise (in North America), an art museum and often an opera house or a concert hall.

ROBERT
CARSEN

'Opera' is the plural of the Latin word 'opus' meaning 'works'. It combines prose, poetry, music, dance, painting, sculpture, costume, lighting and sometimes film, making it the most complex of the performing arts. The opera house, which gives life to these works, is no less significant for what it presents and represents: a crossroads for artists of different nationalities, cultures and languages. It is a building that becomes a symbol for the city in which it exists, but paradoxically it can only exist properly without political or nationalistic boundaries. The word tradition is often erroneously associated with opera, but the only valuable tradition I have noticed related to opera (apart perhaps from a constant search for excellence), is that of innovation and controversy.

When the majority of opera houses were constructed in the eighteenth and nineteenth centuries, the creation of new works was much more frequent than it is today. However we tend to forget that many of the operas that we now consider to be successful keystones of the standard repertoire created a scandal and were misunderstood and rejected at their premieres: *Le nozze di Figaro*, *La traviata*, *Madama Butterfly*, to name just a few. Audiences sometimes also forget – and it is the director's job to make sure that they do not – that works such as these were written because of their creators' desire to dramatize important topics, such as social injustice, sexual politics and colonial imperialism. These works were often expressly written to be controversial, to challenge and also to inspire. And they were written for the opera house.

Forms of cultural expression have diversified hugely over the last 50 years, and new technologies have allowed many forms of the performing arts, including opera, to expand and develop. Opera now not only uses video and film as a regular design tool, but is itself regularly experienced both in the cinema and online. Today everything in our lives is much more 'connected' and we no longer wish to experience art forms individually, but to combine them, to overlap them. Museums, for example, have become ever-expanding living civic spaces, enriched by film cycles, concerts and live performances related to the themes of their temporary exhibitions. Opera has always been ahead of that game, combining art forms by definition to create its unique voice.

That voice combines words and music, the concrete and the abstract, the intellect and the emotion, to make something unique. It attempts to express the inexpressible, and it is precisely its irrational quality that makes it so important. When it works, opera is more powerful than anything that can be found on a stage. I believe sincerely that opera has a long life ahead of it, because it has always understood that the past ideally informs the present in order to become the future.

How important is technology to designing opera today and the future of opera?

DAVID STAPLES

From the very first, the performance of opera has relied on technology: lighting, scenery, effects. This has grown over the years and opera directors and designers have embraced new technologies in their productions, to include projection and virtual reality, for example. This has made opera both relevant and appealing to young audiences. While the audiences for concerts, dance and theatre have been stable over the last decade or so, the audience for opera has increased. I believe a significant part of that increase can be attributed to surtitles that have made opera more accessible and comprehensible. The prospect of augmented reality and other technologies that can enhance the opera experience could work to further expand audiences and their enjoyment.

YUVAL SHARON

Technology will play a critical role in the future development of opera. This may be most obvious for directors and designers creating new productions of standard repertoire: compare moving lights commonly used today with the candles that provided illumination for so long and you get an extreme example of how technical developments have altered the perception of a work. But I am more interested in how technology will alter the creation of new opera: what extensions of the traditional boundaries of opera can now be traversed thanks to technological advances? I think conservative opera-lovers get nervous at the thought of amplification as a technical modification of what they love the most: the unamplified voice in an acoustically perfect space. But why subject all future operas to the same conditions? I think of a theatre like Bayreuth, where Wagner employed pre-electrified amplification – or, more simply put, architecture – to create a new sonic world, not to mention his theatrical inventiveness that required new stagecraft techniques. I believe most strongly in opera's future when I see composers and librettists integrate the latest technology directly into the work they are writing.

What is the role of the opera house in its interaction with the space of a city?

ALEX BEARD

Opera houses are typically located right at the heart of their cities – just look at Milan, Vienna and Paris – where the audiences and leading artists of the day come together in art. Opera houses are places for debate and exchange; they are spaces in which to be seen, to be challenged and to be entertained – a confluence of people and ideas.

However, they are often set at one remove, isolated in their squares, piazzas and grand boulevards from the daily concerns of city life, and energized only for the evening performance. This is changing – many new opera houses are now conceived as spaces for everyone, at the heart of the social and cultural fabric of the city, in and out of performance as so powerfully demonstrated in Oslo. And this concept lies at the core of the Royal Opera House's ambitions for our Open Up building project.

We will create a welcoming new entrance onto the Covent Garden Piazza, inviting visitors to cross the threshold and explore the remarkable creativity at play here. There will be a window onto Bow Street, looking onto a greatly extended public foyer, with an internal piazza reflecting the vibrancy outside. We will present impromptu performances, host learning events, offer public tours, with cafes and restaurants open to all. It will be a place for everyone to make their own connections with opera, at the heart of their city.

244

244
Hopscotch
Directed by Yuval Sharon
Los Angeles, 2015

245
Mittwoch aus Licht by Karlheinz Stockhausen
Birmingham Opera Company, 2012

246
Chorus in *The Death of Klinghoffer* by John Adams
Co-produced by English National Opera and
Metropolitan Opera, New York
Metropolitan Opera House, Lincoln Center,
New York, 17 October 2014

245

246

AFTERWORD

Opera houses are the greatest of theatres, but they have always been more than theatres. The gambling and procuring is thankfully long past, but the debate and exchange continues, reinvented for each generation.

DAVID
STAPLES

Opera houses are large and frequently one of the most significant public buildings in a city. There are expensive investments for a city or government. Today opera houses are often built in prime locations to make a statement: on the fjord in Oslo, on the harbour front in Copenhagen, on the waterfront in Sydney. Such locations often distance the new opera building from the city. A new opera house, concert hall or theatre offers an opportunity to create a new focal point, a meeting place and a place for shared experiences. If appropriately sited and designed, an opera house should be able to contribute to the city's everyday life not only through its performances but also by its presence. Too often the ambition to create a major building defeats the aim of interacting with the city.

How will artists shape the future of opera?

PRETTY
YENDE

The voice is at the centre of all opera, and the voice is power. Even when just used in speech it is always an exchange of energy between speaker and listener. Singing is one of the most powerful gifts one can ever have. To be able to express emotions, ideas and stories through the power of the human voice is something very special. To be part of it and to be able to express my joy through the music is very special for me; because I believe that the whole exchange of lives that happens in a performance, between the performers on stage and the audience, is quite extraordinary. It is a supernatural world that releases an understanding that goes beyond our human understanding, beyond our physical lives. Singing is open to all of humanity, including the people who think this art form doesn't belong to them. Look at my story: I come from Africa, and I heard opera for the first time through the British Airways advert, the 'Flower Duet' from *Lakmé*. Opera got me, without me even knowing French. The impact it had on my life is something that I am now sharing with the whole world on a global stage. The impact of opera is so extraordinary that I needed to find ways to break down the stereotypes around it, and to say that music, especially classical music, is a gift to all of humanity, not just to some.

UNSUK
CHIN

The weight of four hundred years of tradition – including the great number of idiosyncratic twentieth-century operatic masterpieces from Janáček to Ginastera and beyond – remains a vast challenge for the contemporary composer. Besides, writing opera is so very different from writing for other musical genres. A composer, especially a contemporary one, has to give up purism and accept that theatrical impact – with all the sudden dramatic contrasts it entails – calls for a catholic approach as to style: a certain eclecticism is not only desired, but it is a condition sine qua non. This is one reason (writing for voice is another) why avant-garde composition, with its purism and its quest to break with tradition, didn't always fare well with opera, despite many important and fascinating approaches. Luckily, today's composers aren't caught in the midst of ideological turf wars anymore, and are finally in a position to make decisions more freely.

Opera will always be storytelling, though how it will do so will have to differ – in our time of biotechnology, mass media and microprocessors – from the narrative strategies that had been perfectly authentic for the nineteenth century. I presume that creators of opera will be looking for non-linear, labyrinthine, stylized and free-floating ways of narration rather than for naturalistic drama which doesn't usually fit well with contemporary music. Composers may be increasingly drawn to contemporary subject matter, but opera will always be a 'magic mirror' (Ferruccio Busoni), hence, timeless subjects and the restoration of myths will remain important.

Opera houses with regular ensembles will have to continue to foster new work in order to stay alive and kicking; in addition, experimental music theatre should continue to have its own specialist spaces or festivals. It is possible that collaboration between artists from different fields will increase during the composition process, but still, the composers' musical decisions will have to remain at the core of the whole process. How much new media and technology will have an impact on opera remains to be seen. Finding a suitable libretto will always remain a headache and a fascinating challenge, and the same can be said of writing music for an apparatus that is steeped in tradition. Of course, there exist other kinds of challenges and pressures, too: nowadays, the premise that works of art have intrinsic merits and should be subsidized (regardless of success or lack thereof) is becoming less and less commonplace – and this is a worrying development, bearing in mind that producing an opera is expensive and depends heavily on funding.

DAVID HENRY HWANG

As someone who writes, not only opera librettos, but also plays, musical theatre, movies and television shows, I believe I'm aware of the respective advantages and challenges of each form. When I write an opera libretto, I believe one of my responsibilities is to serve the composer. I regard them as the principal artist in our collaboration, similar to the director in movies, the show runner in television, and the playwright in the theatre.

However, I wonder if this paradigm is actually good for contemporary opera. We are currently living through a renaissance in the Broadway musical, which is closer to the centre of American popular culture today than at any time since the 1950s, with *Hamilton* being the most obvious example. I find the distinction between 'high art' and popular culture arbitrary and nonsensical. Writing a libretto for the Royal Opera House does not feel any more 'serious' or important to me than writing the book for a Disney musical. Classical operas were popular works in their day. Moreover, many opera companies now perform musicals, including works by Sondheim or Rodgers & Hammerstein. Someday, I hope a new opera will transfer to Broadway, the West End, or some other commercial venue.

For this to happen, I believe we have to give more weight to the story. When asked the difference between opera and musical theatre, the answer is often that the former is more music-driven, and the latter more story-driven. However, looking again at classical opera, many were written with more focus on story, and librettists playing a more prominent role, than most opera collaborations today. Perhaps new operas need more opportunities to be workshopped, as well as co-productions which budget for rewriting and restaging between venues. Perhaps composers should sometimes alter their music to fit the story, not only the other way around.

Musicals are created as relatively equal collaborations between librettist, lyricist, composer, and sometimes, director. Might this be a better framework for developing and producing new operas today – one which will produce works with greater appeal to audiences now and in the future?

YUVAL SHARON

Opera should be telling specific stories which resonate with the concerns, references and aesthetic experiences of an audience. The way opera companies in different cities collaborate is one of the direst problems in the current landscape of operatic production. Most geographic intersections don't go beyond the level of a co-production: two or more companies creating a single interpretation of a work. This has economic advantages for the producers, and certain productions can play just as well in Los Angeles as they do in Budapest – but I always have a nagging feeling that there are longer-term cultural disadvantages to this approach. The field of ideas becomes narrower, and the relationship to a specific audience is compromised. It may look like dialogue is being fostered, but I think this approach actually prevents real dialogue between cities.

247

248

247
Pretty Yende as Rosina in
Gioachino Rossini's *Il barbiere di Siviglia*
Metropolitan Opera House, Lincoln Center,
New York, 2017

248
Written on Skin
Directed by Katie Mitchell with music by
George Benjamin and libretto by Martin Crimp
Royal Opera House, London, 2013

249
Sally Matthews as Alice in *Alice in Wonderland*
Music by Unsuk Chin and libretto by
David Henry Hwang
Bavarian State Opera, Munich, 2007

249

AFTERWORD

I'd like to see opera collaborating with other art forms, but there is a big issue here. When artists from other disciplines are invited to get involved in an operatic production, the method usually follows a forced compliance into an airtight apparatus. The form of opera and the mode of production stay intact, and it's the chaos of the 'foreign element' that gets tamed by the system and normalized into the recognizable. As an aesthetic methodology and as a social model, this is the wrong way to cultivate the future. The audacity of opera is its astonishing ability to harmonize difference – not through normalization or homogenization, but through polyphony. Opera should be seen as an open matrix, where diverse artists and layers of diverging art forms break apart the expected form. This is where new opera has greater potential over the standard repertory; even a failed experiment in contemporary collaboration will contribute more towards opera's vitality in the twenty-first century than a successful production of a Mozart masterpiece. New attempts to expand the definition of opera, where the inclusion of diverse artistry and perspective can have the most radical formal consequences, will keep the art form as a whole both legitimate and necessary.

How are audiences shaping the future of opera?

FRED
PLOTKIN

Audiences can influence and shape the future of opera by demanding that live performances (rather than televized and cinematic facsimiles) be available to as many people as possible. Only when opera is experienced communally – with the unmistakable beauty of the sound of a human voice singing sublime music while orchestral instruments lend their own voices – can its soul-stirring magnificence be experienced.

Therefore, audiences must support this art form in various ways: teach it to children; purchase tickets to fill theatres; take a friend who has never been to an opera; influence politicians to recognize that it is a democratic rather than elitist art form (as is often incorrectly asserted); and to use public money to support it.

The opera audience must be open to the ideas of new composers, librettists, directors and designers. Not everything they create will be successful (perhaps not initially), but even Verdi and Wagner had operas that failed. We can seek out new young singers but also remember and cherish venerable senior artists who still have so much to give, both on stage and as teachers of the next generation of performers and audiences.

Above all, opera audiences must remember that they too are part of the art form, just as much as the musicians, designers, managers, ticket sellers and ushers. When they are aware of their role, and of their importance, they will have a greater investment in the future of opera.

FIONA
MADDOCKS

An audience is never one thing, never one group of people, with predictable opinions, taste, knowledge or spending power. The idea that this shape-changing entity – elusive and different except at the moment of box office transaction when all must elect to buy a ticket – can or should shape the future of opera might sound democratic but cannot be the way forward.

This is where expertise and imagination count. A creative team in an opera house, planning years ahead, must balance adventure and familiarity, old and new, the availability of singers, the size of a chorus or orchestra for a given work, the likely box office success or otherwise. An audience, whoever they are as individuals, will almost certainly want chiefly that which they know. Their real way to influence the future is to attend in the here and now: to buy tickets, to support a company loyally, to take friends and act as willing advocates for the art form.

Once in the theatre, a first and important way of influencing a particular performance is by preparing, listening, responding, concentrating, being open minded. Everyone has been at a performance where the audience atmosphere feels dead whereas, the night before and with the same performers, the mood was thrilling. It's not all down to performers so let's not blame them. Attentive listening is a vital part of performance.

There are practical avenues a dedicated opera fan might explore. Here are some. Book tickets even for the operas you don't know or didn't like last time you tried. Attend performances by students and give support to young talent; the tickets are cheaper, the repertoire often unusual while standards can be exceptionally high (in the major UK conservatoires especially). You will be witnessing, perhaps spotting, the talents of the future. You might find a way to sponsor, starting at modest prices, a singer or a prop or an entire company. And try using social media responsibly, to share with and enthuse others who might have an incipient interest but are in need of a spur, a helping hand, direction. If they trust your encouragement, they might just take the risk, attend an opera and keep the flame alive.

JOHN
FULLJAMES

I'm struck that amidst these very different perspectives all our contributors share a sense that opera's global future is diverse and eclectic. Opera will be both big and small, in formal spaces and informal ones, inspired both locally and internationally, performed locally and disseminated internationally. Cities are meeting places, and within those cities opera houses are also meeting places. They are refuges from the city in the heart of the city. Within those refuges, opera must tell the stories of today from around the world and use the power of the naked human voice to enable us to see ourselves and each other more clearly.

250
Ensemble in 'Spaceship' at the dress
rehearsal of *Einstein on the Beach*
Composed by Philip Glass and directed
by Robert Wilson
Dorothy Chandler Pavilion, Los Angeles, 2013

Notes

VENICE

1 Busenello 1656, p.37. For a detailed study of this scene, see Heller 1999.

2 There is an extensive bibliography on *L'incoronazione di Poppea* and the interpretive challenges presented by the opera. See Carter 1997, 2002; Fenlon and Miller 1992; Heller 1999, 2000, 2013; McClary 1991; Rosand 1985, 1991, 2007.

3 On the myth of Venice, see Muir 1981, pp.13–61; Grubb 1986; Rosand 2001.

4 On the history of tourism in Venice, see Davis and Marvin 2004.

5 Coryat 1611, p.160.

6 Muir 1981, p.15; Rosand 2001, pp.6–18.

7 On the appropriation of the pagan gods to represent Venice, see Rosand 2001, pp.117–51.

8 Rosand 2001, pp.117–19.

9 Logan 1972, pp.20–37.

10 Howell 1651, p.1.

11 Ibid., p.7.

12 Saint-Didier 1699, pp.42–3.

13 Muir 1981; Howard 2002; Fenlon 2009.

14 Muir 1981, pp.119–34.

15 Koldau and Kurtzman 2002.

16 Fenlon 2009.

17 Coryat 1611, p.173.

18 Ibid., p.250.

19 Fenlon 2007; Goldfarb 2013; Glixon 2013.

20 Fabbri 2007.

21 Howard and Moretti 2009.

22 Feldman 1995.

23 Coryat 1611, p.176.

24 Misson 1699, p.198.

25 Rapp 1976 and Pullan 1968; also Grubb 1986, pp.60–6 for an overview of historiographical issues.

26 Lanaro 2006.

27 Setton 1991, pp.146–71.

28 Weiner 1970.

29 Grubb 1986, pp.55–60.

30 Heller 1999; Bouwsma 1990.

31 Misson 1699, p.186.

32 For an overview of the role of women in Venice as it relates to opera, see Heller 2003.

33 Cited by Heller 2003, pp.51; on Tarabotti see also Weaver 2006 and Heller 2000; see Tarabotti 2004 for a modern translation of Tirannia Paterna; on forced monacalization, see Sperling 1999.

34 Misson 1699, p.195.

35 Wilson 1999.

36 Coryat 1611, p.265.

37 On the domestic arrangements, clothing, and lives of courtesans in the late sixteenth century see Brown 1700, pp.159–88.

38 Coryat 1611, p.265.

39 On the phenomenon of the so-called 'cortegiano honesta', see Rosenthal's 1992 biography of Veronica Franca; on the poetic exchanges involving courtesans, see Quaintance 2015.

40 Coryat 1611, p.166–7.

41 Howell 1651, p.39.

42 Evelyn and Bray 1901, vol.1, p.245.

43 The fundamental study of Venetian opera remains Rosand 1991; for a detailed examination of opera as an industry, see Glixon and Glixon 2006. For an elegant discussion of why opera took hold in Venice, see Romano 2006.

44 Glixon and Glixon 2006 provide case studies illustrating the precarious finances endured by many of the theatres; see particularly chapter 4, pp.66–105.

45 Ibid., pp.1–16.

46 Ibid., pp.17–33.

47 Ibid., pp.229–40.

48 For an overview of Cavalli's contributions in opera, see Rosand 2013.

49 The other two are Le nozze d'Enea con Lavinia (for which only the libretto survives) and Il ritorno d'Ulisse in patria. See Rosand 2007.

50 Glixon and Glixon 2006, p.222–3.

51 Glixon 1995; also Glixon and Glixon 2006, pp.197–204.

52 Heller 2003, pp.176–9.

53 For a discussion of the Incogniti and their relationship to opera, with further bibliography, see Heller 2003, pp.44–81.

54 Rosand 1978; Glixon 1999; Heller 2015.

55 Heller 2015.

56 Busenello and Livingston 1911, p.20, cited by Heller 1999, p.44.

57 Heller 1999, pp.57–62.

58 Heller 2000.

59 Ibid.

60 Rosand 1985; Carter 1997; Heller 1999.

61 Heller 1999, pp.87–90.

62 Heller 2013.

LONDON

1 Chamberlayne 1729.

2 The first biography of Handel was by John Mainwaring (Mainwaring 1760). It was based in part on the composer's own reminiscences. For more recent, document-based biographies of Handel, see Burrows 2012; Harris 2014; Hogwood 1988; Hunter 2015; Keates 2009; Robbins Landon 1984.

3 For a portrait of life in London around the time of Handel's first visit, see Lindsay 1978; Earle 1994; Waller 2000.

4 Most sources estimate the population of London c.1700 to be c.550,000–600,000 (demographia.com/dm–lon31.htm; oldbaileyonline.org/static/Population–history–of–london.jsp; localhistories.org/population. html; londononline.co.uk/factfile/historical/).

5 For Paris, see Roche 1987, p.20; Harding 2002, p.16; Petty in Henry Hull (ed.) 1899, pp.501–9.

6 For Norwich see Corfield 1972, p.267.

7 Brown 1700.

8 Saussure (1726) 1902, pp.164–5.

9 Ward c.1700.

10 Preface to the William Vickers manuscript of 1770–2, quoted in *The New Monthly Magazine and Literary Journal* 1825, vol.9, p.505.

11 For Thomas Britton and his concerts see Harris 2014, pp.118–20. The quotation from *The Diary of Ralph Thoresby* is from vol.II (Hunter 1830), pp.111–12, and dates from 1 June 1712.

12 Uffenbach (1710) 1934.

13 *The Poor Man's Complaint: Or, The Sorrowful Lamentation of Poor Plain–Dealing at this Time of Distress and Trouble* 1690–1700, Pepys Collection IV:300.

14 Defoe's *True-Born Englishman* was first published in 1701.

15 Mainwaring 1760, p.62.

16 See Brewer 2013, and Burrows 1993, ch.XII.

17 For the history of the Haymarket Theatre, see Nalbach 1973; Milhous and Hume 1989.

18 Hogwood 1988, p.50.

19 Ibid.

20 Weiss 2002, pp.66–8.

21 Hogwood 1988, p.51; Milhous and Hume 1989, p.525.

22 See also Monod 2006; Hume 1988; Hume 1998; Hunter 2001.

23 Many of the listed biographies include the quotes from Addison and Steele. See also Weiss 2002, pp.65–72.

24 Addison and Steele 1711, no.V.

25 Ibid.

26 Ibid., no.XIV.

27 Mainwaring 1760, p.120.

28 See Hunter 2015, especially pp.349–60. See also Hunter 2000 in which the author shows it is anachronistic to suggest that Handel was writing his operas for, or even attracting, a 'middle–class' audience. On the contrary, the 'middling sort' in Handel's day constituted a tiny proportion of the English population, few of whom could have afforded tickets, much less a subscription, to the opera (though they may have provided a larger segment of the audiences for his later oratorios). Handel's primary appeal, Hunter insists, at least in his operas, was directed towards a tiny but wealthy aristocracy and the patronage its top echelons could supply, and it was only after his death that he could realistically be regarded as the composer of the 'middle classes'.

29 Hume 1988, p.428.

30 For Curtis Price on *Rinaldo*, see Sadie and Hicks 1987, p.120. The view that *Rinaldo* 'settled the course of Handel's career and the future of opera in England' is from Hogwood 1988, p.65.

31 Mainwaring 1760, pp.76 and 78.

VIENNA

1 As quoted in Gay 1969, p.24.

2 Beales 1985, p.185.

3 Quoted in Williams 1984, p.475.

4 Pezzl 1785, p.332.

5 Steele and Addison 1988, p.199.

6 Quoted in Bernard 1971, p.141.

7 Gugitz 1940, p.71.

8 Ibid., p.9.

9 Ibid., p.10.

10 O'Brien 1969, p.60.

11 Quoted in Bodi 1977, p.41.

12 Sonnenfels 1783–7, vol.IV, p.9.

13 Quoted in Ritter 1970, p.13.

14 Mozart and Anderson 1985, 5 December 1781.

15 Ibid., p.219.

16 Ibid., 23 February 1778.

17 Robbins Landon 1990, p.128.

18 Mozart and Anderson 1985, 4 April 1781.

19 Ibid., 12 May 1781.

20 Pezzl 1789, p.86.

21 Mozart and Anderson 1985, 24 March 1781.

22 Pezzl 1789, p.89.

23 Mozart and Anderson 1985, 22 December 1781.

24 Ibid., 11 April 1781.

25 Bodi 1977, p.77.

26 Winter 1971, p.191.

27 Rosenstruch-Königsberg 1984, p.74.

28 Georg Forster, quoted in Braunbehrens 1966, p.255.

29 Sonnenfels 1783–7, vol.3, p.119.

30 Mozart and Anderson 1985, 16 October 1777.

31 Ibid., 7 February 1778.

32 Lorenzo Da Ponte, preface to published libretto for *Le nozze di Figaro*, in Deutsch 1990, p.273.

MILAN

1 The Risorgimento is a movement of contested length, but is often thought of as the period from c.1815 to c.1870 during which, through military and diplomatic means, Italy achieved statehood, having previously been a collection of independent entities mixed with areas under the control of various foreign powers.

2 Letter dated 9 January 1871; Walker 1984, p.13.

3 See a letter from Lavigna dated 11 December 1833, in Gatti 1931, I, p.74; a similarly worded document dated 24 February 1834 is found in Gatti 1931, I, p.75.

4 Letter dated 8 August 1832, in Abbiati 1959, I, p.113.

5 See Parker 1989, pp.25–7.

6 Franco Abbiati 1959, I, p.415; see also Budden 1973, 1978, 1981, I, p.93.

7 While most of the review Abbiati quotes comes from Ricordi's house journal, the *Gazzetta musicale di Milano*, the passage supposedly referring to 'Va, pensiero' comes from Angelo Lambertini's review of the first performance of *Nabucco* in the *Gazzetta privilegiata di Milano* (10 March 1842). The chorus there referred to as being encored is clearly the concluding hymn, 'Immenso Jeovha'.

8 Walker 1984, p.151.

9 Ibid., p.163.

10 Quoted from Parker 1997, p.27.

11 Ibid., p.93.

12 Parker 1997, pp.92–3.

13 For a detailed account of musical events in Milan during the period, see Parker 1997, pp.83–97.

14 Quoted in Walker 1984, p.46.

15 As Verdi's sometime librettist Francesco Maria Piave predicted, in an letter to the composer Vincenzo Capecelato dated 11 October 1848, 'it's certain that Radeski [Field Marshal Radetzky, commander of the Austrian troops in northern Italy] will want La Scala open in the Carnival season'; Parker 1997, pp.131–2.

16 Abbiati 1959, II, pp.350–1, suggests that the composer attended a La Scala performance of *Giovanna de Gusman* (a censored version of his French opera *Les Vêpres siciliennes*, 1855) in March 1856, and even quotes (undated) letters that seem to suggest this. Unless more information arrives, however, this Milanese visit must remain rather doubtful.

17 Walker 1984, pp.269–70.

18 These negotiations are chronicled in Phillips-Matz 1993, pp.541–4.

19 Ibid., p.554.

20 Walker 1984, p.470.

PARIS

1 Quoted in Giroud 2010, p.161.

2 Blanchard Jerrold 1867, p.64.

3 For more on the figure of the flâneur, see Benjamin, Eiland and McLaughlin 1999, pp.416–55.

4 Gregor-Dellin 1980, p.455.

5 Berlioz 1843, pp.1–2.

6 The articles, each around three full pages in length, were published in the *Revue et Gazette musicale* on 6, 13, 20, 27 June; 11 and 25 July; and 8 August 1852.

7 Chadeuil 1858, p.2.

8 For more on this and other detailed aspects of Wagner's revisions to *Tannhäuser* for Paris, see Abbate 1983, pp.73–123.

9 Ibid., p.88.

10 For more on these concerts, see Willson 2014, pp.287–314.

11 Respectively, Fiorentino 1860, p.2; Champfleury 1860, p.7.

12 Azevedo (1861) 2010, p.236.

13 See Abbate 1983, p.76.

DRESDEN

1   Richard Strauss, 'Reminiscences of the first performance of my Operas', in Schuh 1953, p.150.

2   Lee and Segal 2015, pp.179–81.

3   Kramer 2004.

4   Finney 1991, pp.55–9.

5   Gilman 1988.

6   Richard Strauss, 'Reminiscences of the first performance of my Operas', in Schuh 1953, p.150.

7   Kennedy 1999.

8   Richard Strauss, 'Recollections and Reflections', in Schuh 1953.

9   Gilman 1988.

10 Richard Strauss, 'Recollections and Reflections', in Schuh 1953, p.150.

11 Kennedy 1999, pp.141 and 145.

12 Paul 2014.

13 Jager and Brebbia 2000, p.41.

14 Banerjee, 2003.

15 Woodhead (1903) 1904.

16 Paul 2014.

17 König 1996.

18 Woodhead (1903) 1904.

19 Vincenz and Hesse 2008.

20 Richard Strauss, 'Recollections and Reflections', in Schuh 1953, p.53

21 Dr Emil Jettl quoted in Gilman, 1988.

22 Kultermann, 2006.

23 nytimes.com/1987/01/13/arts/opera–salome –in–milan–staged–by–robert–wilson.html.

24 Interview with Richard Strauss in Dresden Neueste Nachrichten, 9 December 1905.

25 Newspaper review titled 'Salome' in Dresden Anzeige, 10 December 1905, quoted in Bartnig, 2014.

26 Review of the premiere in Dresdner Nachrichten, 11 December 1905.

27 Richard Strauss, 'Recollections and Reflections', in Schuh 1953.

28 Kennedy 1999, pp.141 and 145.

29 Gay 2006.

30 Mitchell 2000, p.433.

31 Dickinson 2001.

32 Honeycutt 1979.

33 Moeller 2014.

34 This translation was taken from Altshuler 2011.

35 Richard Strauss, 'Recollections and Reflections', in Schuh 1953, p.16.

36 Ibid., p.40.

37 Ross 2012.

38 Kultermann 2006.

39 Kustow 2013, p.51.

40 Ibid., p.54.

41 Wilde 1968.

LENINGRAD

1   For instance in Shostakovich's letter to Lev Oborin dated 4 December 1924, see Wilson 2006, p.51.

2   Shostakvich's article appeared in the Leningrad weekly illustrated journal Rabochij I Teatr (The Worker and Theatre) f 20/11/1931.

3   Formerly the Mariinsky Theatre, known by its acronym GATOB (State Theatre of Opera and Ballet), renamed the Kirov Theatre in 1935.

4   Repertoire note for the Boosey and Hawkes' edition of The Nose.

5   Andrei Balanchavadze in Wilson 2006, pp.91–2.

6   Morrison 2004.

7   Wilson 2006, p.104.

8   Letter dated 27 November 1931 as quoted in Kovnatskaya 2006.

9   Russian words ending either with the suffix 'ichestvo' or 'inshchina' denote a pernicious influence. The nearest solution in translation is using the 'ism' suffix in English.

10 Shostakovich 1934.

11 Ibid., see note 10.

12 Taruskin 1997, pp.498–510.

13 Some sources indicate that Leskov's story came to Shostakovich's attention through Zamyatin; the literary scholar Caryl Emerson goes further in suggesting that the composer used Zamyatin's rhapsodic, purified version of the story to create the emotionally charged world of his heroine. See Emerson 2004, pp.198–9.

14 The title was changed to Lady Macbeth of the Mtsensk District in 1967 (see: studfiles.ru/ preview/2781483/).

15 Vishnevskaya 1984, p.252.

16 Ibid.

17 Serbraykova 1971, pp.309–10.

18 Shostakovich 1934b.

19 Ibid.

20 Wilson 2006, p.109.

21 Vishnevskaya 1984, p.355.

22 Shostakovich 1934b.

23 Ibid.

24 Ibid.

25 A Bolshevik and central committee member, purged in 1937.

26 Digonskaya 2012.

27 Ibid.

28 I.I. Sollertinsky, the opera's greatest defender, declared that Lady Macbeth 'was through its force and conviction on a level with Carmen, The Queen of Spades and Wozzeck'. See Sollertinsky 1978, p.25.

29 Shostakovich's letter to Smolich, dated 18 February 1934. Quoted in Yudin 1983, p.92.

30 Shostakovich's Lady Macbeth of Mtsensk District. Restoration of a Masterpiece in programme book for Mstislav Rostropovich's first performance in Russia with original text (St Petersburg, 1996).

31 Markov 1960, pp.223–4.

Bibliography

Abbate 1983
Carolyn Abbate, 'The Parisian "Vénus" and the "Paris" *Tannhäuser*', *Journal of the American Musicological Society* (Spring 1983), vol.36, no.1

Abbiati 1959
Franco Abbiati, *Giuseppe Verdi* (Milan 1959), 4 vols

Addison and Steele 1711
Joseph Addison and Richard Steele, *The Spectator* (London 1711)

Altshuler 2011
Bruce Altshuler, 'Everything is illuminated', *Tate Etc.*, Issue 21: Spring 2011, tate.org.uk/context-comment/articles/everything-illuminated [accessed 14 September 2016]

Azevedo (1861) 2010
Alexis Azevedo, *L'Opinion nationale* (19 March 1861); translation from William Gibbons, 'Music of the Future, Music of the Past: "Tannhäuser" and "Alceste" at the Paris Opéra', *19th-Century Music*, 33/3 (Oakland, Spring 2010)

Banerjee 2003
Anindita Banerjee, 'Electricity: Science Fiction and Modernity in Early Twentieth-Century Russia', *Science Fiction Studies* (2003), vol.30, issue 1

Bartnig 2014
Hella Bartnig, 'Zwischen Opernquerelen und Premierenrausch', *Dresdner Hefte: Richard Strauss in Dresden und die Ära Schuch* (Dresden 2014), vol.118

Beales 1985
Derek Beales (ed.), *History, Society and the Churches* (Cambridge 1985)

Benjamin, Eiland and McLaughlin 1999
Walter Benjamin, *The Arcades Project*, trans. by Howard Eiland and Kevin McLaughlin (Cambridge, Mass. and London 1999)

Berlioz 1843
Hector Berlioz, 'Voyage musical en Allemagne (cinquième lettre)', *Journal des débats* (Paris 12 September 1843)

Bernard 1971
Paul P. Bernard, *Jesuits and Jacobins: Enlightenment and Enlightened Despotism in Austria* (Illinois 1971)

Blanchard Jerrold 1867
W. Blanchard Jerrold, *Paris for the English* (London 1867)

Bodi 1977
Leslie Bodi, *Tauwetter in Wien: Zur Prosa der österreichischen Aufklärung 1781–1795* (Frankfurt 1977)

Bouwsma 1968
William J. Bouwsma, *Venice and the Defense of Republican Liberty: Renaissance Values in the Age of Counter-Reformation* (Berkeley 1968)

Bouwsma 1990
William J. Bouwsma, *A Usable Past: Essays in European Cultural History* (Berkeley 1990)

Braunbehrens 1966
Volkmar Braunbehrens, *Mozart in Wien* (Munich 1966)

Brewer 2013
John Brewer, *The Pleasures of the Imagination: English Culture in the Eighteenth Century* (Oxford and New York 2013)

Brown 1700
Thomas Brown, *Amusements Serious and Comical, Calculated for the Meridian of London* (London 1700)

Brown 1996
Patricia Fortini Brown, *Venice and Antiquity: The Venetian Sense of the Past* (New Haven and London 1996)

Brown 2004
Patricia Fortini Brown, *Private Lives in Renaissance Venice: Art, Architecture, and the Family* (New Haven and London 2004)

Budden 1973, 1978, 1981
Julian Budden, *The Operas of Verdi* (London 1973, 1978, 1981), 3 vols

Burrows 1993
Donald Burrows, 'London: Commercial Wealth and Cultural Expansion', in George J. Buelow (ed.), *Music and Society: The Late Baroque Era: From the 1680s to 1740* (Basingstoke 1993), chapter XII

Burrows 2012
Donald Burrows, *Handel, Master Musician Series* (Oxford 2012)

Busenello 1656
Giovanni Francesco Busenello, *L'ore ociose* (Venice 1656)

Busenello and Livingston 1911
Giovanni Francesco Busenello, *I sonetti morali ed amorosi di Gian Francesco Busenello*, ed. by Arthur Livingston (Venice 1911)

Carter 1997
Tim Carter, 'Re-reading "Poppea": Some Thoughts on Music and Meaning in Monteverdi's Last Opera', *Journal of the Royal Musical Association* (1997), vol.122, no.2

Carter 2002
Tim Carter, *Monteverdi's Musical Theatre* (New Haven and London 2002)

Chadeuil 1858
Gustave Chadeuil, *Le Siècle* (19 February 1858)

Chafe 1991
Eric Chafe, *Monteverdi's Tonal Language* (New York 1991)

Chamberlayne 1729
Edward Chamberlayne, *Angliae Notitia: Or the present state of England* (London 1729)

Champfleury 1860
Champfleury, *Richard Wagner* (Paris 1860)

Corfield 1972
P.J. Corfield, 'A Provincial Capital in the Later Seventeenth Century: The Case of Norwich', in P. Clark and P. Slack (eds), *Crisis and Order in English Towns, 1500–1700: Essays in Urban History* (London 1972)

Coryat 1611
Thomas Coryat, *Coryat's Crudities Hastily gobbled up in five Moneths travels in France, Savoy, Italy, etc.* (London 1611)

Davis and Marvin 2004
Robert C. Davis and Garry R. Marvin, *Venice The Tourist Maze: A Cultural Critique of the World's Most Touristed City* (Berkeley 2004)

Deutsch 1990
Otto Eric Deutsch, *Mozart: A Documentary Biography* (London 1990)

Dickinson 2001
Edward Ross Dickinson, 'Reflections on Feminism and Monism in the Kaiserreich, 1900–1913', *Central European History* (2001), vol.34, no.2

Digonskaya 2012
Olga Digonskaya 'Lady Macbeth and the Bolshoi Theatre', *DSCH Collected articles: Research and Materials* (Moscow 2012), issue IV

Earle 1994
Peter Earle, *A City Full of People: Men and Women of London, 1650–1750* (London 1994)

Emerson 2004
Caryl Emerson, 'Shostakovich and the Russian Literary Tradition', *Shostakovich and His World* (Princeton 2004)

Evelyn and Bray 1901
John Evelyn, *The Diary of John Evelyn*, ed. by William Bray (New York and London 1901)

Fabbri 2007
Paolo Fabbri, *Monteverdi*, trans. by Tim Carter (Cambridge 2007)

Feldman 1995
Martha Feldman, *City Culture and Madrigal at Venice* (Berkeley 1995)

Feldman and Gordon 2006
Martha Feldman and Bonnie Gordon (eds), *The Courtesan's Arts: Cross-Cultural Perspectives* (Oxford 2006)

Fenlon 2007
Iain Fenlon, *The Ceremonial City: History, Memory and Myth in Renaissance Venice* (New Haven 2007)

Fenlon 2009
Iain Fenlon, *Piazza San Marco* (Cambridge, MA 2009)

Fenlon and Miller 1992
Iain Fenlon and Peter N. Miller, *The Song of the Soul: Understanding 'Poppea'* (London 1992)

Finney 1991
Gail Finney, *Women in Modern Drama: Freud, Feminism, and European Theater at the Turn of the Century* (New York 1991)

Fiorentino 1860
P.A. Fiorentino, *Le Constitutionnel* (Paris 1860)

Gatti 1931
Carlo Gatti, *Verdi* (Milan 1931), 2 vols

Gay 1969
Peter Gay, *The Enlightenment: An Interpretation: Volume II, The Science of Freedom* (New York 1969)

Gay 2006
Peter Gay, *Freud: A Life for Our Time*
(New York and London 2006)

Gibbons 2010
William Gibbons, 'Music of the Future, Music of the Past: "Tannhäuser" and "Alceste" at the Paris Opéra', *19th-Century Music* (Spring 2010), vol.33, no.3

Gilman 1988
Sander L. Gilman, 'Strauss, the Pervert, and Avant Garde Opera of the Fin de Siècle', *New German Critique* (Winter 1988), no.43

Giroud 2010
Vincent Giroud, *French Opera: A Short History*
(New Haven 2010)

Glixon 1995
Beth L. Glixon, 'Private Lives of Public Women: Prima Donnas in Mid-Seventeenth-Century Venice', *Music & Letters* (1995), vol.76, no.4

Glixon 1999
Beth L. Glixon, 'More on the Life and Death of Barbara Strozzi', *Musical Quarterly* (1999), vol.83, no.1

Glixon and Glixon 2006
Beth L. Glixon and Jonathan E. Glixon, *Inventing the Business of Opera: The Impresario and His World in Seventeenth-Century Venice* (Oxford and New York 2006)

Glixon 2013
Jonathan L. Glixon, 'Music in Venice: A Historiographical Overview' in Eric R. Dursteler (ed.), *A Companion to Venetian History, 1400–1797* (Leiden 2013)

Goldfarb 2013
Hillard T. Goldfarb, *Art and Music in Venice: From the Renaissance to the Baroque*
(New Haven 2013)

Gregor-Dellin 1980
Martin Gregor-Dellin, *Richard Wagner: sein Leben, sein Werk, sein Jahrhundert* (Munich 1980)

Grubb 1986
Jams S. Grubb, 'When Myths Lose Power: Four Decades of Venetian Historiography', *The Journal of Modern History* (1986), vol.58

Gugitz 1940
Gustav Gugitz, *Das Wiener Kaffeehaus*
(Vienna 1940)

Harding 2002
Vanessa Harding, *The Dead and the Living in Paris and London, 1500–1670* (New York 2002)

Harris 2014
Ellen T. Harris, *George Frideric Handel: A Life with Friends* (New York 2014)

Heller 1999
Wendy Heller, 'Tacitus Incognito: Opera as History in "L'incoronazione di Poppea"', *Journal of the American Musicological Society* (1999), vol.52, no.1

Heller 2000
Wendy Heller, '"O delle donne miserabil sesso": Tarabotti, , and "L'incoronazione di Poppea"', *Il Saggiatore Musicale* (2000), vol.7

Heller 2003
Wendy Heller, *Emblems of Eloquence: Opera and Women's Voices in Seventeenth-Century Venice* (Berkeley 2003)

Heller 2013
Wendy Heller, 'The Veil, the Mask, and the Eunuch: Sight, Sound, and Imperial Erotics in "L'incoronazione di Poppea"' in Rebecca Cypess, Beth L. Glixon and Nathan Link (eds), *Word, Image, and Song* (Rochester, NY 2013), vol.1

Heller 2015
Wendy Heller, 'Barbara Strozzi and the Taming of the Male Poetic Voice', in Dinko Fabris and Margaret K. Murata (eds), *Passaggio in Italia: Music on the Grand Tour in the Seventeenth Century* (Belgium 2015)

Herrmann 2014
Matthias Herrmann, 'Meister-Komponist und Meister-Interpret Richard Strauss und Ernst von Schuch in Dresden', *Dresdner Hefte: Richard Strauss in Dresden und die* Ära *Schuch* (Dresden 2014), vol.118

Hogwood 1988
Christopher Hogwood, *Handel* (London 1988)

Honeycutt 1979
Karen Honeycutt, 'Socialism and Feminism in Imperial Germany', *Signs* (Autumn 1979), vol.5, no.1

Howard 2002
Deborah Howard, *The Architectural History of Venice* (New Haven 2002)

Howard and Moretti 2009
Deborah Howard and Laura Moretti, *Sound and Space in Renaissance Venice: Architecture, Music, Acoustics* (New Haven 2009)

Howell 1651
James Howell, *A Survey of the Signorie of Venice*
(London 1651)

Hume 1988
Robert D. Hume, 'The Sponsorship of Opera in London, 1704–1720', *Modern Philology* (May 1988), vol.85, no.4

Hume 1998
Robert D. Hume, 'The politics of opera in late seventeenth-century London', *Cambridge Opera Journal* (March 1998), vol.10, no.1

Hunter 2000
David Hunter, 'Patronising Handel, Inventing Audiences: The Intersection of Class, Money, Music and History', *Early Music* (February 2000), vol.XVIII, no.1

Hunter 2001
David Hunter, 'Handel Among the Jacobites', *Music and Letters* (2001), vol.82, no.4

Hunter 2015
David Hunter, *The Lives of George Frideric Handel* (Woodbridge 2015)

Hunter 1830
Joseph Hunter (ed.), *The Diary of Ralph Thoresby* (London 1830), vol.II

Jager and Brebbia 2000
W. Jager and C.A. Brebbia (eds), *The Revival of Dresden* (Southampton and Boston, MA 2000)

Keates 2009
Jonathan Keates, *Handel: The Man and his Music*
(London 2009)

Kennedy 1999
Michael Kennedy, *Richard Strauss: Man, Musician, Enigma* (Cambridge 1999)

Koldau and Kurtzman 2002
Linda Maria Koldau and Jeffrey Kurtzman, '*Trombe, Trombe d'argento, Trombe squarciate, Tromboni,* and *Pifferi* in Venetian Processions and Ceremonies of the Sixteenth and Seventeenth Centuries', *Journal of Seventeenth-Century Music* (2002), vol.8, no.1, sscm-jscm.org/v8/no1/kurtzman.html [accessed 8 September 2016]

König 1996
Wolfgang König, 'Science-based industry or industry-based science? Electrical engineering in Germany before World War I', *Technology and Culture* (1996), vol.37

Kovnatskaya 2006
L. Kovnatskaya (ed.), *D.D. Shostakovich Letters to I.I. Sollertinsky* (St Petersburg 2006)

Kramer 2004
Laurence Kramer, *Opera and Modern Culture: Wagner and Strauss* (Berkeley 2004)

Kultermann 2006
Udo Kultermann, 'The "Dance of the Seven Veils": Salome and Erotic Culture around 1900', *Artibus et Historiae* (2006), vol.27, no.53

Kustow 2013
Michael Kustow, *Peter Brook: A Biography*
(London 2013)

Lanaro 2006
Paola Lanaro (ed.), *At the Centre of the Old World: Trade and Manufacturing in Venice and on the Venetian Mainland, 1400–1800* (Toronto 2006)

Lee and Segal 2015
Hyunseon Lee and Naomi Segal (eds), *Opera, Exoticism and Visual Culture* (Bern 2015)

Lindsay 1978
Jack Lindsay, *The Monster City: Defoe's London, 1688–1730* (London and New York 1978)

Logan 1972
Oliver Logan, *Culture and Society in Venice 1470–1790: The Renaissance and its Heritage* (New York 1972)

Mainwaring 1760
John Mainwaring, *Memoirs of the Life of the Late George Frederic Handel* (London 1760)

Markov 1960
Pavel Markov, *Theatre Direction: V.I. Nemirovich – Danchenko and Musical Theatre* (Moscow 1960)

McClary 1991
Susan McClary, 'Constructions of Gender in Monteverdi's Dramatic Music', *Feminine Endings: Music, Gender, and Sexuality* (Minneapolis and Oxford 1991)

Milhous and Hume 1989
Judith Milhous and Robert D. Hume, 'The Haymarket Opera in 1711', *Early Music* (November 1989), vol.XVII, no.4

Misson 1699
Maximilien Misson, *A New Voyage to Italy: with Curious Observations on several other Countries* (London 1699)

Mitchell 2000
Juliet Mitchell, *Psychoanalysis and Feminism: A Radical Reassessment of Freudian Psychoanalysis* (New York 2000)

Moeller 2014
Magdalena M. Moeller, *The Brücke Museum,* Berlin (Munich 2014)

Monod 2006
Paul Monod, 'The Politics of Handel's Early London Operas, 1711–1718', *Journal of Interdisciplinary History* (Winter 2006), vol.XXXVI, no.3

Morrison 2004
Simon Morrison, 'Shostakovich and Industrial Saboteur', *Shostakovich and his World* (Princeton 2004)

Mozart and Anderson 1985
Wolfgang Amadeus Mozart, *The Letters of Mozart and his Family*, trans. by Emily Anderson (London 1985)

Muir 1981
Edward Muir, *Civic Ritual in Renaissance Venice* (Princeton, NJ 1981)

Nalbach 1973
Daniel Nalbach, *The King's Theatre 1704–1867: London's First Italian Opera House*, Society for Theatre Research (London 1973)

O'Brien 1969
Charles O'Brien, 'Ideas of Religious Toleration at the Time of Joseph II', *Transactions of the American Philosophical Society* (1969), New Series, vol.LIX

Parker 1989
Roger Parker, *Studies in Early Verdi 1832–1844: New Information and Perspectives on the Milanese Musical Milieu and the Operas from 'Oberto' to 'Ernani'* (New York and London 1989)

Parker 1997
Roger Parker, *'Arpa d'or dei fatidici vati': The Verdian Patriotic Chorus in the 1840s* (Parma 1997)

Paul 2014
Jürgen Paul, 'Die Kulturstadt Dresden um 1900', *Dresdner Hefte: Richard Strauss in Dresden und die Ära Schuch* (Dresden 2014), vol.118

Petty 1899
Sir William Petty, 'Two Essays in Political Arithmetick, Concerning the People, Housing, Hospitals, &c. London and Paris', in *The Economic Writings of Sir William Petty*, ed. by Charles Henry Hull (New York 1899), vol.2

Pezzl 1785
Johann Pezzl, *Faustin, oder das philosophische Jahrhundert* (Vienna 1785)

Pezzl 1789
Johann Pezzl, *Skizze von Wien* (Vienna and Leipzig 1789)

Phillips-Matz 1993
Mary Jane Phillips-Matz, *Verdi: A Biography* (Oxford 1993)

Pote 1729
Joseph Pote, *The Foreigner's Guide: or a necessary and instructive companion both for the foreigner and native in their tour through the cities of London and Westminster* (London 1729)

Price 1987
Curtis Price, 'English Traditions in Handel's "Rinaldo"', in Stanley Sadie and Anthony Hicks (eds), *Handel Tercentenary Collection* (Basingstoke 1987)

Pullan 1968
Brian Pullan, *Crisis and Change in the Venetian Economy in the Sixteenth and Seventeenth Centuries* (London 1968)

Quaintance 2015
Courtney Quaintance, *Textual Masculinity and the Exchange of Women in Renaissance Venice* (Toronto 2015)

Rapp 1976
Richard Tilden Rapp, *Industry and Economic Decline in Seventeenth-Century Venice* (Cambridge, MA 1976)

Revue et Gazette musicale (June, July and August 1852)

Ritter 1970
Erwin Ritter, 'Johann Baptise von Alxinger and the Austrian Enlightenment', *European University Papers* (Berne 1970), Series 1, vol.XXXIV

Robbins Landon 1984
H.C. Robbins Landon, *Handel and his World* (London 1984)

Robbins Landon 1990
H.C. Robbins Landon (ed.), *The Mozart Compendium* (London 1990)

Roche 1987
Daniel Roche, *The People of Paris: An Essay in Popular Culture in the 18th Century* (Berkeley 1987)

Romano 2006
Dennis Romano, 'Why Opera? The Politics of an Emerging Genre', *The Journal of Interdisciplinary History* (2006), vol.36, no.3

Rosand 2001
David Rosand, *Myths of Venice: The Figuration of a State* (Chapel Hill and London 2001)

Rosand 1978
Ellen Rosand, 'Barbara Strozzi, "Virtuossima cantatrice": The Composer's Voice', *Journal of the American Musicological Society* (1978), vol.31, no.2

Rosand 1985
Ellen Rosand, 'Seneca and the Interpretation of "L'incoronazione di Poppea"', *Journal of the American Musicological Society* (1985), vol.38, no.1

Rosand 1991
Ellen Rosand, *Opera in Seventeenth-Century Venice: The Creation of a Genre* (Berkeley and Los Angeles 1991)

Rosand 2007
Ellen Rosand, *Monteverdi's Last Operas: A Venetian Trilogy* (Berkeley and Los Angeles 2007)

Rosand 2013
Ellen Rosand (ed.), *Reading Cavalli's Operas for the Stage: Manuscript, Edition, Production* (Farnham and Burlington, VT 2013)

Rosenstruch-Königsberg 1984
Edith Rosenstruch-Königsberg, *Freimaurer, Illuminat, Weltburger: Friedrich Munters Reisen und Briefe in ihren europaischen Bezügen* (Berlin 1984)

Rosenthal 1992
Margaret F. Rosenthal, *The Honest Courtesan: Veronica Franca, Citizen and Writer in Sixteenth-Century Venice* (Chicago and London 1992)

Ross 2011
Alex Ross, *Listen to This* (London 2011)

Ross 2012
Alex Ross, *The Rest is Noise: Listening to the Twentieth Century* (London 2012)

Sadie and Hicks 1987
Stanley Sadie and Anthony Hicks (eds), *Handel Tercentenary Collection* (Basingstoke 1987)

Saint-Didier 1699
Alexandre Toussaint de Limojon de Saint-Didier, 'La Ville et la République de Venise' (Paris 1680), trans. by Francis Terne, *The City and Republick of Venice* (London 1699)

Salomé: Strauss, L'Avant Scène Opera No. 240 (2007)

Saussure (1726) 1902
César de Saussure, *A foreign View of England in the reigns of George I and George II,* entry for 29 October 1726 (London 1902)

Schuh 1953
Willy Schuh (ed.), *Recollections and Reflections*, trans. by L. J. Lawrence (London 1953)

Serbraykova 1971
Galina Serbraykova, *About Myself and Others* (Moscow 1971)

Setton 1991
Kenneth Meyer Setton, *Venice, Austria, and the Turks in the Seventeenth Century* (Philadelphia 1991)

Shostakovich 1934
Dmitri Shostakovich, *About My Opera*, MALEGOT programme booklet (Leningrad 1934)

Shostakovich 1934b
Dmitri Shostakovich, *An Introduction to my Opera*, Nemirovch-Danchenko Music Theatre's programme booklet (Moscow 1934)

Shostakovich 1996
Dmitri Shostakovich, *Lady Macbeth of Mtsensk District. Restoration of a Masterpiece* (St Petersburg 1996)

Sollertinsky 1978
I.I. Sollertinsky, *Shostakovich's Creative Path* (Moscow 1978)

Sonnenfels 1783–7
Joseph von Sonnenfels, *Gesammelte Schriften* (Vienna 1783–7)

Sperling 1999
Jutta Gisela Sperling, *Convents and the Body Politic in Late Renaissance Venice* (Chicago and London 1999)

Steele and Addison 1988
Richard Steele and Joseph Addison, *Selections from the Tatler and Spectator* (London 1988)

BIBLIOGRAPHY

Strozzi 1644
Giulio Strozzi, *Le glorie della signora Anna Renzi romana* (Venice 1644)

Strozzi 1652
Giulio Strozzi, *Veremonda L'Amazzonne di Aragona* (Venice 1652)

Tarabotti 2004
Arcangela Tarabotti, *Paternal Tyranny*, ed. and trans. by Letizia Panizza (Chicago 2004)

Taruskin 1997
Richard Taruskin, 'Entr'acte: The Lessons of Lady Macbeth', *Defining Russia Musically: Historical and Hermeneutical Essays* (Princeton 1997)

The Poor Man's Complaint: Or, The Sorrowful Lamentation of Poor Plain-Dealing at this Time of Distress and Trouble (London 1690–1700), Pepys Collection IV:300

Uffenbach (1710) 1934
Zacharias Konrad von Uffenbach, *London in 1710: From the Travels of Zacharias Conrad Von Uffenbach* (London 1934)

Vincenz and Hesse 2008
Kirsten Vincenz and Wolfgang Hesse (eds), *Fotoindustrie und Bilderwelten — Die Heinrich Ernemann AG für Camerafabrikation in Dresden 1889–1926* (Dresden 2008)

Vishnevskaya 1984
Galina Vishnevskaya, *Galina: A Russian Story* (London 1984)

Walker 1984
Frank Walker, *The Man Verdi* (rpt. Chicago, 1984)

Waller 2000
Maureen Waller, *1700: Scenes from London Life* (London 2000)

Walton 2005
Chris Walton, 'Beneath the Seventh Veil: Richard Strauss's "Salome" and Kaiser Wilhelm II', *The Musical Times* (Winter 2005), vol.146, no.1893

Ward c.1700
Ned Ward, *The London Spy* (c.1700)

Weaver 2006
Elissa Weaver (ed.), *Arcangela Tarabotti: A Literary Nun in Baroque Venice* (Longo 2006)

Weiner 1970
Gordon M. Weiner, 'The Demographic Effects of the Venetian Plagues of 1575–77 and 1630–31', *Genus* (1970), vol.26, no.1/2

Weiss 2002
Piero Weiss, *Opera: A History in Documents* (Oxford 2002)

Wilde 1968
Oscar Wilde, *Salomé* (1968)

Williams 1984
E. N. Williams, *The Ancien Régime in Europe* (London 1984)

Willson 2014
Flora Willson, 'Future History: Wagner, Offenbach, and "la musique de l'avenir" in Paris, 1860', *Opera Quarterly* (2014), vol.30, no.4

Wilson 1999
Bronwen Wilson, '"Il bel sesso, e l'austero Senato": The Coronation of Dogaressa Morosina Morsini Grimani', *Renaissance Quarterly* (1999), vol.52, no.1

Wilson 2006
Elizabeth Wilson, *Shostakovich: A Life Remembered* (London 2006)

Winter 1971
Eduard Winter, *Baroque Absolutismus and Aufkläring in der Donaumoarchie* (Vienna 1971)

Woodhead (1903) 1904
Howard Woodhead, 'The First German Municipal Exhibition' (Dresden 1903), *American Journal of Sociology* (1904)

Yudin 1983
Gavriil Yudin (ed.), *Letters to Smolich* (Moscow 1983)

WEBSITES
demographia.com/dm-lon31.htm
[accessed 23 July 2016]

localhistories.org/population.html
[accessed 23 July 2016]

londononline.co.uk/factfile/historical/
[accessed 23 July 2016]

nytimes.com/1987/01/13/arts/opera-salome-in-milan-staged-by-robert-wilson.html
[accessed 10 February 2017]

oldbaileyonline.org/static/Population-history-of-london.jsp [accessed 23 July 2016]

studfiles.ru/preview/2781483/
[accessed 1 November 2016]

Glossary

Archlute — a plucked string instrument slightly larger than a tenor lute

Aria — a solo song usually with accompaniment, found in operas or oratorios

Baritone — a male singing voice pitched between the tenor and bass voice types

Bass — the lowest male singing voice

Bass-baritone — the second lowest male singing voice, especially associated with roles in Wagner operas

Cantata — a piece of music in several movements, involving soloists with or without chorus, usually with instrumental accompaniment and often on a religious or pastoral theme

Castrato — during the seventeenth and eighteenth centuries, a male singer who had been castrated as a boy in order to preserve a soprano or alto voice range

Celesta — a keyboard instrument that makes a bell-like sound from hammers striking metal plates

Chorus — a group of singers who perform the choral parts of an opera or oratorio

Coloratura — an ornate and virtuosic vocal style

Commedia dell'arte — often acknowledged as one of the first forms of early modern professional theatre, Commedia dell'arte originated in sixteenth-century Italy and involved masked stock characters and improvization on common plots

Composizione ideale (free composition) — a compositional style that does not abide by the rules of strict counterpoint

Continuo (instruments) — the accompaniment (usually to Baroque or sometimes Classical music) comprising a bass line, typically played by the cello, harmonized with such instruments as harpsichord, theorbo or lute

Contralto — the lowest female singing voice; the term 'alto' is generally used for the same voice type in choral music

Counterpoint — the setting of multiple musical lines or melodies performed together (generally according to specific rules)

Countertenor — the highest type of male voice in opera, near in pitch range to the alto voice

Deus ex machina — a plot device where a seemingly hopeless situation is suddenly resolved through an unexpected and often supernatural twist

Dramatis personae — the characters in a dramatic work

Ensemble scenes — scenes in an opera (or play) involving several characters interacting (and often singing together)

Entr'acte — a piece of music performed between acts of a play or opera

Forte (f) — an indication to play or sing loudly

Fortissimo (ff) — an indication to play or sing very loudly

Fugue — a composition which starts with a musical subject, a melody or phrase, which is introduced in one part and then repeated in each part in turn with new countermelodies, creating an interweaving pattern of (contrapuntal) imitation

Gesamtkunstwerk — literally meaning 'total work of art', particularly associated with Richard Wagner's aesthetic philosophy; it refers to art made through a combination of several different art forms

Glissando — a musical device involving a slide upwards or downwards between two pitches

Harmony — the sounding of two or more notes at the same time

Harpsichord — a plucked string instrument belonging to the keyboard family

Kapellmeister — director of music (usually of a choir, orchestra or opera company)

Libretto — the text of a musical work

Maestro al cembalo — harpsichordist — there was no conductor in Baroque ensembles and the harpsichordist tended to lead performances from the keyboard

Maestro di capella — director of music (at an institution, usually of a choir or orchestra)

Maestro di musica — director of music

Masquerade — a performance or event involving the wearing of masks

Melody — musical notes played in succession; a tune

Metastasian operas — operas written to the words of the Italian poet and librettist Pietro Metastasio (1698–1782)

Mezzo-soprano — the second highest type of female singing voice, pitched between the soprano and contralto voice types

Opera buffa — a genre of opera whose comedic plot is usually based around domestic drama and romantic intrigue

Opera seria — a genre of opera whose plot is usually drawn from ancient history or literature, and with a serious or tragic theme

Ostinato — a repeated melodic or rhythmic musical phrase

Overture — a piece of orchestral music at the beginning of an opera

Passacaglia — a musical form, often in triple time, based on a repeating bass line

Pasticcio — otherwise known as a pastiche; a genre of opera that uses portions of other composers' work, or reuses some of the composer's previous work, sometimes alongside original composition

Pianissimo (pp) — an indication to play or sing very quietly

Piano (p) — an indication to play or sing quietly

Prima donna — literally meaning 'first lady'; the term refers to the leading female singer in a company, usually a soprano

Quadrille — a dance performed by four couples in a rectangular formation

Recitative — a passage of accompanied singing adopting the free rhythms of natural speech, used for narrative or dialogue in operas or oratorios

Recitativo accompagnato — recitative accompanied by the orchestra

Recitativo secco — recitative accompanied only by continuo

Score — the complete written or printed music for any piece, showing all the individual parts arranged on separate staves

Semi-opera — plays, typically of the Restoration period, which combine spoken and musical episodes

Singspiel — comic opera that includes spoken dialogue between songs, ensembles and choruses; popular in eighteenth-century Germany

Sonnet — a poem of 14 lines, usually in iambic pentameter

Soprano — the highest type of female singing voice

Tenor — a high male voice type pitched higher than a baritone but lower than a countertenor

Theorbo — a plucked string instrument belonging to the lute family

Tutti — all performers in a work or in a section of the orchestra playing at the same time

Zarzuela — a form of Spanish musical comedy or operetta in which passages of speech and song alternate

Contributors

KATE BAILEY
A Senior Exhibition Curator and Producer in the Theatre and Performance Department at the V&A, Kate Bailey is the curator of *Opera: Passion, Power and Politics*. Her previous exhibitions include *Russian Avant-Garde Theatre: War, Revolution and Design* (2014) and the award-winning touring video installation, *Five Truths* (2011).

ALEX BEARD
Alex Beard is the CEO of the Royal Opera House, London. He joined in 2013 following almost 20 years working at the Tate, London, including as its Deputy Director from 2002. He is Chairman of High House Production Park Ltd, and is a board member of 14–18 NOW and the West End Partnership. He was awarded a CBE in 2012 for services to the arts.

ROBERT CARSEN
Canadian director Robert Carsen has worked as an opera, theatre and musical-theatre director and lighting designer all over the world, including in six of the seven cities involved in this exhibition, as well as for six of its seven operas. Recent productions include *Der Rosenkavalier* and *Falstaff* for the Royal Opera House, London, and the Metropolitan Opera in New York, *Die Zauberflöte* at the Paris Opéra, and *Don Giovanni* at Teatro alla Scala, Milan. He has also worked as the artistic director and designer for exhibitions at the Musée d'Orsay and Grand Palais in Paris, the Royal Academy in London and the Art Institute of Chicago.

UNSUK CHIN
Seoul-born composer Unsuk Chin works with some of the most renowned international orchestras, including the Berlin Philharmonic and BBC Symphony Orchestra, and has been championed by conductors including Sir Simon Rattle and Gustavo Dudamel. Her opera *Alice in Wonderland* at the Bavarian State Opera in Munich was named 'World Premiere of the year' by international opera critics in 2007.

PLÁCIDO DOMINGO
Plácido Domingo is a world-renowned artist, recognized not only as one of the finest and most influential singing actors in the history of opera, but also as a respected conductor. As the General Director of Los Angeles Opera he is also a major force as an opera administrator. He turned 76 in January 2017, but his gifts and energy remain undiminished.

JOHN FULLJAMES
John Fulljames has been the Associate Director of Opera for The Royal Opera, London, since 2011. He has directed *La donna del lago*, *Quartett*, *Rise and Fall of the City of Mahagonny* and *Orphée et Eurydice*, which was co-directed with Hofesh Shechter for The Royal Opera. John was the Artistic Director of The Opera Group (now Mahogany Opera Group) between 1997 and 2011, where he worked closely with a wide range of composers and librettists to develop, commission and produce new operas.

WENDY HELLER
Professor Wendy Heller is the Scheide Professor of Music History and Chairman of the Department of Music at Princeton University. She specializes in the study of opera from interdisciplinary perspectives, and her numerous writings on Venetian opera include *Emblems of Eloquence: Opera and Women's Voices in Seventeenth-Century Venice*. Her edition of Francesco Cavalli's *Veremonda, L'amazzone di Aragona* was presented last year at the Schwetzingen Festival.

KASPER HOLTEN
Kasper Holten was Director of the Royal Danish Opera between 2000 and 2011, and afterwards was the Director of Opera for The Royal Opera, London, until 2017. He has directed a feature film of Mozart's *Don Giovanni (Juan)*, as well as opera productions across the world, including at The Royal Opera in London, Vienna State Opera, Deutsche Oper Berlin, Bregenz Festival and Teatro alla Scala, Milan. He received a knighthood in 2003, and a medal Ingenio et Arti from Queen Margrethe II of Denmark in 2011.

TRISTRAM HUNT
Dr Tristram Hunt is the Director of the V&A. A historian, politician, writer and broadcaster, he also served as Labour MP for Stoke-on-Trent Central from 2010 to 2017, and was previously the Shadow Secretary of State and Shadow Minister for Education.

DAVID HENRY HWANG
America's most produced living opera librettist, David Henry Hwang has worked with composers including Philip Glass, Osvaldo Golijov, Unsuk Chin and Bright Sheng. He is also a Tony Award-winning playwright, screenwriter and musical theatre librettist, whose works include *Madama Butterfly*, *Yellow Face*, *Chinglish* and Disney's *Aida*.

MICHAEL LEVINE
Canadian Michael Levine has worked internationally for the past 35 years as a set and costume designer in theatre, opera, dance and film. Recent productions include: *Billy Budd* directed by Deborah Warner for Teatro Real, Madrid; *The Encounter* for the Complicite Theatre; *Wozzeck* directed by Andreas Homoki for Zürich Opera; *Le Petit Prince* choreographed by Guillaume Cote for the National Ballet of Canada; *Benjamin, dernière nuit* directed by John Fulljames for Opéra de Lyon.

FIONA MADDOCKS
Fiona Maddocks is the classical music critic of *The Observer* and a board member of *Opera* magazine. She was the founding editor of *BBC Music Magazine* and has written books on Hildegard of Bingen and Harrison Birtwistle. Her most recent publication is *Music for Life*.

DANIELLE DE NIESE
Through her many recordings on Decca, live opera performances and television exposure, Danielle de Niese has gained wide recognition as a highly respected and popular classical artist, who combines a 'sweet, gleaming soprano' voice, 'phenomenal musicality' and 'sharply comic, yet utterly moving acting'. She has been named 'opera's coolest soprano' by the *New York Times Magazine* and described by *Opera News* as 'not just a superb performer, but a phenomenal one'.

ANTONIO PAPPANO
Sir Antonio Pappano has been Music Director for The Royal Opera in London since 2002, and the Music Director of the Orchestra dell'Accademia Nazionale di Santa Cecilia in Rome since 2005. He has conducted many of the world's most prestigious orchestras, including the Berlin, Vienna, New York and Munich Philharmonic Orchestras. He has also presented several critically acclaimed BBC Television documentaries including *Opera Italia*, *Pappano's Essential Ring Cycle* and *Pappano's Classical Voices*.

ROGER PARKER
Roger Parker is Professor of Music at King's College London, having previously taught at the universities of Cornell, Oxford and Cambridge. He is working on a book about music in London in the 1830s, and is Director of the European Research Council-funded project 'Music in London, 1800–1851'.

FRED PLOTKIN
Fred Plotkin is the author of *Opera 101: A Complete Guide to Learning and Loving Opera* and is also an opera writer for New York Public Radio. He has worked for Teatro alla Scala in Milan and the Metropolitan Opera in New York and has also participated in opera programmes for BBC Radio and the Oxford Literary Festival.

YUVAL SHARON
Described by *The Hollywood Reporter* as 'LA's avant-garde opera darling', director Yuval Sharon has created an unconventional body of work that seeks to expand the operatic form. He is the Artistic Director of The Industry in Los Angeles, and he has worked with Graham Vick on Birmingham Opera Company's *Mittwoch aus Licht* (2012) and directed *The Three Sisters* for the Vienna State Opera. He currently has a three-year residency with the Los Angeles Philharmonic.

DANIEL SNOWMAN
Daniel Snowman is a social and cultural historian whose career has spanned both the academic world and the BBC. His published works include critical portraits of the Amadeus Quartet and Plácido Domingo, a study of the cultural impact of the 'Hitler Emigrés', and *The Gilded Stage: A Social History of Opera*.

DAVID STAPLES
David Staples is a project director and specializes in preliminary planning and feasibility studies for arts venues, planning new opera houses that successfully serve their clients, users and community. The former chairman of the Society of Theatre Consultants and a former board member of the International Society of Performing Arts, he is also a member of the Association of British Theatre Technicians. He has worked with the Oslo Opera House, the Royal Opera House in Muscat, Oman, and the Onassis House of Letters and Arts in Athens.

NICHOLAS TILL
Nicholas Till is a historian, theorist and artist working in opera and music theatre. He is Professor of Opera and Music Theatre at the University of Sussex, and author of *Mozart and Enlightenment: Truth, Virtue and Beauty in Mozart's Operas*, published in 1992. He is currently working on a project to recreate the original programme of entertainment presented at Hoxton Hall music hall in east London in 1863.

GRAHAM VICK

The Director at Glyndebourne between 1992 and 2000, Graham Vick also founded Birmingham Opera Company (BOC) in 1987. His pioneering work with BOC was a milestone for the modernization and development of opera as an art form. Graham Vick has also directed productions in some of the world's major opera houses such as the Metropolitan Opera, New York and Teatro alla Scala, Milan.

FLORA WILLSON

A British Academy Postdoctoral Fellow at King's College London, Flora Willson is currently writing a book about operatic culture in the 1890s. She also writes for *The Guardian*, gives talks at the Royal Opera House, London, and elsewhere, and is a regular guest on BBC Radio 3.

ELIZABETH WILSON

Elizabeth Wilson is a cellist and author, whose work has covered Russian and Soviet music, composers and performers. She has written biographies of the cellists Mstislav Rostropovich and Jacqueline du Pré, as well as the much-acclaimed *Shostakovich: A Life Remembered*. Her books have been published in the UK and US, and have been translated into Japanese, Chinese, Italian and Russian.

PRETTY YENDE

South African soprano Pretty Yende discovered opera at the age of 16 after hearing the 'Flower Duet' from *Lakmé* in a television advert. She subsequently won the International Hans Gabor Belvedere Singing Competition in 2009 and became part of the young artists programme at Teatro alla Scala, Milan. Since then, her many international appearances have included Pamina from *Die Zauberflöte* (Metropolitan Opera, New York), Susanna in *Le nozze di Figaro* (Los Angeles Opera) and Adina in *L'elisir d'amore* (The Royal Opera, London).

SIMONE YOUNG

Simone Young is a conductor of opera and symphonic concerts, and is particularly renowned for her interpretations of Strauss, Wagner, Verdi, Bruckner and Brahms. She has worked as the artistic head of the Opera Australia and the Hamburg State Opera, and performs regularly at the opera houses in Vienna, Berlin, Munich and Zürich among others, as well as on concert podiums across four continents.

Acknowledgements

Opera is a collaborative art form, and we are enormously grateful to everyone who has helped to realize this ambitious project. The first exhibition of its kind, creating *Opera: Passion, Power and Politics* has been a stimulating and challenging journey, tapping into many different resources and networks across cities, cultures and continents. Such an enormous subject could not have been tackled without the support of numerous experts and specialists from across opera's history and practice, all of whom have been incredibly generous with their time and expertise.

Profound thanks go to Jule Rubi, the exhibition research assistant, whose contribution to, and passion for, the subject has helped us every step of the way; to Martin Roth, Alex Beard, Kasper Holten and John Fulljames for their vision and commitment to the project since its inception; and to Robert Carsen, whose experience, knowledge and artistic direction have been crucial in the development of the exhibition. We appreciate the endless support of all our advisors at the Royal Opera House, including Tony Followell, Tom Nelson, John Snelson, Sarah Crabtree and Kate Hopkins.

Our deepest thanks go to our advisors for the exhibition and to the contributors to this book: Professor Chris Baugh, Plácido Domingo, Professor Wendy Heller, Michael Levine, Danielle de Niese, Sir Antonio Pappano, Professor Roger Parker, Professor Ted Rabb, Matthias Schaller, Irina Antonovna Shostakovich, Daniel Snowman, Professor Nicholas Till, Graham Vick, Dr Heather Wiebe, Dr Flora Willson, Elizabeth Wilson, Dr Richard Wistreich, Simone Young, and so many others.

This exhibition would not have been possible without the outstanding work of the core project team: Curious Space designers Patrick Burnier, Anna Jones and Tom Oldham, their project manager Sue Dickinson, sound designer David Sheppard, audio-visual designers Adam Young and Finn Ross from FRAY, lighting designers Paule Constable and Jono Kenyon, Marc Bloom and Nic Carter from Socio Design, Jeremy Hull and Chloe Sutton from Fraser Randall.

It is increasingly important for the V&A to secure sponsors and partners in order to enable us to present such ambitious exhibitions. *Opera: Passion, Power and Politics* has received overwhelming support and we are extremely grateful to our lead sponsor Societe Generale and our sound partner Bowers & Wilkins. We would also like to thank the Blavatnik Family Foundation and The Taylor Family Foundation for their generosity, as well as GRoW @ Annenberg, Bertelsmann and Cockayne Grants for the Arts.

Profound thanks go to our editors Tom Windross and Kirstin Beattie, without whom this book would not be here, as well as to designers Praline, copyeditor Rebeka Cohen, and production manager Emma Woodiwiss; thanks also go to our colleagues Rebecca Lim, Olivia Oldroyd, Amy Higgitt, Sadie Hough, Francesca Sidhu, Nikki Caxton, Zoe Louisos,

Sarah Jameson, Stephanie Cripps, Annabel Wilton and their colleagues from the V&A Exhibitions Department for their amazing work throughout the project; Susan Catcher and all our colleagues from the various Conservation Departments; Bryony Shepherd and Asha McLoughlin for their help on interpretation; our colleagues Emma Jane Avery, Jenny Phelan, Matilda Pye, Laura Carderera, Leanne Manfredi, Faunsia Tucker, Sarah Campbell, Adrian Deakes and their colleagues from the Learning Department for putting together a great programme for the exhibition; and last but not least our warmest thanks go to Sophie Brendel, Jane Rosier, Lucy Hawes, Pandora Ryan, Laura Sears, Stacey Bowles, Joanna Hanna-Grindall, Sophie Hargroves, Kati Price, Joanna Jones, Liz Edmunds, Fred Caws; the Photography Department, Technical Services and Visitor Experience Teams at the V&A.

Alongside these colleagues, we would like to thank all the curators from across the V&A whose help has been invaluable in putting this exhibition together: Tessa Murdoch, Angus Patterson, Kirstin Kennedy, Reino Liefkes, Julius Bryant, Mark Evans, Ana Debenedetti, Ruth Hibbard, Leela Meinertas, Leslie Miller, Nick Humphrey, Susan North, Jennie Lister, Max Donnelly, Kirsty Hassard, Martin Barnes, Susanna Brown and Briony Carlin. Thanks also go our former colleagues who played an important role in the development of the project: Annabel Judd, Daniel Slater and Philip Contos.

We have also benefited greatly from assistants and interns, some of whom have now joined the V&A on a more permanent basis: Yulia Naumova, Matteo Augello, Natalia Karakosta and Alice Beverley; Phoebe Coleman, Martha Clewlow, Jacob Duffell, Philomène Dupleix, Sarah Hardie, Gillian Hopper, Maria Ilyevskaya, Elena Korotkikh, Carla Lariot, Benjamin Levy, Catriona MacDonald, Lisa Osborne, Dorotea Petrucci, Zoe Richards, Camilla Sponza, Sara Tarter and Zhongli Zhao.

The V&A Theatre and Performance Department has been a rewarding environment in which to develop such a project, and we are grateful to our colleagues for their advice and support. On behalf of everyone at the Museum we would like to thank Dr Tristram Hunt, Director of the V&A, Bill Sherman, Head of Collections and Research, David Bickle, Director of Design, Exhibitions and FuturePlan, Linda Lloyd-Jones, Head of Exhibitions, and Joanna Norman, Deputy Head of Research, for their tremendous support.

Picture Credits

By plate number. All images © Victoria and Albert Museum, London. Except:

2 © Glyndebourne Productions/ Mike Hoban
3 © Liz Lauren. Chicago Opera Theater, 2004
4 © Gérard Amsellem-Lyon
5 © 2008 David Leventi. Courtesy of Rick Wester Fine Art, New York
6 © Trust Doria Pamphilj
8 © Palazzo Ducale, Venice/ Bridgeman Images
9 © 2017. Photo Scala, Florence – courtesy of the Ministero Beni e Att. Culturali
10 © 2017. DeAgostini Picture Library/Scala, Florence
11 Royal Collection Trust/© Her Majesty Queen Elizabeth II 2016
12 © Heritage Images/Hulton Fine Art Collection/Getty Images
20 © Courtesy of the Trustees of Sir John Soane's Museum, London/ Bridgeman Images
23 © Royal Academy of Music/ Lebrecht Music & Arts
25 © Fondazione Scientifica Querini Stampalia
26 © Biblioteca Nazionale Marciana
27 © 2017. Photo Scala, Florence/ bpk, Bildagentur fuer Kunst, Kultur und Geschichte, Berlin
28 © Musée d'art et d'histoire, Ville de Genève, Photo: Flora Bevilacqua/ inv. nº 1841-0001
29 © Biblioteca Nazionale Marciana
31 © Biblioteca Nazionale Marciana
32 © Musée d'art et d'histoire, Ville de Genève, Photo: Jacot-Descombes Bettina/inv. nº 1974-0011
39 © Vincent Pontet
41 © Bill Cooper/ArenaPAL
42 © Bill Cooper/ArenaPAL
43 © Bill Cooper/ArenaPAL
44 © Rob Moore, 2005
45 © 2017. Photo Scala Florence/ Heritage Images 918
46 © RIBA Library Drawings and Archives Collections
48 © Fitzwilliam Museum, Cambridge
49 © The Trustees of the British Museum
51 © Foundling Museum, London/ Bridgeman Images
55 © British Library, London/ Bridgeman Images
57 © British Library, London/ Bridgeman Images
58 Private collection
59 © The Trustees of the British Museum
61 Staatsbibliothek zu Berlin – Preußischer Kulturbesitz, Abteilung Historische Drucke, Yq 9301 (R)
62 © Fitzwilliam Museum, Cambridge/Bridgeman Images
64 © Science Museum/Science and Society Picture Library
66 © British Library, London/ Bridgeman Images
67 © Tate, London 2015
69 © The Trustees of the British Museum
80 © British Library, London/ Bridgeman Images
81 © Clive Barda, 2004
82 © Bill Cooper/Royal Opera House/ArenaPAL
83 © Robbie Jack – Corbis /Corbis Entertainment/Getty Images
84 © Wiener Staatsoper/Michael Pöhn
85 © G. Nimatallah/Bridgeman Images
86 © Leemage/Corbis Historical/ Getty Images
88 © Internationale Stiftung Mozarteum (ISM)
90 © Wien Bibliothek
91 © The Cleveland Museum of Art, The Edward B. Greene Collection 1942.1142
93 © 2017. Photo Austrian Archives/ Scala Florence
94 © Wien Bibliothek
95 © DEA/A. DAGLI ORTI/Agostini Picture Library/Getty Images
96 © Leemage/Universal Images Group/Getty Images
97 © KHM-Museumsverband, Theatermuseum Vienna
98 © KHM-Museumsverband, Theatermuseum Vienna
99 © KHM-Museumsverband, Theatermuseum Vienna
100 © British Library, London/ Bridgeman Images
101 © KHM-Museumsverband, Theatermuseum Vienna
103 National Museum, Prague, Czech Republic
104 © British Library, London/ Bridgeman Images
107 © 2014 Christie's Images Limited
110 © Museum of London
115 © British Library, London/ Bridgeman Images
116 © ROH/Catherine Ashmore, 2013
117 © ROH/Catherine Ashmore, 2013
118 © 2015 ROH. Photographed by Catherine Ashmore
119 © 2008 David Leventi. Courtesy of Rick Wester Fine Art, New York
120 © Comune di Milano – Palazzo Morando – Costume Moda Immagine
121 © Museo Teatrale alla Scala
122 © Museo Teatrale alla Scala
124 © Ricordi & C. S.r.l. Milan
125 © Museo Teatrale alla Scala
126 © British Library, London/ Bridgeman Images
127 Courtesy of Biblioteca Braidense
128 © Comune di Milano – Palazzo Moriggia – Museo del Risorgimento
130 © Museo Teatrale alla Scala
131 © Museo Teatrale alla Scala
132 © Museo Teatrale alla Scala
133 © Museo Teatrale alla Scala
134 © Museo Teatrale alla Scala
135 © A. Dagli Orti/Bridgeman Images
137 © Ricordi & C. S.r.l. Milan
138 © Ricordi & C. S.r.l. Milan
139 © Ricordi & C. S.r.l. Milan
140 Image courtesy of Buckingham
142 © DEA/G. CIGOLINI/De Agostini/Getty Images
143 © 2017. DeAgostini Picture Library/Scala, Florence
144 © Bibliothèque Nationale de France
145 © 2016 ROH. Photographed by Clive Barda
146 © 2016 ROH. Photographed by Clive Barda
147 © Robbie Jack/Corbis Entertainment/Getty Images
148 © 2009 David Leventi. Courtesy of Rick Wester Fine Art, New York
151 © The Bowes Museum, Barnard Castle, Co. Durham
152 © Musée d'Orsay, Paris/ Bridgeman Images
159 © Bibliothèque Nationale de France
160 © Bibliothèque Nationale de France
161 © Tallandier/Bridgeman Images
162 © National Gallery, London/ Bridgeman Images
163 © Los Angeles County Museum of Art/Bridgeman Images
164 © Bibliothèque Nationale de France
165 © 2017. Copyright The National Gallery, London/Scala, Florence
167 © The Bowes Museum, Barnard Castle, Co. Durham
171 © Bibliothèque Nationale de France
172 © Bibliothèque Nationale de France
173 © Bibliothèque Nationale de France
174 © 2017. Photo Scala, Florence/ bpk, Bildagentur fuer Kunst, Kultur und Geschichte, Berlin
175 © Monika Ritterhaus
176 © Robbie Jack – Corbis/Corbis Entertainment/Getty Images
177 © Ralph Brinkhoff
178 © ullstein bild/Getty Images
179 © 2017. Digital image, The Museum of Modern Art, New York/Scala, Florence
180 © KHM-Museumsverband, Theatermuseum Vienna
182 Private Collection Richard-Strauss-Archive
183 © 2017. Photo Scala, Florence/ bpk, Bildagentur fuer Kunst, Kultur und Geschichte, Berlin
184 © RIBA Library Drawings and Archives Collections
185 © SLUB Dresden/Deutsche Fotothek/Regine Richter
186 © bpk/Staatliche Kunstsammlungen Dresden/ Jürgen Karpinski
187 Private Collection Richard-Strauss-Archive
188 © Hôpital de la Salpêtrière, Paris/ Bridgeman Images
189 © ullstein bild/Getty Images
191 © 2017. Digital image, The Museum of Modern Art, New York/Scala, Florence
193 © Deutsche Fotothek
194 © KHM-Museumsverband, Theatermuseum Vienna
196 © Fortuny y Madrazo Mariano, Localisation: Paris, Musée d'Orsay, conservé au Musée du Louvre. Photo © RMN-Grand Palais (Musée d'Orsay)/Tony Querrec Salomé portant la tête de saint Jean-Baptiste
197 © Salvador Dali, Fundació Gala-Salvador Dalí, DACS 2017
201 Andrezj Majewski
202 © Archivo Gianni Versace
203 © Erich Heckel/DACS 2017
205 © British Library, London/ Bridgeman Images
206 © Hiroyuki Ito/Hulton Archive/ Getty Images
207 © Mats Bäcker
208 © Hiroyuki Ito/Hulton Archive/ Getty Images
209 © Nikolai Krusser
210 © The State Museum of the History of St Petersburg
211 Courtesy of Russian Theatre Museum, St Petersburg
213 © Mikhailovsky Theatre, St Petersburg
214 © Rodchenko & Stepanova Archive, DACS, RAO 2017
215 Courtesy of Russian Theatre Museum, St Petersburg
216 Courtesy of Russian Theatre Museum, St Petersburg
217 © Shostakovich Museum, Moscow
218 © British Library, London/ Bridgeman Images
219 © State Russian Museum, St Petersburg/Bridgeman Images
220 © Bridgeman Images
221 © Tate, London 2015
222 © Irina Antonovna Shostakovich
223 © St Petersburg Museum of Theatre and Music
224 © St Petersburg Museum of Theatre and Music
225 © St Petersburg Museum of Theatre and Music
226 © Tate, London 2015
227 © Mikhailovsky Theatre, St Petersburg
228 © Mikhailovsky Theatre, St Petersburg
229 © Mikhailovsky Theatre, St Petersburg
230 Courtesy of Library of Congress
232 © The State Museum of the History of St Petersburg
233 © Vera Mukhina
235 © Mikhailovsky Theatre, St Petersburg
236 © St Petersburg Museum of Theatre and Music
237 © St Petersburg Museum of Theatre and Music
238 © State Tretyakov Gallery, Moscow/Bridgeman Images
240 © 2015 ROH. Photographed by Clive Barda
241 © Erik Berg
242 © kokkai/Getty Images
243 © Mendowong Photography/ Moment/Getty Images
244 Photograph by Angie Smith for The New Yorker
245 Photograph by Helen Maybanks
246 © Jack Vartoogian/Archive Photos/Getty Images
247 © Jack Vartoogian/Archive Photos/Getty Images
248 ©ROH/Stephen Cummiskey, 2013
249 © Johannes Simon/Staff/Getty Images
250 © Lawrence K. Ho/Los Angeles Times/Getty Images

Index